Mindfulness, Bliss, and Beyond

Mindfulness, Bliss, and Beyond

A Meditator's Handbook

Ajahn Brahm

foreword by Jack Kornfield

Wisdom Publications, Inc.
199 Elm Street
Somerville MA 02144 USA
www.wisdomexperience.org

© 2006, 2014 Ajahn Brahm

Library of Congress Cataloging-in-Publication Data
Ajahn Brahm, 1951–
  Mindfulness, bliss & beyond : a meditator's handbook / Ajahn Brahm.
    p. cm.
  Includes bibliographical references and index.
  ISBN 0-86171-275-7 (pbk. : alk. paper)
  1. Meditation—Buddhism. I. Title. II. Title: Mindfulness, bliss, and beyond.
BQ5612.A43 2006
294.3'4435—dc22

                                    2006019444

ISBN 978-0-86171-275-5   ebook ISBN 978-0-86171-983-9

25 24 23 22 21
12 11   10   9   8

Cover design by Tony Lulek. Special thanks to Gopa.
Interior design by Gopa & Ted2, Inc. Set in Bembo 10.8/15

Printed in the United States of America.

MIX
Paper from
responsible sources
FSC® C011935

Please visit www.fscus.org.

Contents

✦ ✦ ✦ ───────────────────────────────

Foreword

✦ ✦ ✦ ──

Y OU HOLD IN YOUR HANDS a truly helpful and sophisticated manual of meditation written by a monk with deep and wide-ranging experience. Ajahn Brahm is one of a new generation of Westerners who have studied, practiced, and mastered an important range of Buddhist teachings and now offer them to sincere practitioners across the modern world.

In *Mindfulness, Bliss, and Beyond* you will find a thorough set of teachings for developing and deepening meditation, aimed particularly at attaining absorption, or *jhāna samādhi,* and opening to the insights that can follow from it. Ajahn Brahm offers a careful and subtle understanding of how to transform initial difficulties and how to incline the mind toward rapture, happiness, light, and the profound steadiness of jhāna. Then he turns this concentrated attention to illuminate the emptiness of self that brings liberating understanding. These are beautiful teachings.

While I acknowledge with pleasure the fruit of Ajahn Brahm's rich experience as a guide for meditators, Ajahn Brahm presents this way of developing jhāna and insight as the real true way the Buddha taught and therefore the best way. It is an excellent way. But the Buddha also taught many other equally good ways to meditate and employed many skillful means to help students awaken. The teachings of Thich Nhat Hanh, the Dalai Lama, Ajahn Buddhadāsa, and Sunlun Sayadaw are among a wide spectrum of masters who offer different and equally liberating perspectives. Together they comprise a rich mandala of living Dharma, of which Ajahn Brahm reveals one important facet.

So, those of you interested in the practice of jhāna and the depths of the Buddhist path: read this book carefully. And try its practices. Much will be gained from its rich and wise words and even more from the experiences it points to. And as the Buddha and Ajahn Brahm both advise, test them out, use them, and learn from them, but do not cling to them. Let them lead you to the liberation beyond all clinging, the sure heart's release. May these teachings bring understanding, benefit, and blessings to all.

With metta,

Jack Kornfield
Spirit Rock Center
Woodacre, California

Abbreviations

✦ ✦ ✦

Buddhist Texts in Pāli		Numbered by:
AN	*Aṅguttara Nikāya*	division & sutta no.
Dhp	*Dhammapada*	verse no.
Dhp-a	*Dhammapada-aṭṭhakathā*	volume & page no. in Pali Text Society (PTS) edition
DN	*Dīgha Nikāya*	sutta, section, & verse no. in *The Long Discourses of the Buddha*
Ja	*Jātaka*	volume & page no. in PTS edition
Miln	*Milindapañha*	chapter & dilemma no. in PTS edition
MN	*Majjhima Nikāya*	sutta & section no. in *The Middle Length Discourses of the Buddha*
SN	*Saṃyutta Nikāya*	chapter & sutta no.
Sn	*Sutta Nipāta*	verse no.
Th-a	*Paramatthadīpanī (Theragāthā-aṭṭhakathā)*	volume & page no. in PTS edition
Thag	*Theragāthā*	verse no.
Thig	*Therīgāthā*	verse no.
Ud	*Udāna*	chapter & sutta no.
Vin	*Vinaya*	volume, chapter, section, & subsection no. in PTS edition
Vsm	*Visuddhimagga*	chapter & section no. in *The Path of Purification*

Acknowledgments

✦ ✦ ✦

Fᴵʀsᴛ, I ᴡɪsʜ ᴛᴏ ᴀᴄᴋɴᴏᴡʟᴇᴅɢᴇ Cūlaka Bhikkhu (Dr. Jacob Meddin) who turned his tiny monk's hut into something resembling a third-world sweatshop, working long hours over many months, even though in poor health, to produce the first versions of these instructions for the Buddhist Society of Western Australia's in-house Dhamma Journal. My thanks also go to Ron Storey, who typed out the manuscript so many times that he must now know these teachings by heart, and to Nissarano Bhikkhu, who organized the index. Next, I convey long overdue appreciation to my first meditation teacher, Nai Boonman of the Samatha Society in U.K., who revealed the beauty and importance of jhāna to me while I was till a long-haired student at Cambridge University in 1970. But most of all, I express my infinite gratitude to the teacher under whose instructions I happily lived for nine years in Northeast Thailand, Venerable Ajahn Chah, who not only explained the path to liberation so clearly, but who also lived the path so totally, to the very end.

Last but not least, my thanks go to all at Wisdom Publications, including David, Rod, and my copyeditor John LeRoy, for all their hard work bringing this volume to completion. May their good karma give them good health so that they will be able to work even harder on my next book.

Introduction:
The Big Picture

✦ ✦ ✦ ——————————————————————

M EDITATION IS *the* way of letting go. In meditation you let go of the complex world outside in order to reach a powerful peace within. In all types of mysticism and in many spiritual traditions, meditation is the path to a pure and empowered mind. The experience of this pure mind, released from the world, is incredibly blissful. It is a bliss better than sex.

In practicing meditation there will be some hard work, especially at the beginning, but if you are persistent, meditation will lead you to some very beautiful and meaningful states. It is a law of nature that without effort one does not make progress. Whether you are a layperson or a monk or nun, without effort you get nowhere.

Effort alone is not sufficient. Effort needs to be skillful. This means directing your energy to just the right places and sustaining it until the task is complete. Skillful effort neither hinders nor disturbs; instead it produces the beautiful peace of deep meditation.

The Goal of Meditation

To know where your effort should be directed in meditation, you must have a clear understanding of the goal. The goal of this meditation is beautiful silence, stillness, and clarity of mind. If you can understand that goal, then the place to apply your effort and the means to achieve the goal become much clearer. The effort is directed to letting go, to developing a mind that inclines to abandoning. One of the many simple but profound statements of the Buddha is that "a meditator who makes letting go the main object easily achieves *samādhi,*" that is, attentive stillness, the goal of meditation (SN 48,9).[1] Such a meditator gains these states of inner bliss almost automatically. The Buddha was saying that the major cause for attaining deep meditation and reaching these powerful states is the ability to abandon, to let go, to renounce.

Letting Go of Our Burdens

During meditation, we should not develop a mind that accumulates and holds on to things. Instead we should develop a mind that is willing to let go, to give up all burdens. In our ordinary lives we have to carry the burden of many duties, like so many heavy suitcases, but within the period of meditation such baggage is unnecessary. In meditation, unload as much baggage as you can. Think of duties and achievements as heavy weights pressing upon you. Abandon them freely without looking back.

This attitude of mind that inclines to giving up will lead you into deep meditation. Even during the beginning stages of your meditation, see if you can generate the energy of renunciation—the willingness to give things away. As you give things away in your mind, you will feel much lighter and more free. In meditation, abandoning occurs in stages, step by step.

Meditators are like birds that soar through the sky and rise to the peaks. Birds never carry suitcases! Skillful meditators soar free from all their burdens and rise to the beautiful peaks of their minds. It is on such summits of perception that meditators will understand, from their own direct experience, the meaning of what we call "mind." At the same time they will also understand the nature of what we call "self," "God," "the world," "the universe," the whole lot. It's there that they become enlightened—not in the realm of thought, but on the soaring summits of silence within their mind.

The Plan of the Book

Part 1 of this book, "The Happiness of Meditation," is for those who want to meditate in order to relieve some of the heaviness of life but, because of obstacles or disinclination, will not pursue meditation into the bliss states and enlightenment. Here I demonstrate that, even for the beginner, meditation when practiced correctly generates considerable happiness. Chapters 1 and 2 deal with the first steps of meditation in a clear and systematic way. They are a revised version of a little booklet of mine titled *The Basic Method of Meditation*.[2] Chapters 3 and 4 identify the problems that can occur in meditation and show how these obstacles, once recognized, are easily overcome. In chapters 5 and 6 I explain mindfulness in a unique way and then extend the meditator's repertoire by presenting three more methods of meditation, all supportive of the path to inner peace. Then in chapters 7 and 8 I bring into play some of the classic teachings of the Buddha, namely, the discourses on *ānāpānasati* (mindfulness of breathing) and *satipaṭṭhāna* (focuses of mindfulness), in order to validate the instructions so far and enrich them with the insightful descriptions of the Buddha himself.

The second part, "To Bliss and Beyond," is a guided tour through the world of timeless Buddhist rapture. It describes how meditation literally implodes into the supreme bliss of the jhānas and how such states of letting go lift the veil of our five senses to reveal the awesome world of the mind, the magic inner garden where enlightenment is reached. Chapters 9, 10, and 11 cast open the world of the pure mind with a detailed account of the experience of jhāna, giving precise step-by-step instructions on how to enter these amazing states. Next, chapters 12 and 13 continue the ascent of the peaks of spiritual experience by narrating how insight based on jhāna unlocks the gates to the orchard of wisdom. Then in chapters 14 and 15 I describe how the task of life is brought to a grand finale, giving precise and authentic details on what enlightenment is and how it is achieved.

The conclusion, "Letting Go to the End," is the book's "reentry vehicle" that returns the reader from the otherworldly realms of jhāna and nibbāna back to ordinary life—although not without a final leap toward the unconditioned as a sort of memento of our journey.

How to Use This Book

This book has three purposes. First, it serves as a course in Buddhist meditation. Meditators who read the book carefully and carry out its instructions conscientiously will receive a progressive and complete course in meditation, one ultimately based on the traditions and sometimes even the actual words of the Buddha himself. These profound, time-honored teachings are presented here in a manner that is compatible with Western thought.

Second, this book is a troubleshooting guide. It is structured to help surmount specific problems in practice. If, for example, ill will is an obstruction, the reader can turn to chapter 3, "The Hindrances to Meditation I," where one finds the advice to practice loving-kindness meditation *(mettā)* to overcome ill will. Other problem-solving advice is less common—even rare and hard to come by. Chapter 5, "The Quality of Mindfulness," is a good example. The details of how to set up a "gatekeeper" to both monitor and protect your meditation are invaluable instructions.

The third function of this book is to enable readers to explore aspects of Buddhist meditation that they know little about. It provides information that may be hard to find. Chapters 9–12 on the deep states of meditation bliss *(jhāna)* are a good example. Although the jhānas are fundamental to the Buddha's meditation instructions, they are generally not well understood these days.

It was with some trepidation that I sent this book to the publisher. When I began to practice meditation in London during the late 1960s, a visiting Japanese Zen monk told me, "According to the law of karma, anyone who writes a book on Buddhism will spend his or her next seven lifetimes as a donkey!" This had me worried. Whether it is true or not, it is my conviction that anyone who follows the instructions in this book will escape all rebirth, not only rebirth among those with long ears.

In the *Mahāsaccaka Sutta* (MN 36) the Buddha relates, "I considered:...'Could that [jhāna] be the path to enlightenment?' Then, following on that memory, came the realization, 'That is the path to enlightenment.'"[3]

Part 1
The Happiness of Meditation

The Basic Method
of Meditation I

1

♦ ♦ ♦

IN THIS CHAPTER we will cover the four initial stages of meditation. You may wish to go through the initial stages quickly, but be very careful if you do. If you pass through the initial steps too quickly, you may find that the preparatory work has not been completed. It's like trying to build a house on a makeshift foundation—the structure goes up very quickly, but it may come down too soon! You would be wise to spend a lot of time making the groundwork and foundations solid. Then, when you proceed to the higher stories—the bliss states of meditation—they will be stable.

Stage One:
Present-Moment Awareness

When I teach meditation, I like to begin at the simple stage of giving up the baggage of past and future. You may think that this is an easy thing to do, but it is not. Abandoning the past means not thinking about your work, your family, your commitments, your responsibilities, your good or bad times in childhood, and so on. You abandon all past experiences by showing no interest in them at all. During meditation you become someone who has no history. You do not think about where you live, where you were born, who your parents were, or what your upbringing was like. All of that history you renounce. In this way, if you are meditating with others, everyone becomes equal—just a meditator. It becomes unimportant whether you are an old hand at meditation or just a beginner.

If we abandon all that history, we are equal and free. We free ourselves of some of the concerns, perceptions, and thoughts that limit us, that stop us from developing the peace born of letting go. Every part of our history is finally released, even the memory of what happened just a moment ago. Whatever has happened no longer interests us, and we let it go. It no longer reverberates in our mind.

I describe this as developing a mind like a padded cell. When any experience, perception, or thought hits the wall of this cell, it does not bounce back. It just sinks into the padding and stops. The past does not echo in our consciousness. Some people think that if they contemplate the past, they can somehow learn from it and solve their problems. But when we gaze at the past we invariably look through a distorted lens. Whatever we think it was like, in truth it was not quite like that at all! This is why people argue about what happened even a few moments ago.

It is well known to police who investigate traffic accidents that two different eyewitnesses, both completely honest, may give conflicting accounts of the same accident. When we see just how unreliable our memory is, we will not overvalue the past. We can bury it, just as we bury a person who has died. We bury the coffin or cremate the corpse, and it is done with.

Do not linger on the past. Do not keep carrying around coffins full of dead moments. If you do, you weigh yourself down with heavy burdens that do not really belong to you. When you let go of the past, you will be free in the present moment. As for the future—the anticipations, fears, plans, and expectations—let that go too. The Buddha once said, "Whatever you think it will be, it will always be something different" (MN 113,21). This future is known by the wise as uncertain, unknown, and unpredictable. It is often useless to anticipate the future, and in meditation it is always a great waste of time.

The Mind Is Wonderful and Strange

When you work with your mind, you find that it is so strange. The mind can do wonderful and unexpected things. Meditators who are having a difficult time achieving a peaceful state of mind sometimes start thinking, "Here we go again, another hour of frustration." But often something strange happens: although they are anticipating failure, they reach a very peaceful meditative state.

Recently I heard about a man on his first ten-day retreat. After the first day, he was in such pain that he asked to go home. The teacher said, "Stay one more day and the pain will disappear, I promise." So he stayed another day, but the pain only got worse. So again he wanted to go home. The teacher repeated his instruction, "Just one more day and the pain will go." He stayed for a third day, but the pain was even worse. Every evening for each of the first nine days he would go to the teacher and ask to go home. And the teacher would say, "Just one more day and the pain will disappear." To his complete surprise, on the first sit in the morning of the final day, the pain disappeared and it did not come back. He could sit for long periods with no pain at all. He was amazed at how wonderful this mind is and how it can produce such unexpected results. So you cannot know the future. It can be so strange, so weird, so completely beyond what you would expect. Experiences such as this man's can give you the wisdom and courage to abandon all thoughts and expectations about the future.

When you think during your meditation, "How many more minutes are there to go? How much longer do I have to endure this?" that is just wandering off into the future. The pain could disappear in a twinkling. You simply cannot anticipate when that is going to happen.

During a retreat you may think that none of your meditations were any good. But in the next meditation session you might sit down and everything becomes so peaceful and easy. "Wow!" you think. "Now I can meditate!" But then the next meditation is as awful as the first ones. What's going on here?

My first meditation teacher told me something that at the time sounded quite strange. He said that *there is no such thing as a bad meditation*. He was right. All those meditations that you call bad or frustrating are where you do the hard work for your "wages." It's like a person who on Monday works all day but gets no money at the end of the day. "What am I doing this for?" he thinks. He works all day Tuesday and still gets nothing. Another bad day. All day Wednesday and Thursday he works, and still nothing to show for it. Four bad days in a row. Then along comes Friday.

He does exactly the same work as before, and at the end of the day the boss gives him his wages. Wow! Why can't every day be a payday?

Why can't every meditation be a payday? Do you understand the simile? During the difficult meditations you build up your credit, the reason for your success. In the hard meditations you build up your strength, which creates the momentum for peace. Then when there is enough credit, the mind goes into a good meditation, and it is a payday. But you must remember that it was in the so-called bad meditations that most of the work was done.

The Past and Future Are Burdens

In one retreat that I gave, during an interview a woman told me that she had been angry with me all day, but for two different reasons. In her early meditations she was having a difficult time and was angry with me for not ringing the bell to end the meditation early enough. In the later meditations she got into beautiful, peaceful states and was angry with me for ringing the bell too soon. The sessions were all the same length, exactly one hour.

When you anticipate the future by thinking, "How many more minutes until the bell rings?" you torture yourself. So be very careful not to pick up the heavy burden of "How many more minutes to go?" or "What should I do next?" If that is what you are thinking, you are not paying attention to what is happening now. You are asking for trouble. You are not doing the meditation.

In this stage of meditation keep your attention right in the present moment, to the point where you don't even know what day it is or what time it is. Morning? afternoon?—don't know! All you know is what moment it is *right now*. In this way, you arrive at this beautiful "monastery time," where you are just meditating in the moment. You're not aware of how many minutes have gone or how many remain. You cannot even remember what day it is.

Once as a young monk in Thailand, I had actually forgotten what year it was! It is marvelous to live in the realm that is timeless, a realm so much more free than the time-driven world we usually live in. In the timeless realm, you experience *this* moment—just as all wise beings have been experiencing *this* moment for thousands of years. You have arrived at the reality of now.

The reality of now is magnificent and awesome. When you have abandoned all past and all future, it is as if you have come alive. You are here. You are mindful. This is the first stage of meditation, just this mindfulness sustained only in the present. Reaching this stage, you have done a great deal. You have let go of the first burden that stops deep meditation. So it is important to put forth a lot of effort to make this first stage strong, firm, and well established.

Stage Two: Silent Present-Moment Awareness

In the introduction I outlined the goal of this meditation: beautiful silence, stillness, and clarity of mind pregnant with the most profound insights. You have let go of the first burden that stops deep meditation. Now you should proceed to the even more beautiful and truthful silence of the mind.

Silence Means No Commentary

In discussing stage two it is helpful to clarify the difference between experiencing the silent awareness of the present moment and thinking about it. The simile of watching a tennis match on TV helps. You may notice that two matches are occurring simultaneously: the match that you see on the screen and the match that you hear being described by the commentator. The commentary is often biased. If an Australian is playing an American, for example, an Australian sportscaster is likely to provide a very different commentary from an American one. In this simile, watching the TV screen with no commentary stands for silent awareness in meditation, and paying attention to the commentary stands for thinking about it. You should realize that you are much closer to truth when you observe without commentary, when you experience just the silent awareness of the present moment.

Sometimes we assume it is through the inner commentary that we know the world. Actually, that inner speech does not know the world at all. It is the inner speech that spins the delusions that cause suffering. Inner speech causes us to be angry with our enemies and to form dangerous attachments to our loved ones. Inner speech causes all of life's problems. It constructs fear and guilt, anxiety and depression. It builds these illusions as deftly as the skillful actor manipulates the audience to create terror or tears. So if you seek truth, you should value silent awareness and, when meditating, consider it more important than any thought.

It is the high value that one gives to one's own thoughts that is the main obstacle to silent awareness. Wisely removing the importance that one gives to thinking, and realizing the greater accuracy of silent awareness, opens the door to inner silence.

An effective way to overcome the inner commentary is to develop a refined present-moment awareness. You watch every moment so closely that you simply don't have the time to comment about what has just happened. A thought is often an opinion on what has just happened: "That was good." "That was gross." "What was that?" All of these comments are about the previous experience. When you are noting or making a comment about an experience that has just passed, you are not paying attention to the experience that has just arrived. You are dealing with old visitors and neglecting the new arrivals.

To develop this metaphor, imagine your mind to be a host at a party, meeting the guests as they come in the door. If one guest comes in and you start talking with this person about this or that, then you are not doing your duty of paying attention to every guest who enters. Since a guest comes in the door every moment, you must greet each one and then immediately greet the next. You cannot afford to engage even in the shortest conversation with any guest, since this would mean missing the one coming in next. In meditation, experiences come one by one through the doors of our senses into the mind. If you greet one experience with mindfulness and then start a conversation with it, you will miss the next experience following right behind.

When you are perfectly in the moment with every experience, with every guest that comes into your mind, then you simply do not have the space for inner speech. You cannot chatter to yourself because you are completely taken up with mindfully greeting everything just as it arrives. This is refining present-moment awareness to the level that it becomes silent awareness of the present in every moment.

In developing inner silence you are giving up another great burden. It is as if you have been carrying a heavy rucksack on your back for thirty or fifty years continuously, and during that time you have wearily trudged for many, many miles. Now you have had the courage and found the wisdom to take that rucksack off and put it on the ground for a while. You feel so immensely relieved, so light, and so free, now that you are unburdened.

Another useful technique for developing inner silence is recognizing the space between thoughts, or between periods of inner chatter. Attend closely with sharp mindfulness when one thought ends and before another thought begins—*there!* That is silent awareness! It may be only momentary at first, but as you recognize that fleeting silence you become accustomed to it. And as you become accustomed to it, the silence lasts longer. You begin to enjoy the silence, once you have found it at last, and that is why it grows. But remember, silence is shy. If silence hears you talking about her, she vanishes immediately!

Silence Is Delightful

It would be marvelous for each one of us if we could abandon all inner speech and abide in silent awareness of the present moment long enough to realize how delightful it is. Silence is so much more productive of wisdom and clarity than thinking. When one realizes that, silence becomes more attractive and important. The mind inclines toward it, seeks it out constantly, to the point where it engages in the thinking process only if it is really necessary, only if there is some point to it. Once we have realized that most of our thinking is really pointless, that it gets us nowhere and only gives us headaches, we gladly and easily spend much time in inner quiet. This second stage of the meditation, then, is *silent present-moment awareness*. We may want to spend much time developing just these first two stages, because if we can reach this point, we have come a long way indeed in our meditation. In that silent awareness of "just now," we experience much peace, joy, and consequent wisdom.

Stage Three: Silent Present-Moment Awareness of the Breath

If we want to go further, then instead of being silently aware of whatever comes into the mind, we choose silent present-moment awareness of just one thing. That one thing can be the experience of breathing, the idea of loving-kindness *(mettā)*, a colored circle visualized in the mind *(kasiṇa)*, or several other less common focal points for awareness. Here I will describe *silent present-moment awareness of the breath*.

Unity versus Diversity

Choosing to fix one's attention on one thing is letting go of diversity and moving to its opposite, unity. As the mind begins to unify and sustain attention on just one thing, the experience of peace, bliss, and power increases significantly. Here we discover that the diversity of consciousness is another heavy burden. It is like having six telephones on your desk ringing at the same time. Letting go of this diversity and permitting only one telephone (a private line at that) on your desk is such a relief that it generates bliss. The understanding that diversity is a heavy burden is crucial to being able to focus on the breath.

Careful Patience Is the Fastest Way

If you have developed silent awareness of the present moment carefully for long periods of time, then you will find it quite easy to turn that awareness onto the breath and follow that breath from moment to moment without interruption. This is because the two major obstacles to breath meditation have already been overcome. The first of these two obstacles is the mind's tendency to go off into the past or future, and the second obstacle is inner speech. This is why I teach the two preliminary stages of present-moment awareness and silent present-moment awareness as a solid preparation for deeper meditation on the breath.

It often happens that meditators start breath meditation when their minds are still jumping around between past and future, and when awareness is being drowned out by inner commentary. Without proper preparation they find breath meditation difficult, even impossible, and give up in frustration. They give up because they did not start at the right place. They did not perform the preparatory work before taking up the breath as a focus of their attention. However, if your mind has been well prepared by completing these first two stages, then when you turn to the breath you will be able to sustain your attention on it with ease. If you find it difficult to attend to your breath, this is a sign that you rushed the first two stages. Go back to the preliminary exercises. Careful patience is the fastest way!

It Does Not Matter Where You Watch the Breath

When you focus on the breath, you focus on the experience of the breath happening now. You experience what the breath is doing, whether it is going in, going out, or is in between. Some teachers say to watch the breath at the tip of the nose, some say to watch it at the abdomen, and some say to move it here and then move it there. I have found through experience that it does not matter where you watch the breath. In fact it is best not to locate the breath anywhere. If you locate the breath at the tip of your nose then it becomes "nose awareness," not breath awareness, and if you locate it at your abdomen then it becomes "abdomen awareness." Just ask yourself right now: "Am I breathing in or breathing out? How do I know?" There! The experience that tells you what the breath is doing, that is what you focus on. Let go of the concern about where this experience is located. Just focus on the experience itself.

The Tendency to Control Breathing

A common problem at this stage is the tendency to control the breathing, and this makes the breathing uncomfortable. To overcome this difficulty, imagine that you are just a passenger in a car looking through the window at your breath. You are not the driver, nor a backseat driver. So stop giving orders, let go, and enjoy the ride. Let the breath do the breathing and simply watch.

When you know the breath is going in or going out for about one hundred breaths in a row, not missing one, then you have achieved what I call the third stage of this meditation, which involves sustained attention on the breath. This again is more peaceful and joyful than the previous stage. To go deeper, you aim next for full sustained attention on the breath.

Stage Four: Full Sustained Attention on the Breath

The fourth stage occurs when your attention expands to take in every single moment of the breath. You know the in-breath at the very first moment, when the first sensation of inbreathing arises. Then you observe as those sensations develop gradually through the whole course of one in-breath, not missing even a moment of the in-breath. When that in-breath finishes, you know that moment. You see in your mind that last movement of the in-breath. You then see the next moment as a pause between breaths, and then many more moments of pause until the out-breath begins. You see the first moment of outbreathing and each subsequent sensation as the out-breath evolves, until the out-breath disappears when its function is complete. All this is done in silence and in the present moment.

Getting Out of the Way

You experience every part of each in-breath and out-breath continuously for many hundred breaths in a row. That is why this stage is called full sustained attention on the breath. You cannot reach this stage through force, through holding or gripping. You can attain this degree of stillness only by letting go of everything in the entire universe except for this momentary experience of the breath happening silently. Actually "you" do not reach this stage, the mind does. The mind does the work itself. The mind recognizes this stage to be a very peaceful and pleasant place to abide, just being alone with the breath. This is where the doer, the major part of one's ego, starts to disappear.

One finds that progress happens effortlessly at this stage of meditation. We just have to get out of the way, let go, and watch it all happen. The mind will automatically incline, if we only let it, toward this very simple, peaceful, and delicious unity of being alone with one thing, just being with the breath in each and every moment. This is the unity of mind, the unity in the moment, the unity in stillness.

The Beginning of the Beautiful Breath

The fourth stage is what I call the "springboard" of meditation, because from it one may dive into the blissful states. When we simply maintain this unity of consciousness by not interfering, the breath will begin to disappear. The breath appears to fade away as the mind focuses instead on what is at the center of the experience of breath, which is awesome peace, freedom, and bliss.

At this stage I introduce the term "beautiful breath." Here the mind recognizes that this peaceful breath is extraordinarily beautiful. We are aware of this beautiful breath continuously, moment after moment, with no break in the chain of experience. We are aware only of the beautiful breath, without effort and for a very long time.

Now as I will explain further in the next chapter, when the breath disappears, all that is left is "the beautiful." Disembodied beauty becomes the sole object of the mind. The mind is now taking the mind as its own object. We are no longer aware of the breath, body, thought, sound, or outside world. All that we are aware of is beauty, peace, bliss, light, or whatever our perception will later call it. We are experiencing only beauty, continuously, effortlessly, with *nothing* being beautiful! We have long ago let go of chatter, let go of descriptions and assessments. Here the mind is so still that it cannot say anything. One is just beginning to experience the first flowering of bliss in the mind. That bliss will develop, grow, and become very firm and strong. And then one may enter into those states of meditation called the *jhānas*.

I have described the first four stages of meditation. Each stage must be well developed before going on to the next. Please take a lot of time with these four initial stages, making them all firm and stable before proceeding. You should be able to maintain with ease the fourth stage, full sustained attention on the breath, during every moment of the breath without a single break for two or three hundred breaths in succession. I am not saying you should count the breaths during this stage; I am just giving an indication of the approximate span of time that one should be able to stay in stage four before proceeding further. In meditation, as I indicated earlier, careful patience is the fastest way!

The Basic Method
of Meditation II   2

◆ ◆ ◆

I N THIS CHAPTER we will consider three more advanced stages
of meditation: stage five, full sustained attention on the beautiful
breath; stage six, experiencing the beautiful nimitta; and stage seven, jhāna.

Stage Five: Full Sustained
Attention on the Beautiful Breath

The fifth stage is called *full sustained attention on the beautiful breath*. Often
this stage flows naturally and seamlessly from the previous stage. As
briefly discussed in the previous chapter, when one's full attention rests
easily and continuously on the experience of breathing with nothing
interrupting the even flow of awareness, the breath calms down. It
changes from a coarse, ordinary breath to a very smooth and peaceful "beautiful breath." The mind recognizes this beautiful breath and
delights in it. It experiences a deepening of contentment. It is happy just
to be watching this beautiful breath, and it does not need to be forced.

Do Nothing

"You" do not do anything. If you try to do something at this stage, you
will disturb the whole process. The beauty will be lost. It's like landing
on a snake's head in the game of snakes and ladders—you must go back
many squares. From this stage of meditation on, the doer has to disappear. You are just a knower, passively observing.

A helpful trick at this stage is to break the inner silence for a moment
and gently say to yourself: "calm." That's all. At this stage of the

meditation, the mind is usually so sensitive that just a little nudge causes it to follow the instruction obediently. The breath calms down and the beautiful breath emerges.

When we are passively observing the beautiful breath in the moment, the perception of "in" (breath) or "out" (breath), or the beginning, middle, or end of a breath, should be allowed to disappear. All that remains will be the experience of the beautiful breath happening now. The mind is not concerned with what part of its cycle the breath is in or where in the body it occurs. Here we are simplifying the object of meditation. We are experiencing breath in the moment, stripped of all unnecessary details. We are moving beyond the duality of "in" and "out" and are just aware of a beautiful breath that appears smooth and continuous, hardly changing at all.

Do absolutely nothing and see how smooth, beautiful, and timeless the breath can be. See how calm you can allow it to be. Take time to savor the sweetness of the beautiful breath—ever calmer, ever sweeter.

Only "the Beautiful" Is Left

Soon the breath will disappear, not when you want it to but when there is enough calm, leaving only the sign of "the beautiful."

A well-known passage from English literature might help clarify the experience of one's breath disappearing. In Lewis Carroll's *Alice in Wonderland*,[4] Alice is startled to see the Cheshire Cat sitting on a bough of a nearby tree and grinning from ear to ear. Like all the strange creatures in Wonderland, the Cheshire Cat has the eloquence of a politician. Not only does the cat get the better of Alice in the ensuing conversation, but it also suddenly disappears and then, without warning, just as suddenly reappears.

Alice said, "…and I wish you wouldn't keep appearing and vanishing so suddenly: you make one quite giddy!"

"All right," said the Cat; and this time it vanished quite slowly, beginning with the end of the tail, and ending with the grin, which remained some time after the rest of it had gone.

"Well! I've often seen a cat without a grin," thought Alice;

"but a grin without a cat! It's the most curious thing I ever saw in all my life!"

This story is an eerily accurate analogy for the meditation experience. Just as the Cheshire Cat disappeared and left only its grin, so the meditator's body and breath disappear, leaving only the beautiful. For Alice, it was the most curious thing she ever saw in all her life. For the meditator it is also strange, to clearly experience a free-floating beauty with nothing to embody it, not even a breath.

The beautiful, or more precisely the sign of the beautiful, is the next stage on this meditation path. The Pāli word for "sign" is *nimitta*. So this next stage is called "experiencing the beautiful nimitta."

Stage Six:
Experiencing the Beautiful Nimitta

This sixth stage is achieved when one lets go of the body, thought, and the five senses (including the awareness of the breath) so completely that only a beautiful mental sign, a nimitta, remains.

This pure mental object is a real object in the landscape of the mind *(citta)*, and when it appears for the first time, it is extremely strange. One simply has not experienced anything like it before. Nevertheless, the mental activity we call perception searches through its memory bank of life experiences for something even a little bit similar. For most meditators, this disembodied beauty, this mental joy, is perceived as a beautiful light. Some see a white light, some a golden star, some a blue pearl, and so on. But it is not a light. The eyes are closed, and the sight consciousness has long been turned off. It is the mind consciousness freed for the first time from the world of the five senses. It is like the full moon—here standing for the radiant mind, coming out from behind the clouds—here standing for the world of the five senses. It is the mind manifesting—it is not a light, but for most it appears as a light. It is perceived as a light because this imperfect description is the best that perception can offer.

For other meditators, perception chooses to describe this first appearance of mind in terms of a physical sensation such as intense tranquillity or ecstasy. Again, the body consciousness (that which experiences pleasure and pain, heat and cold, and so on) has long since closed down, so this is not a physical feeling. It is just perceived as being similar to pleasure. Although some meditators experience sensations while others see light, the important fact is that they are all describing the same phenomenon. They all experience the same pure mental object, and these different details are added by their different perceptions.

The Qualities of a Nimitta

One can recognize a nimitta by the following six features: (1) it appears only after the fifth stage of the meditation, after the meditator has been with the beautiful breath for a long time; (2) it appears when the breath disappears; (3) it comes only when the external five senses of sight, hearing, smell, taste, and touch are completely absent; (4) it manifests only in the silent mind, when descriptive thought (inner speech) is totally absent; (5) it is strange but powerfully attractive; and (6) it is a beautifully simple object. I mention these features so that you may distinguish real nimittas from imaginary ones.

Sometimes when the nimitta first arises it may appear dull. In this case, one should immediately go back to the previous stage of the meditation, full sustained attention on the beautiful breath. One has moved to the nimitta too soon. Sometimes the nimitta is bright but unstable, flashing on and off like a lighthouse beacon and then disappearing. This too shows that the meditator has left the beautiful breath too early. One must be able to sustain one's attention on the beautiful breath with ease for a long, long time before the mind is capable of maintaining clear attention on the far more subtle nimitta. So you should train the mind on the beautiful breath. Train it patiently and diligently. Then when it is time to go on to the nimitta, it will be bright, stable, and easy to sustain.

Letting Go

The main reason why the nimitta can appear dull is that the depth of contentment is too shallow. You are still wanting something. Usually you want the bright nimitta or you want jhāna. Remember—and this is important—jhānas are states of letting go, incredibly deep states of contentment. So give away the hungry mind. Develop contentment on the beautiful breath, and nimittas and jhānas will happen by themselves.

Put another way, the nimitta is unstable because you, the doer, just will not stop interfering. The doer is the controller, the backseat driver, always getting involved where it does not belong and messing everything up. Meditation is a natural process of coming to rest, and it requires you to get out of the way completely. Deep meditation only occurs when you really let go. This means *really* letting go—to the point that the process becomes inaccessible to the doer.

A skillful means to achieve such profound letting go is to deliberately offer a gift of confidence to the nimitta. Very gently interrupt the silence for a moment and whisper, inside your mind, that you are giving complete trust to the nimitta, so that the doer can relinquish all control and just disappear. The mind, represented here by the nimitta before you, will then take over the process as you watch.

You do not need to do anything here, because the intense beauty of the nimitta is more than capable of holding your attention without your assistance. Be careful here not to start asking questions like "What is this?" "Is this jhāna?" "What should I do next?" which all come from the doer trying to get involved again. Questioning disturbs the process. You may assess everything once the journey is over. A good scientist only assesses the experiment at the end, when all the data are in.

There is no need to pay attention to the shape or edges of the nimitta: "Is it round or oval?" "Is the edge clear or fuzzy?" These are all unnecessary queries, which just lead to more diversity, more duality of inside and outside, and more disturbance. Let the mind incline where it wants, which is usually to the center of the nimitta. The center is where the most beautiful part lies, where the light is most brilliant and pure. Let go and just enjoy the ride as the attention gets drawn right into the center, or as the light expands and envelops you totally. Let the mind merge into the bliss. Then let the seventh stage of this path of meditation, the jhāna, occur.

Stage Seven: Jhāna

There are two common obstacles at the door into jhāna: exhilaration and fear. In exhilaration, the mind becomes excited: "Wow, this is it!" If the mind thinks like this, then the jhāna is unlikely to happen. This "wow!" response needs to be subdued in favor of absolute passivity. You can leave all the wows until after emerging from the jhāna, where they properly belong.

The more likely obstacle, though, is fear. Fear arises from the recognition of the sheer power and bliss of the jhāna, or else at the recognition that to go fully inside the jhāna something must be left behind—*you!* The doer is silent before entering the jhāna, but it is still there. Inside the jhāna, however, the doer is completely gone. Only the knower is still functioning. One is fully aware, but all the controls are now beyond reach. One cannot even form a single thought, let alone make a decision. The will is frozen, and this can be scary for beginners, who have never had the experience of being so stripped of control and yet so fully awake. The fear is of surrendering an essential part of one's identity.

This fear can be overcome through confidence in the Buddha's teachings, and through recognizing and being drawn to the enticing bliss just ahead. The Buddha often said that this bliss of jhāna should not be feared but should be followed, developed, and practiced often (e.g., *Laṭukikopama Sutta*, MN 66,21). So before fear arises, offer your full confidence to that bliss, and maintain faith in the Buddha's teachings and the example of the noble disciples. Trust the Dhamma, the Buddha's teachings, and let the jhāna warmly embrace you in an effortless, bodiless, ego-less, and blissful experience that will be the most profound of your life. Have the courage to fully relinquish control for a while and experience all this for yourself.

The Qualities of Jhānas

A jhāna will last a long time. It does not deserve to be called jhāna if it lasts only a few minutes. The higher jhānas usually persist for many hours. Once inside, there is no choice. One will emerge from the jhāna only when the mind is ready to come out, when the accumulated "fuel" of relinquishment is all used up. Each jhāna is such a still and satisfying state of consciousness that its very nature is to persist for a very long time.

Another feature of jhāna is that it occurs only after the nimitta is discerned, as described above. Furthermore, one should know that during any jhāna it is impossible to experience the body (e.g., physical pain), hear a sound from outside, or produce any thought—not even a "good" thought. There is just a clear singleness of perception, an experience of nondual bliss that continues unchanging for a very long time. This is not a trance but a state of heightened awareness. I say this so that you may know for yourself whether what you take to be a jhāna is real or imaginary.

I will give particular attention to the jhāna in chapters 9 through 11.

The Great Vipassanā versus Samatha Debate

Some traditions speak of two types of meditation, insight meditation (*vipassanā*) and calm meditation *(samatha)*. In fact the two are indivisible facets of the same process. Calm is the peaceful happiness born of meditation; insight is the clear understanding born of the same meditation. Calm leads to insight and insight leads to calm.

For those who are misled to conceive of all the instructions offered here as "just samatha practice" (calming) without regard to vipassanā (insight), please know that this is neither vipassanā nor samatha. It is called *bhāvanā* (mental development). This method was taught by the Buddha (AN IV,125–27; MN 151,13–19) and repeated in the forest tradition of Northeast Thailand, with which my teacher, Ven. Ajahn Chah, was associated. Ajahn Chah often said that samatha and vipassanā cannot be separated, nor can the pair be developed apart from right view, right thought, right moral conduct, and so forth. Samatha and vipassanā, Ajahn Chah said, are like two sides of one hand. In the original Buddhist tradition they are inseparable. Indeed, to make progress in the seven stages of meditation I have described, the meditator needs an understanding and acceptance of the Buddha's teachings, and one's virtue must be pure.

Insight meditation is an inherent part of the method of meditation described so far. In particular, this meditation can produce insight or understanding in three important areas: insight into problems affecting daily happiness, insight into the way of meditation, and insight into the nature of "you."

Insight into Problems Affecting Daily Happiness

When a problem arises—a death, a sickness, some other type of loss, or even a hurtful argument—it is not only painful but confusing. It is like being lost in dense and dangerous jungle. When one is lost in the forest, one should climb to the top of a tall tree or tower and look for a distant landmark, such as a river or road that leads to safety. Having gained perspective and an overview of the situation, confusion vanishes.

In this simile, the jungle stands for the tangled problems of daily life. Climbing to the top of a tower or tree refers to the practice of meditation, which leads to the calm, cool air where insight or perspective is gained. Thus if you have a heavy problem, do not think about it endlessly. Then you are merely wandering around lost in your jungle. Instead, carefully follow the instructions for the method of meditation described in this chapter and the previous one, and you will leave your problem behind. You will rise above your jungle, and from that vantage point you will gain insight into what is to be done. The answer will appear out of the calm.

Insight into the Way of Meditation

At the end of each meditation session, spend two or three minutes reviewing all that has happened during that session. There is no need to "take notes" (that is, remind oneself to remember) during the meditation, because you will find it easy to remember the important features at the end. Was it peaceful or frustrating? Now ask yourself why. What did you do to experience peace, or what caused the feeling of frustration? If your mind wandered off into fantasy land, was that peaceful and useful? Such reviewing and inquiry *only at the end of the session* generates insight into how to meditate and what meditation is. No one starts out as a perfect meditator.

The insights gained by reviewing your meditation at the end of each session will deepen your experience of meditation and overcome hindrances. Developing this type of insight into your meditation is important, and I will come back to it in part 2.

Suffice it to say at this point that you need insight to achieve each of the stages I have described. To be able to let go of your thoughts, for example, you need some insight into what "letting go" is. The further you develop these stages, the more profound your insight will be. And if you reach as far as jhāna, then it will change your whole understanding.

By the way, these insights into the way of meditation also work for problems in daily life. This is because the tendencies that create obstacles in meditation are the same clumsy attitudes that cause difficulties in life. Meditation is like a gym in which you develop the powerful mental muscles of calm and insight, which you then use both in further meditation and in daily life to bring happiness and success.

Insight into the Nature of "You"

The deepest and most elusive insight is into who you really are. This insight is gained not through belief or thinking but only by meditation, by becoming absolutely still, releasing the mind, and then knowing the mind. The Buddha compared the mind to the full moon at night hidden behind clouds. The clouds stand for the activity of the five senses and thought. In deep meditation, the five senses recede to reveal the pure and radiant mind. In jhāna, you can actually observe the pure mind.

In order to know the inner secrets of the mind, one must continue to observe it in the stillness of jhāna, with no thought at all, for a very long time. One simile tells of a thousand-petaled lotus that closes its petals at night and opens them at dawn. When the first rays of the morning sun warm the outermost row of petals, they begin to open, which allows the sun to warm the next row of petals. Soon those petals open too, and the sun's warmth falls on the next row, and so on. But if a cloud appears and obscures the sun, then the lotus closes its petals. It takes a long period of unbroken sunshine to warm the lotus enough to open the innermost row of petals and reveal its secrets.

The lotus in this simile stands for the mind; the sun's warmth stands for still attention; and the cloud stands for a thought or mental agitation that destroys the stillness. I shall develop this simile later. For now, let me say that these inner secrets are beyond your imagining. Some meditators stop at an inner row of petals and mistakenly think, "This is it." Then the stillness breaks and the lotus closes in a twinkling. This is false enlightenment. When your meditation is so profound that you can remain in stillness for several hours, observing the mind freed from the hindrances, and watching the innermost row of petals open fully to reveal the jewel in the heart of the lotus, then you will realize the ultimate insight, the truth of who you are. Find out for yourself!

In the previous chapter, I counseled that patience is the fastest way to proceed. This also holds true for the three stages of meditation discussed in this chapter. These are all stages of letting go, each dependent upon the ones preceding. In the end, to enter into jhāna one has to really let go. This is a profound letting go made possible by careful and diligent practice.

There is much more to meditation than I have covered so far. In these two chapters only the basic method has been described: seven stages that culminate in the first jhāna. Much more needs to be said about the hindrances, qualities of mindfulness, other meditation objects, and more. Let us begin our detailed study by turning our attention to the five hindrances and how they are overcome.

The Hindrances
to Meditation I

3

I N THIS CHAPTER and the next I will explain in detail the five hindrances, obstacles that you will meet in your meditation and that you should learn to overcome. These obstacles to deep meditation are called in the Pāli language *nīvarana*. Literally that means "closing a door" or "obstructing entering into something," and this is exactly what the hindrances do. They stop you from entering into the deep absorption states, or jhānas. They also obstruct or weaken wisdom and strengthen delusion. So if one is going to say anything in Buddhism about the enemies to meditation, one can say that the five hindrances are Public Enemy Number One. *They stop people from becoming enlightened,* and it's precisely for this reason that understanding these five hindrances and overcoming them is crucial. When you don't fully understand them, you cannot overcome them.

Some teachers fail to explain the hindrances clearly enough, especially the hindrances that are very subtle. These refined hindrances prevent you from getting into deep meditation. If you do not even try to identify them and surpass them, then they will hold sway over your mind. You will be obstructed from enjoying the bliss of the mind and from developing the great insights of enlightenment.

Basically, these five hindrances stand between you and enlightenment. When you know them, you have a good chance of overcoming them. If you have not achieved the jhānas yet, it means you have not fully understood these five hindrances. If you have gotten into such deep states, then you have overcome the hindrances. It's as simple as that.

The Buddha named the five hindrances as follows: sensory desire (*kāma-cchanda*), ill will (*vyāpāda*), sloth and torpor (*thīna-middha*), rest-lessness and remorse (*uddhacca-kukkucca*), and doubt (*vicikicchā*). This is the usual order in which the Buddha lists them, and this is the order in which they will be presented here, too.

The First Hindrance—Sensory Desire

Kāma-cchanda, or sensory desire, is first on the list of hindrances because of its importance. It is the major obstacle preventing one from entering deep meditation. Few meditators fully understand its scope. It is not just sensory desire as that term is commonly understood. First of all, the Pāli word *kāma* means anything pertaining to the five senses of sight, hearing, smell, taste, and touch. *Chanda* means to delight in or agree with. Together the compound kāma-cchanda means "delight, interest, involvement with the world of the five senses."

For example, when we are meditating and hear a sound, why can't we simply ignore it? Why does it disturb us so? Many years ago in Thai-land the local villages surrounding our monastery held a party. The noise from the loudspeakers was so loud that it seemed to destroy the peace in our monastery. So we complained to our teacher, Ajahn Chah, that the noise was disturbing our meditation. The great master replied, "It is not the noise that disturbs you, it is you who disturb the noise!"

In the above example kāma-cchanda was the mind getting involved with the sound. Similarly, when your meditation is interrupted by a pain in your legs, say, then it is not the pain that disturbs you but it is you who disturb the pain. If you had been mindful, you would have seen your awareness go out to your body, becoming interested in sensations again. That was kāma-cchanda at work.

It is difficult to overcome kāma-cchanda because we are so attached to our five senses and their affairs. Whatever we are attached to we find impossible to release. To understand this attachment it is useful to examine the connection between our five senses and our body. It is commonly claimed that the five senses are there to protect our body, but insight will tell you the opposite: that the body is there to provide

a vehicle for your five senses to play in the world. You will also notice
that when the five senses disappear so does your body. Letting go of one
means letting go of the other.

Abandoning Kāma-cchanda Little by Little

You can't simply decide to let go of the five senses and the body through
a single effort of will. The abandoning of kāma-cchanda in meditation is
achieved little by little. You start by choosing a comfortable, quiet place
in which to meditate. You may sit on a chair if it is more comfortable
for you, remembering that even the Buddha sat on a chair sometimes.
When you first close your eyes you will be unable to feel much of the
body. In the same way that it takes a few minutes to see when you go
out from a well-lit room into the dark, so it takes a few minutes to
become sensitive to your bodily feelings. Thus the final adjustments to
our body posture are made a few minutes after closing our eyes.

Indulging kāma-cchanda in this way will subdue it for a while. Your
body will feel comfortable and the five senses satisfied, but not for long.
You must use this initial freedom to start placing the mind beyond the
reach of the five senses. You begin with present-moment awareness. Most
if not all of our past and future is occupied by the affairs of our five senses.
Our memories are of physical sensations, tastes, sounds, smells, or sights.
Our plans are likewise filled with five-sense business. Through achieving
present-moment awareness we cut off much of kāma-cchanda.

The next stage of meditation is silent present-moment awareness. In
this you abandon all thought. The Buddha identified an aspect of kāma-
cchanda that is called *kāma-vitakka,* meaning thinking about the five-sense
world. For the new meditator, the most obvious form of kāma-vitakka is
sexual fantasy. One can use up many hours, especially on a long retreat,
with this type of kāma-vitakka. This obstacle to progress in meditation is
transcended by realizing, through insight or faith, that total freedom from
the five senses (i.e., jhāna) is more ecstatic and profound than the very
best of sexual experiences. A monk or nun gives up their sexuality not
out of fear or repression, but out of recognition of something superior.
Even thoughts about lunch belong to kāma-vitakka. They disturb the

silence. And few meditators realize that noting bodily sensations, for example thinking to oneself "breath going in" or "hearing a sound" or "feeling a stabbing pain," is also part of kāma-vitakka and a hindrance to progress.

Lao Tzu, the great Taoist sage, would allow one student to accompany him on his evening walk, as long as the student maintained silence. One evening, as they reached a mountain ridge, the student remarked, "What a beautiful sunset." Lao Tzu never let that student accompany him again. When others asked why, the master explained, "When that student said, 'What a beautiful sunset,' he was no longer watching the sunset, he was only watching the words." That is why you have to abandon noting, for watching the words is not being mindful of the thing it tries in vain to describe.

In silent present-moment awareness it is as if the world of the five senses is now confined in a cage, unable to roam or create any mischief. Next, in order to abandon the five senses completely and with them the body, you choose to focus your mindfulness on a small part of the five-sense world to the exclusion of the rest. You focus your mindfulness on the physical sensation of the breath, paying no attention to other sensations in your body, nor to sounds and so on. The breath becomes the stepping stone from the world of the five senses over to the realm of the mind.

When you succeed in full sustained attention on the breath you will notice the absence of any sound. You never recognize the moment that hearing stops because its nature is to fade away gradually. Such a fading, like physical death, is a process not an event. Usually you discover when reviewing the meditation at the end of the sitting (as advised in chapter 2) that for a certain period your mind was impervious to any sound. You also notice that your body had disappeared, that you could not feel your hands, nor did you receive any messages from your legs. All that you knew was the feeling of the breath.

Some meditators become alarmed when parts of their body seem to vanish. This shows their strong attachment to their body. This is kāma-cchanda at work, hindering progress in their meditation. Usually you soon become familiar with the fading away of bodily sensations and start to delight in the wonderful tranquillity beyond their reach. It is the freedom and joy born of letting go that repeatedly encourages you to abandon your attachments.

Soon the breath disappears and the awesome nimitta fills your mind. It is only at this stage that you have fully abandoned kāma-cchanda, your involvement in the world of the five senses. For when the nimitta is established, all five senses are extinguished, and your body is out of range. The first and major hindrance has now been overcome and it is blissful. You are at the door of the jhānas. This is the method for abandoning kāma-cchanda little by little. It is why the stages of meditation are taught in this way. As the Buddha said in the Jātakas (Ja 4,173) "the more you abandon the five-sense world, the more you experience bliss. If you want to experience complete bliss, then completely abandon the five-sense world."

The Second Hindrance—Ill Will

The second hindrance, ill will or *vyāpāda,* is also a major obstacles to deep meditation, especially for Western meditators. The usual understanding of this second hindrance is anger toward another person. But that is not the full extent of ill will, because it is more likely to be toward yourself or even toward the meditation object.

Ill Will toward Yourself

Ill will toward yourself can manifest as not allowing yourself to bliss out, become peaceful, or become successful in meditation. There are many people who have very deep guilt complexes. This is mostly a Western trait because of the way that many of us have been brought up.

Ill will toward yourself is something that you should watch out for in meditation. It may be the main hindrance that is stopping you from getting deep into meditation. This problem was pointed out to me quite a few years ago when one of the Western nuns was telling me about her meditation. Often she got very deep in her meditation, almost into jhānas. She was at the door, she said, and the thing that stopped her was the feeling that she did not deserve this happiness! It was ill will toward herself that stopped her, the reluctance to allow herself bliss. I've seen that in many people since. Sometimes when the meditation gets peaceful, when happiness comes up, we think that there must be something wrong. We have ill will toward ourselves, so we don't permit ourselves to be happy and free.

In the nun's case, she saw very clearly that the only thing between her and jhānas was a subtle form of the hindrance of ill will. She didn't think she deserved so much bliss. *You do deserve so much bliss.* Why should you not? There's nothing against it. There are some kinds of bliss in this world that are illegal. There are others that break the Buddhist precepts, cause disease, or have terrible side effects. But jhānas have no bad side effects, they're not illegal, and the Buddha specifically encouraged them.

If you look very carefully at the way you meditate, you may find that you encounter the hindrance of ill will, but not at that last step before jhānas. You encounter it at some earlier stage of meditation when you do not allow yourself delight. Maybe you prefer to sit through pain rather than enjoy peace and happiness. Perhaps you think that you do not deserve happiness, bliss, and freedom.

An aversion to inner happiness is a sure sign of guilt. When someone is found guilty, punishment usually follows, maybe imposed by a court of law. Guilt and punishment are inseparable in our culture and in our minds. If we feel guilty about something, the next thing we think of is punishing ourselves—denying ourselves some type of pleasure, happiness, or freedom. People in the West just keep on seeking punishment. It's crazy!

Goodwill toward Yourself

To overcome that hindrance do some loving-kindness meditation. Give yourself a break. Say to yourself, "The door to my heart is open to all of me. I allow myself happiness. I allow myself peace. I have goodwill toward myself, enough goodwill to let myself become peaceful and to bliss out on this meditation." If you find it hard to extend loving-kindness toward yourself, ask why. There may be a deep-seated guilt complex inside, and you still expect punishment. You haven't given yourself unconditional forgiveness.

A beautiful ethic of Buddhism is that it does not matter what anyone else does to you or how long they have done it to you; it doesn't matter how unfair, cruel, or undeserving their treatment has been—you may still forgive them absolutely. I hear people saying that sometimes there are things you cannot forgive. That's not Buddhism! *There's nothing, absolutely nothing, you can't forgive in Buddhism.* Some years ago, a demented man went to a primary school in Scotland and killed many small children. At the religious service after the massacre, a prominent cleric asked God not to forgive this man, arguing that some things you cannot forgive! My heart sank when I heard that a religious leader would not offer forgiveness and show the way to heal people's pain in the aftermath of tragedy.

As far as Buddhism is concerned, you can forgive everything. Your forgiveness is healing. Your forgiveness solves old problems and never creates new ones. But because of ingrained attitudes you may have toward yourself, you cannot forgive yourself. Sometimes the problem is buried deep inside. Sometimes you've forgotten it. You just know there is something inside of you that you feel guilty about, that you can't forgive. You have some reason for denying yourself freedom, jhāna, and enlightenment. That ill will toward yourself may be the main reason why your meditation is not successful. Check that one out.

Ill Will toward the Meditation Object

Ill will toward the meditation object is a common problem for people who have been meditating on the breath without much success yet. I say "yet" because it's only a matter of time. *Everyone* will have success if they follow the instructions. But if you haven't succeeded yet, you may have some ill will toward meditation or the meditation object. You may sit down and think, "Oh, here we go again," "This is going to be difficult," "I don't really want to do this," "I have to do this because it's what meditators do," or "I've got to be a good Buddhist, and this is what Buddhists are supposed to do." If you start the meditation with ill will toward meditation, doing it but not liking it, then it's not going to work. You are putting a hindrance in front of yourself straightaway.

I love meditation. I enjoy it so much. Once when I led a meditation retreat I said to my fellow monks upon arriving, "Great, a meditation retreat!" I got up early every morning really looking forward to it. "Wow, I'm on meditation retreat. I don't have to do all the other stuff that I do in the monastery." I love meditation so much, and I've got so much goodwill toward it that there isn't the slightest bit of aversion. Basically I'm a "meditation junkie," and if you've got that sort of attitude, then you find that the mind, as the Buddha said, "leaps toward meditation" (AN IX, 41).

I like to use this simile: you are walking down the street when you see a dear old friend on the opposite side of the road. You've had such good times together. It doesn't matter where you are going or what you are supposed to be doing, you can't help but rush across the street, grab your friend by the hand, and give your friend a hug. "Come for a cup of coffee. I don't care if I'll be late for an appointment. It's such a long time since I've seen you. Come on, let's have some time together." Meditation is like a dear old friend that you want to spend time with. You're willing to drop everything else. If I see a meditation a mile away I just run toward it and give it a good old hug and take it for a cup of coffee somewhere. And as for the meditation object, the breath, we've had such good times together, my breath and I. We're the best of mates. If you regard the breath with that sort of goodwill, you can see why it's so easy to watch the breath in your meditation.

The opposite, of course, is when you know you have to be with this frigging breath and you don't like it. You've had so much difficulty with this breath. You see it coming along on the other side of the street and you think, "Oh my God, here it is again." You try to duck away and hide behind a lamppost so it doesn't see you. You just want to escape. Unfortunately people do develop such ill will toward the breath. If it's not pointed out to them, they will regard meditation as a chore. There's no happiness in it. It becomes something like going to the gym. "If there's no pain, then there's no gain." You lift weights until it really hurts, because you think you are going to get somewhere that way. If that's the way you enter meditation, then you've got no hope.

So cultivate goodwill toward the meditation object. Program yourself to delight in this meditation. Think, "Wow! Beautiful! All I've got to do is just sit and do nothing else—nothing to build, no letters to write, no phone calls to make. I just need to sit here and be with my good old friend, my breath." If you can do that you've abandoned the hindrance of ill will, and you've developed the opposite—loving-kindness toward your breath.

I use the following method to overcome any ill will toward my breath. I look upon my breath like a newborn son or daughter. Would you leave your baby at the shopping mall and just forget it? Would you drop it as you're walking on the road? Would you lose sight of it for long? Why is it that we can't keep our attention on the breath? Again this is because we lack kindness toward our breath, we don't delight in it, and we don't appreciate it. If you appreciated your breath as much as your child or someone else who is very, very dear to you and very vulnerable, you would never drop, forget, or abandon it. You would always be mindful of it. But if you have ill will toward the breath, you'll find yourself wandering off and forgetting it. You're trying to lose it, because you don't like it all that much. That's why you lose your meditation object.

To sum up, ill will is a hindrance, and you overcome that hindrance by compassion to all others, forgiveness toward yourself, loving-kindness toward the meditation object, goodwill toward the meditation, and friendship toward the breath. You can have loving-kindness toward silence and the present moment too. When you care for these friends who reside in the mind, you overcome any aversion toward them as meditation objects. *When you have loving-kindness toward the meditation object, you do not need much effort to hold it.* You just love it so much that it becomes effortless to be with.

The Hindrances to Meditation II 4

♦ ♦ ♦

W E TURN NOW to the remaining three hindrances—sloth and torpor *(thīna-middha)*, restlessness and remorse *(uddhacca-kukkucca)*, and doubt *(vicikicchā)*—and then examine what happens when the hindrances are overcome.

The Third Hindrance—Sloth and Torpor

The third hindrance is sloth and torpor. I don't need to describe it in detail, because I'm sure we know it all too well through our experience of meditation. We sit in meditation and don't really know what we are watching, whether it's the present moment, silence, the breath, or whatever. This is because the mind is dull. It's as if there are no lights turned on inside. It's all gray and blurry.

Making Peace with Sloth and Torpor

The most profound and effective way of overcoming sloth and torpor is to make peace with the dullness and stop fighting it! When I was a young monk in the forest monasteries in Thailand and became sleepy during the 3:15 A.M. sitting, I would struggle like hell to overpower the dullness. I would usually fail. But when I did succeed in overcoming my sleepiness, restlessness would replace it. So I would calm down the restlessness and fall back into sloth and torpor. My meditation was like a pendulum swinging between extremes and never finding the middle. It took many years to understand what was going on.

The Buddha advocated investigation, not fighting. So I examined where my sloth and torpor came from. I had been meditating at 3:15 in the morning, having slept very little, I was malnourished, an English monk in a hot tropical jungle—what would you expect! The dullness was the effect of natural causes. I let go and made peace with my sleepiness. I stopped fighting and let my head droop. Who knows, I might even have snored. When I stopped fighting sloth and torpor it did not last all that long. Moreover, when it passed I was left with peace and not with restlessness. I had found the middle of my pendulum swing and I could observe my breath easily from then on.

Dullness in meditation is the result of a tired mind, usually one that has been overworking. Fighting that dullness makes you even more exhausted. Resting allows the energy to return to the mind. To understand this process, I will now introduce the two halves of the mind: *the knower* and *the doer*. The knower is the passive half of the mind that simply receives information. The doer is the active half that responds with evaluating, thinking, and controlling. The knower and the doer share the same source of mental energy. Thus, when you are doing a lot, when you have a busy lifestyle and are struggling to get on, the doer consumes most of your mental energy, leaving only a pittance for the knower. When the knower is starved of mental energy you experience dullness.

At a retreat I led in Sydney a few years ago, a retreatant arrived late from her high-stress job as an executive in the city. In her first sitting that evening her mind was almost as dead as a corpse. So I gave her my special teaching on how to overcome her sloth and torpor: I told her to rest. For the next three days she slept in until dawn, went back to bed again after breakfast, and had a long nap after lunch. What a brilliant meditator! After three days of no fighting, giving hardly any mental energy to the doer but letting it flow to the knower, her mind brightened up. In another three days she had caught up with the rest of the group in her progress through the stages. By the end of the retreat she was way ahead and one of the star meditators of that retreat.

The most profound and effective way to overcome sloth and torpor is to stop fighting your mind. Stop trying to change things and instead let things be. Make peace not war with sloth and torpor. Then your mental energy will be freed to flow into the knower, and your sloth and torpor will naturally disappear.

Giving Value to Awareness

Another method for overcoming sloth and torpor is to give more value to awareness. All Buddhist traditions say that human life is valuable and precious, especially a life like this one where you have encountered the Buddha's teachings. Now you have the opportunity to practice. You may not realize how many lifetimes it has taken and how much merit you've had to accumulate just to get where you are now. You've invested lifetimes of good karma to get this close to the Dhamma. Reflecting like this means you will incline less to sloth and torpor and more to bright awareness.

The path of meditation sometimes comes to a fork in the road. The left path leads to sloth and torpor while the right path leads to bright awareness. With experience you will recognize this fork. This is the point in meditation where you can choose between the alley to sloth and torpor or the highway to mindful stillness. Taking the left path you give up both the doer and the knower. Taking the right path you let go of the doer but keep the knower. When you value awareness you will automatically choose the right path of bright awareness.

Sloth and Torpor and Ill Will

Sometimes sloth and torpor is the result of ill will, the second hindrance. When I used to visit Australian prisons to teach meditation, I would often hear the following prison proverb: "an extra hour of sleep is an hour off your sentence." People who don't like where they are will try to escape into dullness. In the same way, meditators who easily get negative will tend to drift into sloth and torpor. Ill will is the problem.

In our monastery in Thailand we would meditate all night once a week. During those all-night sittings, sloth and torpor would regularly conquer me an hour or two after midnight. Since it was my first year as a monk, I reflected that less than twelve months previously I would spend all night at parties, rock concerts, and clubs. I recalled that I never experienced sloth and torpor when listening to the music of the Doors at 2 A.M. Why? It became clear that when you are enjoying what you are doing then you don't tend to get sloth and torpor, but when you don't like what you are doing then sloth and torpor comes in. I did not like those all-night sits. I thought they were a stupid idea. I did them because I had to. I had ill will, and that was the cause of my sloth and torpor. When I changed my attitude and put joy into the all-night sittings, making them fun, then sloth and torpor rarely came. So you should investigate whether your sloth and torpor is the result of an attitude problem—the attitude of ill will.

Using Fear

When I was a lay Buddhist I attended a Zen retreat in the north of England. It was very early in the morning, and the meditation hall was freezing cold. People had their blankets around them. When you meditate with a blanket anywhere close to you, you tend to get sleepy. The teacher was walking up and down with a big stick, and the fellow next to me who had started nodding got hit. Everyone's sloth and torpor suddenly disappeared right then. We only needed one person to get hit and that was enough. The problem was that the fear that woke me up remained with me, preventing further progress. Experience teaches that you can't generate wholesome states like peace and freedom by using unwholesome methods like fear or violence.

In the old forest tradition of northeast Thailand, monks would meditate in dangerous places such as platforms high in the trees, on the edge of cliffs, or in jungles full of tigers. The ones who survived said they got good meditation, but you never heard from the monks that didn't survive!

The Fourth Hindrance— Restlessness and Remorse

The next hindrance, restlessness and remorse *(uddhacca-kukkucca),* is among the most subtle of hindrances. The main component of this hindrance is restlessness of mind. But first let me briefly address the matter of remorse.

Remorse

Remorse is the result of hurtful things that you may have done or said. In other words, it is a result of bad conduct. If any remorse comes up in meditation, instead of dwelling on it, you should forgive yourself. Everyone makes mistakes. The wise are not people who never make mistakes, but those who forgive themselves and learn from their mistakes. Some people have so much remorse that they think they can never become enlightened.

The story of Angulimāla is a well-known story in the Buddhist scriptures (MN 86). Angulimāla was a serial killer. He killed 999 people. He cut off a finger from each of his victims and put them in a garland he hung around his neck. The one-thousandth victim was to be the Buddha but, of course, you can't kill a buddha. Instead the Buddha "killed him," killed his bad ways, killed his defilements. Angulimāla became a Buddhist monk. Even a serial killer like Angulimāla could achieve the jhānas and become fully enlightened. So have you ever killed anybody? Are you a serial killer? You probably haven't done anything like that. If such people can become enlightened, surely you can. No matter what bad things you've done in your past or what you feel remorseful about, always remember Angulimāla. Then you won't feel so bad about yourself. Forgiveness, letting go of the past, is what overcomes remorse.

Restlessness

Restlessness arises because we do not appreciate the beauty of contentment. We do not acknowledge the sheer pleasure of doing nothing. We have a faultfinding mind rather than a mind that appreciates what's already there. *Restlessness in meditation is always a sign of not finding joy in what's here.* Whether we find joy or not depends on the way we train our perception. It's within our power to change the way we look at things. We can look at a glass of water and perceive it as very beautiful, or we can think of it as ordinary. In meditation, we can see the breath as dull and routine, or we can see it as very beautiful and unique. If we look upon the breath as something of great value, then we won't get restless. We won't go around looking for something else. That's what restlessness is, going around looking for something else to do, something else to think about, somewhere else to go—anywhere but here and now. Restlessness is one of the major hindrances, along with sensory desire. Restlessness makes it so hard to sit still for very long.

I begin meditation with present-moment awareness, just to overcome the coarse restlessness that says, "I want to be somewhere other than right here, right now." No matter what this place is, no matter how comfortable you make it, restlessness will always say it's not good enough. It looks at your meditation cushion and says it's too big or too small, too hard or too wide. It looks upon a meditation retreat center and says, "It's not good enough. We should have three meals a day. We should have room service."

Contentment is the opposite of a faultfinding mind. You should develop the perception of contentment with whatever you have, wherever you are, as much as you can.

Beware of finding fault in your meditation. Sometimes you may think, "I'm not going deep enough. I've been watching the present moment for so long, and I'm not getting anywhere." That thought is the very cause of restlessness. It doesn't matter how the meditation is going in your opinion. Be absolutely content with it and it will go deeper. If you're dissatisfied with your progress, then you're only making it worse. So learn to be content with the present moment. Forget about jhānas, just be content to be here and now, in this moment. As that contentment deepens, it will actually give rise to jhānas.

Watch the silence and be content to be silent. If you're truly content, you don't need to say anything. Don't most inner conversations take the form of complaining, attempting to change things, or wanting to do something else? Or escaping into the world of thoughts and ideas? Thinking indicates a lack of contentment. If you're truly contented, then you're still and quiet. See if you can deepen your contentment, because it is the antidote for restlessness.

Even if you have an ache in the body and don't feel well, you can change your perception and regard that as something quite fascinating, even beautiful. See if you can be content with the ache or pain. See if you can allow it to be. A few times during my life as a monk I have been in quite severe pain. Instead of trying to escape, which is restlessness, I turned my mind around to completely accept the pain and be content with it. I have found that it is possible to be content with even severe pain. If you can do that, the worst part of the pain disappears along with the restlessness. There's no wanting to get rid of it. You're completely still with the feeling. The restlessness that accompanies pain is probably the worst part. Get rid of restlessness through contentment, and you can even have fun with pain.

Develop contentment with whatever you have—the present moment, the silence, the breath. Wherever you are, develop that contentment, and from that contentment—out of the very center of that contentment—you'll find your meditation will deepen. So if you ever see restlessness in your mind, remember the word *contentment*. Contentment looks for what is right, and it can keep you still. But restlessness will always make you a slave. There is a simile that the Buddha used (MN 39,14). Restlessness is like having a tyrannical master or mistress always telling you: "Go and get this," "Go and do that," "That's not right," "Clean that up better," and never giving you a moment of rest. That tyrant is the faultfinding mind. Subdue this tyrant through contentment.

After you've overcome the more general forms of restlessness, a very refined form often occurs at the deeper stages of meditation. I am referring to the time when you first see a nimitta. Because of restlessness, you just can't leave it alone. You mess around with it. You aren't content with the nimitta as it appears right now. You want something more. You get excited. Restlessness is one of the hindrances that can easily destroy the nimitta. You've arrived already. You don't have to do any more. Just leave it alone. Be content with it and it will develop by itself. That's what contentment is—complete nondoing, just sitting there watching a nimitta blossom into a jhāna. If it takes an hour, if it takes five minutes, if it never even happens, you're content. That's the way to get into jhānas. If the nimitta comes and goes, that's a sign of restlessness in the mind. If you can sustain attention effortlessly, restlessness has been overcome.

The Fifth Hindrance—Doubt

The last of the hindrances is called doubt *(vicikicchā)*. Doubt can be toward the teaching, about the teacher, or toward yourself.

Regarding doubt toward the teaching, you should have enough confidence by now to know that some beautiful results come from practicing meditation. You may have experienced many of them already. Allow those positive experiences to strengthen your confidence that meditation is worthwhile. Sitting in meditation, developing the mind in stillness, and especially developing the mind in jhānas are all tremendously worthwhile and will give you clarity, happiness, and understanding of the Buddha's teachings.

With regard to teachers, they are often like coaches of sports teams. Their job is to teach from their own experience and, more important, to inspire students with words and deeds. But before you put your confidence in a teacher, check them out. Observe their behavior and see for yourself if they are practicing what they preach. If they really know what they are talking about, then they will be ethical, restrained, and inspiring. Only if teachers lead by example—a good example, that is—should you place your confidence in them.

Self-doubt—which thinks, "I'm hopeless, I can't do this, I'm useless, I'm sure everyone else who practices meditation, except me, has got jhānas and is already enlightened"—is often overcome with the help of a teacher who inspires and encourages you. It's the teacher's job to say, "Yes, you can achieve all of these things. Many other people have achieved them, so why not you?" Give yourself encouragement. Have confidence that you can achieve whatever you want. In fact, if you have sufficient determination and confidence, then it's only a matter of time before you succeed. The only people who fail are those who give up.

Doubt can also be directed toward what you are experiencing now: "What is this? Is this jhāna? Is this present-moment awareness?" Such doubts are hindrances. They are inappropriate during meditation. Just make the mind as peaceful as you can. Let go and enjoy the peace and happiness. Afterward, you can review the meditation and ask, "What was that? That was really interesting. What was happening there?" That's when you'll find out whether or not it was a jhāna. If while meditating the thought "Is this jhāna?" arises, then it cannot be jhāna! Thoughts like that can't come up within these deep states of stillness. Only afterward, when you review those states, can you look back and say, "Ah, that was a jhāna."

If you get into any difficulty in your meditation, stop and ask yourself, "Which of the hindrances is this?" Find out what the cause is. Once you know the cause, then you can remember the solution and apply it. If it's sensory desire, just take the attention away from the five senses little by little and apply it to the breath or the mind. If it's ill will, do some loving-kindness. For sloth and torpor, remember "give value to awareness." If it's restlessness and remorse, remember "contentment, contentment, contentment" or practice forgiveness. And if it's doubt, be confident and be inspired by the teachings. Whenever you meditate, apply the solutions methodically. That way, the obstacles you experience won't create long-term barriers. They're things that you can recognize, overcome, and move beyond.

The Workshop of the Hindrances

Having discussed the five hindrances separately, I will now point out that they all emanate from a single source. They are generated by the control freak inside of you that refuses to let things go.

Meditators fail to overcome the hindrances because they look for them in the wrong place. It is crucial to success in meditation to understand that the hindrances are to be seen at work in the space between the knower and the known. The hindrances' source is the doer, their result is lack of progress, but their workshop is the space between the mind and its meditation object. Essentially, the five hindrances are a relationship problem.

Skillful meditators observing their breath also pay attention to *how* they watch their breath. If you see expectation between you and your breath, then you are watching the breath with desire, part of the first hindrance. If you notice aggression in the space in between, then you are watching the breath with the second hindrance, ill will. Or if you recognize fear in that space, maybe anxiety about losing awareness of the breath, then you are meditating with a combination of hindrances. For a time you may appear to be successful, able to keep the breath in mind for several minutes, but you will find that you are blocked from going deeper. You have been watching the wrong thing. Your main task in meditation is to notice these hindrances and knock them out. Thereby you earn each successive stage in meditation, rather than trying to steal the prize of each stage by an act of will.

In every stage of this meditation you cannot go wrong when you put peace or kindness in the space between you and whatever you are aware of. When a sexual fantasy is occurring, put peace in the space and the daydream will soon run out of fuel. Make peace not war with the dullness. Place kindness between the observer and your aching body. And agree to a ceasefire in the battle between you and your wandering mind. Stop controlling and start to let go.

Just as a house is built of thousands of bricks laid one by one, so the house of peace (i.e., jhāna) is built of thousands of moments of peace made one by one. When moment after moment you place peace or gentleness or kindness in the space between, then the sexual fantasies are no longer needed, pain fades away, dullness turns to brightness, restlessness runs out of gas, and jhāna simply happens.

In summary, notice that the five hindrances occur in the space between the observer and the observed. So place peace and loving-kindness in that space. Don't just be mindful, but develop what I call *unconditional mindfulness,* the awareness that never controls or even interferes with whatever it knows. Then all the hindrances will be undermined and soon fade.

The Simile of the Snake

Many meditators complain of a pet hindrance, a problem in meditation

that blocks them again and again. Recurring hindrances can be overcome using a method derived from the following simile of the snake.

In my early years as a forest monk in Thailand, I would often return
to my hut late at night barefoot because there weren't any sandals, and I
would use the light of the stars to guide me because there were no bat-
teries for my flashlight. Though the jungle paths were shared with many
snakes, I never got bitten. I knew they were there in great numbers and
that they were very dangerous, so I walked very carefully on the lookout
for them. If I saw a suspicious dark band on the path, though it could
have been a stick, I would leap over it or else go by another route. Thus
I successfully avoided the danger.

In the same way, on the path of meditation there are many dangerous
hindrances waiting to grab you and disable your progress. If you would
only remember that they are prowling and that they are dangerous, then
you would be on the lookout for them and never get caught.

Your pet hindrance is like the most abundant species of snake, one
that has caught you many times already. So at the beginning of each
sitting remind yourself of that pet hindrance. Alert yourself to its danger. Then you will be on the lookout for it, in the space between the
knower and the known, throughout your meditation sitting. Using this
method you'll rarely get caught.

The Nālāgiri Strategy

Some meditators claim to experience all the five hindrances at once and
in great force! At the time they think they might go crazy. To help such
meditators with their acute and intense attack of all hindrances, I teach
the Nālāgiri Strategy based on a well-known episode from the life of
the Buddha.

Enemies tried to kill the Buddha by releasing an intoxicated bull
elephant named Nālāgiri in the narrow street where the Buddha was
walking for alms. Those who saw the mad elephant charging shouted
warnings to the Buddha and his following of monks to quickly get out
of the way. All the monks fled except for the Buddha and his faithful
attendant Ven. Ānanda. Ānanda bravely moved in front of his master,

ready to protect his beloved teacher by sacrificing his own life. Gently the Buddha pushed Ven. Ānanda to the side and faced the immensely powerful charging elephant alone. The Buddha certainly possessed psychic powers, and I believe he could have grabbed the great elephant by the trunk, twirled him three times in the air above his head, and thrown him over the river Ganges hundreds of miles away! But that is not the way of a buddha. Instead he used loving-kindness/letting go. Perhaps the Buddha thought something like "Dear Nālāgiri, the door of my heart is open to you no matter what you ever do to me. You may swat me with your trunk or crush me under your feet, but I will give you no ill will. I will love you unconditionally." The Buddha gently placed peace in the space between him and the dangerous elephant. Such is the irresistible power of authentic loving-kindness/letting go that in a few seconds the elephant's rage had subsided, and Nālāgiri was meekly bowing before the Compassionate One, having his trunk gently stroked "There Nālāgiri, there…"

There are times in some meditators' practice when their mind is as crazy as an intoxicated bull elephant charging around smashing everything. In such situations please remember the Nālāgiri Strategy. Don't use force to subdue your raging bull elephant of a mind. Instead use loving-kindness/letting go: "Dear crazy mind of mine, the door of my heart is fully open to you no matter what you ever do to me. You may destroy or crush me, but I will give you no ill will. I love you, my mind, no matter what you ever do." Make peace with your crazy mind instead of fighting it. Such is the power of authentic loving-kindness/ letting go that in a surprisingly short time, the mind will be released from its rage and stand meekly before you as your soft mindfulness gently strokes it "There mind, there…"

When the Hindrances Are Knocked Out

The question often arises as to how long the hindrances remain knocked out. When they are overcome, does that mean forever or just during your meditation?

At first, you overcome them temporarily. When you emerge from a deep meditation, you'll notice that those hindrances have been gone for a long time. The mind is very sharp, very still. You can keep your attention on one thing for a long time, and you have no ill will at all. You can't get angry with someone even if they hit you over the head. You aren't interested in sensory pleasures like sex. This is the result of good meditation. But after a while, depending on the depth and the length of that meditation, the hindrances come back again. It's like they're in the boxing ring and they've just been knocked out. They are "unconscious" for a while. Eventually they come round again and start playing their tricks. But at least you know what it is like to have overcome those hindrances. The more you return to those deep stages—the more often the hindrances get knocked out—the more sickly and weak they become. Then it's the job of the enlightenment insights to overcome those weakened hindrances once and for all. This is the age-old path of Buddhism. You knock out the five hindrances through meditation practice in order to provide an opportunity for wisdom. Wisdom will then see through these weakened hindrances and destroy them. *When the hindrances have been completely abandoned, you're enlightened.* And if you are enlightened, there is no difficulty in getting into jhānas because the obstacles are gone. What was between you and jhānas has been completely eradicated.

The Quality
of Mindfulness

5

MINDFULNESS is one of the spiritual faculties *(indriya)* that create success in meditation. If it's not fully understood and fully practiced, you can waste a lot of time in your meditation.

Setting Up the Gatekeeper

Mindfulness is not just being aware, being awake, or being fully conscious of what's occurring around you. Mindfulness also guides the awareness to specific areas, remembers the instructions, and initiates a response. In a simile the Buddha used, mindfulness is like a person who guards a door or gate (AN VII,63).

Imagine that you are a wealthy person with a gatekeeper guarding your mansion. One evening, before going to the temple to practice meditation, you tell the gatekeeper to be mindful of burglars. When you return home, your loving-kindness suddenly vanishes when you find your house has been burgled. "Didn't I tell you to be mindful!" you scream at the gatekeeper. "But I was mindful," pleads the gatekeeper. "I gave attention to the burglars as they broke in, and I was clearly attentive as they walked out with your plasma-screen TV and state-of-the-art sound system. I mindfully watched them go in several times, and my mind did not wander as I observed them take all your antique furniture and priceless jewelry."

Would you be happy with such an explanation of mindfulness? A wise gatekeeper knows that mindfulness is more than bare attention. A wise gatekeeper has to remember the instructions and perform them with diligence. If he sees a thief trying to break in, then he must stop the burglar or else call in the police.

In the same way, a wise meditator must do more than just give bare attention to whatever comes into and goes out of the mind. The wise meditator must remember the instructions and act on them with diligence. For instance, the Buddha gave an instruction about "right effort," the sixth factor of the noble eightfold path. When wise meditators practicing mindfulness observe an unwholesome state trying to break in, they try to stop the defilement. And if the unwholesome state does slip in, they try to evict it. Unwholesome states such as sexual desire or anger are like burglars or sweet-talking con artists, who will rob you of your peace, wisdom, and happiness. There are, then, these two aspects of mindfulness: awareness and remembering the instructions.

In the Buddhist suttas, the same Pāli word *sati* is used for both awareness and memory. A person who has good mindfulness is also a person who has a good memory. If we pay full attention to what we are doing, this awareness creates an imprint in our mind. It becomes easy to remember. For example, suppose you come very close to having a serious car accident. Because of the danger, your mindfulness suddenly becomes extremely sharp. And because of the intensity of that mindfulness, you remember the event very clearly. When you go to sleep that night you might not be able to forget it. This shows the connection between awareness and memory. The more you are paying attention to what you're doing, the better you remember it. Again, these two things go together, awareness and memory.

If we have gatekeepers who have developed awareness, they will pay attention to the instructions that they are given. If they give full attention to the instructions, they will be able to remember them and act on them diligently. So we should give ourselves clear instructions paying full attention; then we will remember what we are supposed to be doing. The teacher's job is also to give clear instructions to help us in guiding the mind. When the training in meditation is methodical and each stage is well defined, then our gatekeepers have the clarity they need.

Instructing the Gatekeeper

At the beginning of the meditation, please remember that there's a gate-keeper inside—something that can be aware of what's happening and remember instructions. Tell that gatekeeper something like "Now is the time to be aware of the present moment." Tell the gatekeeper this three times. If you repeat something, you're more likely to remember it. Maybe when you were at school and couldn't spell a word, you had to write it out a hundred times. You never forget it after that, because when you repeat something it takes more effort, and mindful-ness becomes stronger. What's easy to do doesn't require much mind-fulness. So make it difficult for yourself by repeating instructions: "I will be aware of the present moment. I will be aware of the present moment. I will be aware of the present moment."

With the gatekeeper, like any other servant or worker, you don't have to keep giving the same instruction every second or two. Just give that instruction to the gatekeeper three times at the beginning, then let the gatekeeper get on with the task. Trust the gatekeeper to know its job.

Instruct your gatekeeper as you would instruct a taxi driver. You just say clearly where you want to go, then you can sit back, relax, and enjoy the ride. You trust that the driver knows how to get there. But imagine what would happen if you kept telling the driver every few seconds, "Go slower...go faster...turn left here...now go into third gear...look in your mirror...keep to the right." After driving a few hundred yards the taxi driver would throw you out. No wonder then, when meditators keep giving instructions to their gatekeeper every few seconds, their minds rebel and refuse to cooperate.

Let the mind get on with the job of being in the present moment. Don't keep interfering with it. Give the mind clear instructions and then let go and watch. If you establish mindfulness in this way, you will find that your mind will do what it's told. It will still make mistakes now and again, but the instructions that you've given will ensure that as soon as it starts to wander off into the past or the future, mindfulness will remember to return to the present moment. For you, the onlooker, it's something that happens automatically. You just watch the gatekeeper do the work without giving any more instructions. This is knowing the mind and working with its nature.

I encourage you to play games with the mind to learn its capabilities. I was told on my first meditation retreat that there is no need to set the alarm for getting up in the morning. The teacher told us instead to say to ourselves before going to bed, "I'm going to get up at five minutes to five." It worked every morning. I didn't need to keep looking at my clock to check if it was five to five yet, and when I woke up and looked at my clock it was five minutes to five, give or take a minute or two. It's amazing how the mind works. I don't know how it remembered, but it did. So try programming your mind: "Now is the time to watch the present moment. Be in the present moment. Be in the present moment." That's all you need to do. Then you can let the mind do the work.

It's also important to clearly instruct the gatekeeper who is allowed in and who is not. It's not enough just to have the guest list. If the gatekeeper hasn't got a list of who's forbidden, it could easily make mistakes.

The Gatekeeper at Stage One

In the first of these meditation stages, present-moment awareness, the guest list—who's allowed in—is anything happening now. It can be the sound of a bird. It can be the sound of a truck in the distance. It can be the wind. It can be someone coughing or banging the door. It doesn't matter. If it is something happening now, then it is a guest of present-moment awareness. It can be the breath. It can be a nimitta. It can be a jhāna. That's all part of the present moment. So be very clear on who is allowed in, and welcome your guests.

You should also be very clear on what's not allowed in. Who are the gatecrashers to present-moment awareness? Those enemies are any thought, any perception, any view of the past or the future. That is, any looking back or any looking forward. It's important to know those gatecrashers and to articulate them clearly when you instruct your gatekeeper. Say to yourself three times at the start of your meditation, "I'll be aware of the present moment, and I'll not go off into the past or the future." Instructing the gatekeeper about the dangers as well as the goals, helps mindfulness do its task. When a gatecrasher appears, mindfulness knows, "This is not what I'm supposed to be doing." Mindfulness then discards that thought or perception of the past or the future.

The Gatekeeper at Stage Two

In the second stage of silent present-moment awareness, the goal is silence, and the gatecrasher is inner speech. So you tell the mind very clearly at the beginning of that stage: "I'll be silently aware in the present moment and will discard all inner speech." Repeat this two more times. That way you establish mindfulness. You give your meditation the possibility of success because you've instructed your gatekeeper clearly.

The Gatekeeper at Stage Three

In the third stage, silent present-moment awareness of the breath, the only invited guest is the breath in the present moment. Who are the gatecrashers? They are everything other than the breath, which includes sounds outside, feelings in the body, or thoughts about lunch or dinner or whatever. Everything other than the breath is a gatecrasher. So you should tell yourself three times: "I will be aware of the breath in the present moment and discard all other perceptions and thoughts." Once again, having told the mind very clearly both what it is supposed to do and not do, you can let the mind get on with its work. You just look on. When a thought other than the breath comes up, such as hearing the sound of a lawnmower outside, the mind knows immediately that it's not supposed to be doing this and it turns away automatically. This is training the mind in mindfulness. It's fascinating to watch the mind when it is well trained. When it has been given clear instructions, it remembers what to do, it knows what it's doing, and the meditation becomes smooth and appears effortless.

The meditation, however, is not completely effortless. You're putting in some effort but at the right time, when it's going to be effective. It's like growing a tree. There are times when you put effort in and times when you let things be. You plant the seed, you water it, and you fertilize it. But most of the time, when you're growing a tree, your job is just to guard it, to make sure that nothing interferes with the process. The seed has its instructions; it just needs the chance. In the same way, don't keep interfering with the mind. Don't keep prodding it and pushing it and telling it to do things, because otherwise after a while it will just rebel. "Leave me alone. Look, I'm trying to do my job. Get out of the way," says the mind. And if you don't leave the mind alone quickly, your meditation is shot!

The Gatekeeper at Stage Four

In the fourth stage of the meditation—full sustained attention on the breath—the gatekeeper is told to be aware of the whole breath in every moment and not allow other things to intrude on this smooth, continuous awareness: "I shall be aware of the whole breath continually, and disregard anything other than the breath." By instructing the gatekeeper very carefully and clearly, you give mindfulness a chance to succeed. You only have to tell yourself the message three times at the beginning of the stage and just see what happens.

If you give yourself these instructions and after one or two minutes you find you're drifting off focus, there are two possible reasons. Either you didn't instruct yourself carefully enough or you have very weak mindfulness. If you have weak mindfulness, then every three or four minutes you should repeat the instructions. There's no need to repeat the instructions every ten or fifteen seconds. Repeating the instructions too often causes a disturbance in meditation, which never gives meditation a chance to succeed and instead gives rise to restlessness and despair.

If you give yourself the instructions very carefully, you'll remember them. Stage by stage, your mindfulness will deepen. You will notice that mindfulness begins with a large territory in which to roam—the present moment. Then the range allowed to mindfulness is gradually reduced. Mindfulness focuses on what is silent in the present moment, discarding all that belongs to inner speech. Then instead of just silence in the present moment, everything is discarded other than the silent awareness of the breath in the present moment. Then everything is discarded other than the full awareness of the breath, from the very beginning of the in-breath to the end of the in-breath, from the very beginning of the out-breath to the end of the out-breath. In each successive stage mindfulness reduces its spread to gain more power.

Samādhi—Attentive Stillness

In stage three, awareness of the breath, you just have to notice part of each in-breath and part of each out-breath. Once you've noticed part of the in-breath, then the mind can go wandering off somewhere else, but it has to be "home" again in time to catch the next out-breath. Once it's seen the breath going out, then it can go off and observe other things, until it has to come home again to catch the breath going in. Mindfulness still has other places where it can go. It is tied to the breath, but on a long leash. But in stage four, full awareness of the breath, you need to completely lock the awareness into the breathing and go nowhere else. This fourth stage is so important in meditation because here you fully grab hold of your meditation object for the first time. Mindfulness is confined to one small area of existence—your momentary breath. You are focusing your awareness instead of allowing it to go all over the place. When mindfulness is focused it becomes strong. It's like using a magnifying glass to start a fire—you're concentrating all the energy on one thing. This attentive stillness that is able to sustain awareness on one thing is called *samādhi*. No need to call it "concentration," because concentration misses so much of what is really important in the meaning of samādhi.

Samādhi is the attentive stillness that is able to sustain attention on one thing, and it is not uncommon. Take, for example, a surgeon performing an operation. Surgeons tell me that sometimes they spend many hours on one operation. They're on their feet throughout, but they never feel tired because they have to sustain their attention on the end of the scalpel. Just one little mistake, one lapse of attentive stillness, and their patient can die. Surgeons performing operations develop a type of samādhi. They don't feel any pain in their legs, because all their attention is on the end of the knife. Surgeons attain this level of samādhi because they have to. There's only one thing in the world that they're concerned with—just this part of the operation that is happening now. This example tells us an important message about samādhi: *if it's really important, you can do it.*

Arousing Energy

Another factor needed for mindfulness is energy. You need energy at each stage, and that energy is aroused by putting everything you have into what you're doing. Don't keep anything back for the next moment. One of the mistakes that people make—especially with mental energy—is thinking, "If I put a lot of energy into this moment, I'll have nothing left for the next moment." It doesn't work that way with the mind. The more energy you put into this moment, the more you have for the next.

There is a limitless store of mental energy, and if you put a lot of energy into what you are doing right now, you'll find that in the next moment, the next five minutes, or the next hour you're really awake and alert. That's why Ajahn Chah, my teacher, used to say that whatever you're doing, put all your mind into it. Then you will build up energy. If, however, you think, "Oh, I don't really need to put energy into this moment," then you will become dull and won't enjoy anything in life.

When eating, put energy into every mindful mouthful. See how much you can notice. Then you'll enjoy it more! The gatecrasher to mindfulness when you are eating is thinking about something else. Sometimes you don't even know what you are putting into your mouth. No wonder so many people suffer from indigestion! Whatever it is that you are doing, know what you are doing, and energy will be aroused.

Turning Up the Lights

As you build up mindfulness and it gets sharper, you will realize that you are emerging from a world that has been very dim. As you get more and more mindful, it's as if someone has turned on the lights in the room, or the sun has come out, illuminating the surroundings. You see so much more of what's around you. It's like shining a spotlight on reality, and you begin to see the subtle beauty of rich colors, delightful shapes, and deep textures. It all appears very beautiful and wonderful. When mindfulness becomes powerful, it generates not only insight but also bliss.

When you have developed powerful mindfulness, it's like going out into a beautiful garden in the brilliant sunshine. It's energizing and inspiring. Possessing strong mindfulness, such brightness of mind, if you then focus it on a small part of the world, then you will see so deeply into its nature. The experience of bright and focused awareness is wonderful and amazing! You see much more beauty and truth than you ever imagined.

So developing mindfulness is like turning up the lights of the mind. When you sustain mindfulness on one thing instead of letting it wander all over the place, mindfulness builds up its own energy. You begin to see into things very deeply and wonderfully.

Building Up the Muscles of Insight

Empowering mindfulness builds up the muscles of insight. Just take any object such as a leaf on a bush and sustain your attention on that one leaf. Let mindfulness become still until you see not just a green leaf but a whole world. Then you'll understand the power of mindfulness. When you can sustain mindfulness on one thing, you will know how it illuminates and reveals the beauty in that object. It becomes fascinating just how much you can see, how much detail and color and texture there is in a tiny leaf! This is where mindfulness playfully engages with its object, seeing ever new insights into its nature. But if you start wondering about what you're going to have for dinner, you stop seeing deeply into the leaf. Or if you start getting dull, or if you start worrying, "Are people looking at me? Do they think I'm a bit strange?"—then the spell of sustained attention will break. If you can sustain your attention on one thing, however, you'll be amazed by what you see.

If you develop attentive stillness, the ability to sustain mindfulness on one thing for long periods of time, then you will gain the ability to delve into something with insight and to see deeply into its nature. If you want to discover for yourself the deep truths of existence, not taking it on faith from the books or from teachers, then this is how you find out. This is how to achieve enlightenment experiences. You develop powerful mindfulness and point it at some interesting and rich source of wisdom—especially at the mind. If you can sustain attention on your mind and dive into it, you will find a treasure chest of priceless jewels that we call deep insight.

To summarize so far, this is the way of mindfulness: what it actually is, how to develop it and, in particular, how to set up mindfulness at every stage of your meditation. Give your gatekeeper clear instructions so that mindfulness knows what to do. Then sit back and watch this mind do its job. That's all you need to do.

The Different Levels of Mindfulness Revisited

One of the marvelous things about meditation is that as you develop your mindfulness, you discover it has different levels. You realize that your normal mindfulness is too dull and useless for wisdom; it has very little sharpness or power at all. When you make progress in meditation, your mindfulness gets sharper and more powerful. By this I mean that you can sustain attention on very fine areas, and the mindfulness is very bright. And as you deepen the meditation, mindfulness becomes ever more powerful, agile, and sharp.

Sometimes it happens that meditators lose the object of awareness. If the breath is your object, you lose the breath. What has happened is that the breath has become fine and subtle, but the mindfulness is still too coarse. It hasn't been able to keep up with the development of the breath. When that happens, you should go back to the previous stage. This can occur at any time, but especially within full sustained attention on the breath at stage four.

Sometimes the breath disappears and a nimitta can come up, but you can't sustain that nimitta. This is because the quality of mindfulness necessary to sustain a nimitta must be very refined, and you haven't yet built up that level of power. So you must return to the stage before the nimitta comes up. Go back to full awareness of the beautiful breath, which is a coarser object than the nimitta, and let mindfulness develop its strength on that. When your mindfulness is fully developed at the fifth stage, it has the power to handle the more refined nimitta. You will find as mindfulness becomes sharper and more powerful, it can sustain attention even on the most subtle of objects. But first you have to learn how to sustain attention on the coarser meditation objects. At each of these successive stages the mindfulness has a higher quality to it, far more agile and sharp than at the previous stage. The mindfulness required to hold a nimitta is like the skill required of a surgeon operating on the brain, while the mindfulness required to hold the breath at stage three is like the skill required for peeling potatoes. You need quite a different refinement at the subtle level. If you move straight from peeling potatoes into being a brain surgeon, you're going to make a mess. The same applies if you move too quickly from the breath to the nimitta. You're going to lose it.

With development, you can experience immovable mindfulness, the mindfulness that is on one thing entirely—very clear, very sharp. The Buddha said this reaches its peak in the fourth jhāna. That's the pinnacle of mindfulness, where you experience complete equanimity. You're just fully aware and unmoving. That's as powerful as mindfulness can get. Once you have experienced that level of mindfulness, then you will know for yourself how ridiculous it is to think you can become enlightened without jhāna. Without such powerful mindfulness, you will be unable to achieve powerful insights. So you begin to realize from your own experience what mindfulness can be and the level of mindfulness you need to become enlightened.

As you see, mindfulness in daily life is one thing and mindfulness in deep meditation something else. Mindfulness has different degrees of power, subtlety, and penetration. Just as there are many types of knives—blunt ones and sharp ones, potato peelers and scalpels—so it is with mindfulness.

So develop a sharp and powerful mindfulness that you can use to dig deeply into the nature of your mind and uncover the beautiful treasures of impermanence *(anicca),* suffering *(dukkha),* and no-self *(anattā).* When

I say that these are beautiful treasures, some people object: How can suffering be a treasure? How can impermanence and no-self be treasures? Such people want something seemingly marvelous and uplifting like beauty, transcendence, cosmic consciousness, or the essence of all being. But that's why they can't find the real treasures. They don't know what they're looking for.

Using Variety to Freshen Up Our Meditation 6

I N THIS CHAPTER I will present three different types of meditation: loving-kindness, letting be, and walking meditation. In these three meditations the method is mostly the same as in breath meditation, the main difference being where you focus your attention. You will find these methods helpful because they will add variety to your meditation practice. If you keep plugging away at only one type of meditation, you might become so bored that you drift off into dullness or you might lose all interest and give up altogether. You need happiness in your meditation practice, not only as the glue that fixes mindfulness onto its object, but also as the entertainment factor that will keep you returning to meditate. The motto of physical fitness might be "no pain—no gain," but the motto of meditation is "no joy—no mindfulness."

Loving-Kindness Meditation

The Buddha's word for loving-kindness is *mettā*. It refers to an emotion, to that feeling of goodwill that can sustain thoughts wishing happiness for another, and that is willing to forgive any fault. My favorite expression of mettā is encompassed by the words "the door of my heart is fully open to you, forever, whoever you are and whatever you have done." Mettā is love without a self, arising from inspiration, expecting nothing back in return, and without any conditions. The Buddha compared mettā to a mother's love for her child (Sn 149). A mother might not always like her child or agree with everything it does, but she will always care for her child and wish it only happiness. Such an openhearted, non-discriminating, and liberating kindness is mettā.

In mettā meditation you focus your attention on the feeling of loving-kindness, developing that delightful emotion until it fills the whole mind. The way this is achieved can be compared to the way you light a campfire. You start with paper or anything else that is easy to light. Then you add kindling, small twigs, or strips of wood. When the kindling is on fire you add thicker pieces of wood, and after a time the thick logs. Once the fire is roaring and very hot, you can even put on wet and sappy logs and they are soon alight.

Mettā can accurately be compared with a warm and radiant fire burning in your heart. You cannot expect to light the fire of loving-kindness by starting with a difficult object, no more than you can expect to light a campfire by striking a match under a thick log. So do not begin mettā meditation by spreading mettā to yourself or to an enemy. Instead begin by spreading loving-kindness to something that is easy to ignite with loving-kindness.

I prepare myself for mettā meditation by grounding my mindfulness in the present moment, establishing stage one of the meditation method described in chapter 1. Then I initiate mettā meditation by imagining a little kitten. I like cats, especially kittens, so my imaginary kitten is to loving-kindness as gas is to a flame. I only need to think of my little kitten and my heart lights up with mettā. I continue to visualize my imaginary friend, picturing it as abandoned, hungry, and very afraid. In its short span of life it has only known rejection, violence, and loneliness. I imagine its bones sticking out from its emaciated body, its fur soiled with grime and some blood, and its body rigid with terror. I consider that if I don't care for this vulnerable little being then no one will, and it will die such a horrible, lonely, terrified death. I feel that kitten's pain fully, in all its forms, and my heart opens up releasing a flood of compassion. I will care for that little kitten. I will protect it and feed it. I imagine myself looking deeply into its anxious eyes, trying to melt its apprehension with the mettā flowing through my own eyes. I reach out to it slowly, reassuringly, never losing eye contact. Gently, I pick up that little kitten and bring it to my chest. I remove the kitten's cold with the warmth from my own body, I take away its fear with the softness of my embrace, and I feel the kitten's trust grow. I speak to the kitten on my chest: "Little being, never feel alone again. Never feel so afraid. I will always look after you, be your protector and friend. I love you, little kitten. Wherever you go, whatever you do, my heart will always welcome you. I give you my limitless loving-kindness always." I feel my kitten become warm, relax, and finally purr.

This is but an outline of how I begin my meditation on mettā. I usually take much more time. I use my imagination and inner commentary (inner speech) to paint a picture in my mind, to create a scenario where the first flames of mettā can arise. At the end of the mental exercise, my eyes still closed, I focus the attention on the region around my heart and feel the first warm glow of the emotion of loving-kindness.

My kitten is like the paper that you use to start the campfire. You may not like kittens, so choose something else, a puppy or a baby perhaps. Whatever you choose as your first object of mettā, make it an imaginary being and not a real one. In your mind you can make a kitten or a puppy or a baby into anything you like. You have more freedom to generate mettā when you make use of a fantasy creature rather than one from the real world. My imaginary kitten purrs at the right time and never poops in my lap. Having chosen your first object, use your powers of imagination to create a story around that being that arouses your loving-kindness. With practice this innovative method becomes one of the most successful and enjoyable ways to begin mettā meditation.

Some years ago a female student complained to me that this method did not work for her. She regarded small animals, especially mischievous kittens, as little pests, nor did she like crying-and-wailing nappy-soiling babies. She had a severe case of what I now call "mettā-block." She went on to tell me that in her apartment in Sydney she had been growing some flowers in pots. So I suggested that she choose one of her plants as her first object of mettā. She imagined a seedling so delicate and tender. It was so fragile that it needed all her care, love, and protection to survive. She directed all her motherly instincts to that vulnerable little potted plant, nurturing and feeding her friend until it burst from its bud to repay her kindness with a beautiful, fragrant flower. She really took to that method. That was the first time mettā meditation worked for her. During the retreat when this happened, she said it was the only session when she wasn't waiting for me to ring the bell.

After the first flames of mettā have been established in this way, let go of your imaginary creature and put in its place a real person, someone very close to you emotionally such as your partner, a well-loved relation, or even your very best friend. It must be someone for whom it is easy to generate and sustain loving-kindness. In the metaphor of the campfire, they will be the thin pieces of wood called kindling. Once again use your inner speech to paint a picture around them in your mind. They too need your friendship and love. They are also emotionally vulnerable, subject to the disappointments and frustrations of life. Using you inner commentary say: "Dearest friend, I sincerely wish you happiness. May your body be free from pain and your mind find contentment. I give you my love with no conditions. I'll always be there for you. You will always have a place in my heart. I truly care for you"—or similar words of your own design. Use whatever phrases arouse the warm glow of mettā in your heart. Stay with this person. Imagine they are right before you until the mettā grows bright and constant around them. Now briefly place your attention on your body near your heart and feel the physical sensation associated with mettā. You will find it feels delightful.

Let go of the image of that person and substitute that of another close acquaintance, creating the feeling of mettā around them by using your inner speech in the same way: "May you live in happiness…" Imagine them right before you until the mettā glows bright and constant around them.

Next substitute an entire group of people, perhaps all the people who live in your house. Develop the caring glow of mettā around them in the same way: "May you be well and happy…" In the simile of the campfire, you are now putting on the logs.

See if you can imagine mettā to be a golden radiance emanating from a beautiful white lotus flower in the middle of your heart. Allow that radiance of loving-kindness to expand in all directions, embracing more and more living beings until it becomes boundless, filling up all that you can imagine. "May all living beings, near or far, great or small, be happy and at peace…" Bathe the whole universe in the warmth of the golden light of loving-kindness. Stay there for a while.

In the simile of the campfire, the fire is now roaring and very hot and can now burn the wet and sappy logs. Think about your enemy. Visualize someone who has hurt you badly. You will be astonished that your mettā is now strong enough for you to forgive them. You are now able to share the healing golden glow of loving-kindness with them as well: "Friend, whatever you have done to me, revenge will not help either of us, so instead I wish you well. I sincerely wish you freedom from the pain of the past and joy in all your future. May the beauty of this unconditional loving-kindness reach you as well, bringing you happiness and contentment." When the fire of mettā burns strong, nothing can withstand it. Next, there is one final "wet and sappy stick" to be tossed into the fire of mettā. Most meditators find that the hardest person to give loving-kindness to…is themselves.

Imagine that you are looking at yourself in a mirror. Say with your inner speech and with total sincerity: "I wish myself well. I now give myself the gift of happiness. Too long the door of my heart has been closed to me; now I open it. No matter what I have done, or will ever do, the door to my own love and respect is always open to me. I forgive myself unreservedly. Come home. I now give myself the love that does not judge. I care for this vulnerable being called 'me.' I embrace all of me with the loving-kindness of mettā." Invent your own words here to let the warmth of loving-kindness sink deep inside of you, to the part that is most frightened. Let it melt all resistance until you are at one with mettā, unlimited loving-kindness, like a mother's care for her child.

Before you end the mettā meditation, pause for a minute or two and reflect on how you feel inside. Notice the effect that this meditation has had on you. Mettā meditation can produce heavenly bliss.

To bring the meditation to an elegant conclusion, once more imagine mettā as a golden glow radiating from the beautiful white lotus located in your heart. Visualize the golden radiance being drawn back into the lotus, leaving the warmth outside. When the golden glow becomes like a condensed ball of incandescent energy in the center of the white lotus, imagine the petals closing around the ball of mettā, guarding the seed of loving-kindness within your heart, ready to be released again in your next mettā meditation. Open your eyes and get up slowly.

A Softening of the Mind

Mettā meditation softens the mind and turns it toward care, goodwill, and acceptance. You become more selfless, less concerned with your own needs and more willing to peacefully interact with others. The emotion that is mettā feels delightful and pure. As you develop it repeatedly, it soon remains constant in your heart. You become a compassionate person, and your kindness is a source of joy to all beings and to yourself.

Mettā enables you to embrace another being just as they are. Most people find this impossible because of their faultfinding mind. They only see part of the whole, the part that is flawed, and refuse to accept it. Loving-kindness, on the other hand, embraces the wholeness of something and accepts it as it is. Through the practice of mettā meditation, you find yourself becoming less conscious of the faults in yourself and other beings, and more able to embrace them just the way they are. This ability to see the beauty in an object and ignore its flaws is a powerful aid to all types of meditation. To sustain your attention in the present moment, for example, you must accept the way things are now, embracing this moment and not being critical. When you persist in finding faults in the present moment, you will find you cannot remain there.

It is possible to combine mettā meditation with breath meditation. When you begin stage three, awareness of the breath, you observe your breath with loving-kindness. You think something like "breath, the door of my heart is open to you no matter how you feel, no matter what you do." You will soon be looking at your breathing with compassion, embracing it as it is instead of finding fault. By adding mettā to the process of awareness, you have no expectations, since the breath seems more than good enough. Because of loving-kindness, you soon feel this attractive warmth toward the breath that brings joy to every in-breath and out-breath. It becomes so nice to watch your breath that in a very short time you have reached stage five, the beautiful breath.

Taking Mettā into Jhāna

Jhānas are emotional summits and not intellectual heights. You cannot think your way into a jhāna, you can only feel your way in. To succeed you require familiarity with your emotional world, enough to trust in it silently without any controlling. Perhaps this is why female meditators seem to enter jhāna more easily than males. Mettā meditation trains everyone to become more at ease with the power of emotions. Sometimes you may cry during mettā meditation, even weep uncontrollably. If so, let it come. On the path to nibbāna we all have to learn to embrace the intensity of the purest emotions, and the jhānas are the purest of all. Therefore mettā meditation makes jhāna more accessible.

You can even take mettā meditation directly into jhāna. When you have reached the stage described above where you are radiating this limitless golden glow of loving-kindness throughout the whole universe, drenching every sentient being with the immense power of your boundless love, then take the next step. Forget about all beings and ignore where the power is coming from. Focus your attention instead on the experience of mettā in itself. This step often happens automatically with no decision coming from you. The meditation object is being simplified, freed from the perception of separate beings. All that remains in your mind is what I call disembodied mettā, similar to the disembodied grin of the Cheshire Cat in the simile in chapter 2. You experience this as a blissful sphere of gorgeous golden light in your mind's eye. It is a nimitta. It's the mettā nimitta.

A nimitta that is generated through mettā meditation is always incredibly beautiful, only sometimes it isn't so stable. Excitement is the usual problem. However, its nature is so alluring that you cannot resist hanging out with such intense bliss. Thus, in a short time the brilliant golden mettā nimitta becomes still and you fall into jhāna. This is how mettā meditation takes you into jhāna.

Spreading Mettā after Deep Samādhi

Many years ago in my monastery in Perth, we were chanting the Buddha's verses for spreading loving-kindness. The chant lasts only five minutes. I had been meditating deeply beforehand, and when we began chanting my mind engaged with mettā so completely that I was unable to continue with the chanting. Boundless mettā was pouring out of me in a torrent in all directions, and I became happily immersed there. I never did complete those verses. My mind had been made so soft and pliant by my earlier meditations that the Buddha's original words on how to spread loving-kindness triggered an irrepressible outpouring of mettā.

Experiences such as this taught me that you should first train your mind in samādhi, attentive stillness, and then you can spread loving-kindness so powerfully. After establishing samādhi you can *zap* anyone anywhere with superpower mettā! At the end of the meditation retreats that I lead, I invite my students to try this out. Many of my students have powerful minds at the conclusion of a retreat. I lead them in a mettā meditation, and when I feel their power is strong enough, I invite them to *zap* an absent friend with superpower mettā. I prefer them to choose someone a long distance from the retreat center. Then I look at the clock and note the time. At the end of the mettā session I inform my students of that time and suggest that they later contact that friend and inquire what they were doing then or how they were feeling. Many of my students call me on the phone in the following days to excitedly tell me: "It worked!" When you send loving-kindness from a mind empowered by samādhi, it will be received. Try it out for yourself.

Letting Be

Sometimes instead of taking loving-kindness or the breath as my object, I look at my mind and realize the best thing it needs at the moment is just to let things be. Basically, letting-be meditation is simply this second stage of breath meditation, just silent awareness of the present moment. It has to be silent, because to really let things be means you give no orders and have no complaints; you've got nothing to talk about. Letting be happens in the present moment. You're aware of things as they appear right now, and you allow them to come in or stay or go, whenever they want. Letting-be meditation is like sitting in a room, and whoever comes in the door, you let in. They can stay as long as they like. Even if they are terrible demons, you allow them to come in and sit down. You are not at all fazed. If the Buddha himself enters in all his glory, you just sit here just the same, completely equanimous. "Come in if you want." "You can go whenever." Whatever comes into your mind, the beautiful or the gross, you stand back and let it be, with no reactions at all—quietly observing and practicing silent awareness in the present moment. This is letting-be meditation.

The Garden Simile

Many Americans have gardens in their homes where they often spend many hours working. But a garden is to be enjoyed, not just to be worked in. So I advise my students that they should frequently go sit in their own garden and enjoy its great beauty.

The least adept of my students believe that they must mow the grass, prune the bushes, water the flower bed, rake the leaves, and get the garden perfect before they can sit down to enjoy it. Of course, the garden never is perfect, no matter how hard they work. So they never get to rest.

Mediocre students, on the other hand, refrain from work. Instead they sit in their garden and begin to think. "The grass needs mowing and the bushes should be pruned. The flowers are looking dry and the leaves really need raking, and a native bush would look better over there," and so on. They spend their time pondering how to make their garden perfect rather than simply enjoying it. They too find no peace.

The third type of student is the wise meditator. They have done a lot of work in their garden, but now is their time for rest. They say, "The lawn could be mown, the bushes could be pruned, the flowers could be watered and the leaves raked—but not now! The garden is good enough as it is." And they can rest a while, not feeling guilty about unfinished business.

Letting-be meditation is just the same. Don't try to make everything perfect or tie up all those loose ends before you let things be. Life is never perfect and duties are never finished. Letting be is having the courage to sit quietly and rest the mind in the midst of imperfection.

Letting Be Can Become Quite Powerful

Letting-be meditation can become quite powerful. If your breath meditation or mettā meditation or any other type of meditation isn't working, very often it's because the foundation is incorrect. So just do the letting-be meditation. You can "sit out in the garden" and just let things be. Whatever is happening, that's OK. Whatever you're experiencing is fine—no preference, no choice, no good or bad, no argument, and no commentary. Just let things be. You can have a little bit of a inner speech, but only a commentary about "letting be." Just be with what is. Just be with thoughts concerned with the meditation subject, but not about anything else. That way the meditation comes close to complete silent awareness of the present moment.

If I'm in pain, if I have a headache, stomachache, or some other ache, or if the mosquitoes are biting, I say, "Just let it be." I don't argue with it, don't get upset about it. I just watch the feelings in my body as the mosquito pushes its nose into my flesh and itching sensations follow. "Just let things be." If you're lying in bed at night and you can't go to sleep: "Let it be." Or if there's a pain that won't go away: "Just let it be." Just be with it. Don't try running away. If demons have come into your room, you're not going to push them out, but you're not going to invite them to stay either. You're just going to let them be. Letting be is the practice of equanimity.

Walking Meditation

Walking meditation is wonderful, especially in the early morning. Often when you get up early in the morning, in particular when you're not used to getting up so early, you're quite tired and the mind isn't bright. One of the advantages of walking meditation is that you can't nod off while you're walking. So if you're tired, walking meditation is very good to do. It brings up some energy, and also you can get very peaceful.

Walking meditation was both praised and practiced by the Buddha. If you read the *suttas* (teachings in the Pāli canon), you find that the Buddha would usually do walking meditation in the early morning. He wouldn't be sitting; he'd be walking.

Many monks and nuns have become enlightened on the walking meditation path. It's a very effective way of developing both calm and insight (but not to the extent of jhāna). For some monks that I know in Thailand, their main practice is walking meditation. They do very little sitting. They do a lot of walking, and many get tremendously powerful insights while they're walking.

Another benefit of walking meditation is that it is especially suitable for those who have physical discomfort when sitting for long periods. If you find it difficult to sit in meditation because of pains in the body, walking meditation can be a very effective alternative.

Don't consider walking meditation as a "second-class" meditation. If you want to spend most of your meditation time this way, please do so. But do it well and do it carefully. See if you can develop the happiness born of serenity as you're walking back and forth.

Setting Up Walking Meditation

Choose a clear, straight path between twenty to thirty paces long. This can be a corridor in a house, a path in the garden, or just a track on the grass. Use whatever is available, even if it's a bit less than twenty paces long. If it's comfortable to do so, walk without shoes, enjoying the contact of your bare feet on the ground.

Stand at one end of your path. Compose the mind. Relax the body and begin walking. Walk back and forth at a pace that seems natural to you. While you are walking, clasp your hands comfortably in front of you, and rest your gaze on the ground about two meters ahead. Be careful not to look around. If you're doing walking meditation, it's a waste of time to look here and there, because that would be distracting.

The Stages of Meditation Apply Here Too

The first four stages of meditation described in the first two chapters apply here as well. But in walking meditation attention eventually comes to rest on the feet rather than the breath.

At first, aim to develop present-moment awareness, as in stage one. Use the techniques described there to reach the state of just walking, easily, in the here and now. When you feel that you have settled into the present moment, where thoughts concerning the past and future are absent from the mind, then aim to develop silent walking in the present moment. Just as described earlier in stage two, gradually let go of all thinking. Walk without any inner speech. Make use of some of the techniques described in chapter 1 to reach this stage of silent walking.

Once the inner commentary has slowed to a bare trickle of inner speech, deliberately focus your attention on the feeling of movement in the feet and lower legs. Do so to the extent that you clearly notice every step on the path. Know every left step, know every right step—one after the other without missing any. Know every step as you turn around at the end of the path. The famous Chinese saying that the "journey of one thousand miles begins with a single step" is helpful here. Such a journey is in fact only one step long—the step that you are walking now. So just be silently aware of this "one step," and let everything else go. When you have completed ten return trips up and down the path without missing a single left or right step, then you have fulfilled stage three of the walking meditation and may proceed to the next stage.

Now increase the attention so that you notice every feeling of movement in the left step, from the very beginning when the left foot starts to move and lift up from the ground. Notice as it goes up, forward, down, and then rests on the ground again, taking the weight of the body. Develop this continuous awareness of the left step, and then similar smooth, unbroken awareness of the right step. Do this throughout every step to the end of the path. And as you turn around, notice every feeling in the turning-around procedure, not missing a movement.

When you can walk for fifteen minutes comfortably sustaining the attention on every moment of walking, without a single break, then you have reached the fourth stage of walking meditation, full sustained awareness of walking. At this point the process of walking so fully occupies the attention that the mind cannot be distracted. You know when this happens, because the mind goes into a state of samādhi, or attentive stillness, and becomes very peaceful.

Samādhi on the Walking Path

Even the sound of the birds disappears as your attention is fully focused on the experience of walking. Your attention is easily settled, content, and sustained on one thing. You will find this a very pleasant experience indeed.

As your mindfulness increases, you will know more and more of the sensations of walking. Then you find that walking does have this sense of beauty and peace to it. Every step becomes a "beautiful step." And it can very easily absorb all your attention as you become fascinated by just walking. You can receive a great deal of samādhi through walking meditation in this way. That samādhi is experienced as peacefulness, a sense of stillness, a sense of the mind being very comfortable and very happy in its own corner.

I started my walking meditation practice when I was first ordained as a monk in a temple in Bangkok. I would choose a path and quite naturally, without forcing it, I'd walk very slowly. (You don't need to walk fast, and you don't need to walk slowly. Just do what feels comfortable.) I used to get into beautiful samādhi states during walking meditation. I recall once being disturbed because I'd been walking too long. I hadn't noticed the time pass, and I was needed to go to an important ceremony. One of the monks had been sent to get me. I recall this monk came up to me and said, "Brahmavamso, you've got to come to a *dāna*" (an alms offering). I was looking at a space about two meters ahead. My hands were clasped in front of me. When I heard the monk's voice, it seemed as if it came from a thousand miles away because I was so absorbed into my walking meditation. He repeated, "Brahmavamso, you have to come now!" It took me more than a minute to actually lift my gaze from the ground and to turn it around to the side where this senior monk was trying to get my attention. And as I met his eyes, all I could say was

"What?" It took such a long time to get out of that samādhi and react at normal speed. The mind was so cool and so peaceful and so still.

I hope you experience this peacefulness for yourself when you try walking meditation. Many people who practice walking meditation for the first time say, "This is amazing. Beautiful." Just slowing down gives you a sense of peace. You become calm just by watching the sensations as you walk. So walking meditation is another type of meditation that I suggest you experiment with.

Choosing the Right Meditation for the Right Time

Wherever you have choice you may also find confusion. Now that you have read about several different methods of meditation, which one should you choose? The following simile will answer this question.

Apprentice carpenters begin by learning how to use their various tools until they are familiar with what each tool can do. Master carpenters who are about to make some furniture will first examine the wood they have to work with. A piece of timber straight from the lumberyard will have to be sawn to size. Then it must be planed to remove the marks from the saw. Sanding comes next, beginning with the coarsest grade of sandpaper, then a medium grade, then the finest grade of glass paper. Finally oil or wax is rubbed into the wood with a soft polishing cloth. Thus a piece of rough timber from the lumberyard is transformed by the master carpenter into a beautiful, smooth piece of furniture.

Sometimes a carpenter begins with a piece of wood that has already been planed or sanded. The master carpenter examines the wood and quickly knows that all it needs is a light sanding and then a polishing with the oil and cloth. On rare occasions, the master carpenter starts out with such a smooth piece of wood that no sanding is required, just a vigorous polishing. Such are the skills of a master carpenter.

In the same way, apprentice meditators begin by learning how to use the various methods of meditation until they are familiar with what each can do. Master meditators who are about to begin meditating will first examine the state of mind that they are to work with. If they have been very busy, they know that they will be starting out with quite a coarse mind. So they may start with a simple letting-be meditation. Perhaps they see that their body is stiff, so they choose to do some walking meditation. When they see that their mind is not so rough, they take up present-moment awareness and then silent present-moment awareness. Master meditators know from experience when their mind is able to watch the breath or ready to begin mettā meditation. They know when to apply the finer tools such as full sustained awareness of the breath or of the beautiful breath. Meditation masters become so proficient in their craft that they know the right time to turn to the nimitta and how to polish it deftly until the mind enters jhāna. Thus a coarse mind straight from the busy office is transformed by the master meditator into the most beautiful, smooth, and radiant mind.

Sometimes meditation masters begin with a mind that is already cool and mindful. They examine their state of mind and quickly know that they can bypass present-moment awareness and silence and go straight to the breath or to mettā. They may even see that their mind is so joyfully at peace that they can easily begin with awareness of the beautiful breath. On rare occasions, master meditators realize that they already possess such a poised and powerful mind that they can arouse a nimitta within a few seconds and quickly enter a jhāna. Such are the skills of a meditation master.

Foolish carpenters, in a mad rush, take a coarse piece of wood and begin rubbing it with a polishing cloth! They waste much time and destroy many fine cloths. In the same way, inept meditators, in a rush of arrogance, don't even take time to notice the coarseness of their mind and try to use mindfulness of the breathing from the very beginning. They waste much time and create many problems for themselves.

So, please become familiar with the various types of meditation until you know when and how they should be used. Then every time you meditate, begin by examining the mind you have to work with, and you will understand which meditation method to use. You will become a doctor of meditation, diagnosing accurately before treating effectively.

The Beautiful Breath 7

THE ESSENCE OF BUDDHISM is in the enlightenment of the Buddha. Many centuries ago in India, the wandering monk Gautama remembered a childhood experience of the first jhāna and realized that jhāna was the way to awakening (MN 36). He went to a quiet stretch of forest on the banks of a great river, sat on a cushion of grass under a shady fig tree, and meditated. The method of meditation that he used was *ānāpāna-sati,* mindfulness of the in and out breaths. Through this practice he entered jhāna, emerged, and quickly gained the insights of enlightenment. Henceforth he was called the Buddha.

The Buddha continued to teach ānāpānasati for the remainder of his life. It was the method that had given him enlightenment, the meditation practice *par excellence,* and he imparted that same method to all his disciples both in the monastery and in the city. This foremost method of meditation is bequeathed to us today in the original Buddhist texts as part of many suttas, but in particular as the *Ānāpānasati Sutta* of the Majjhima collection (MN 118).

The Buddha described the practice of ānāpānasati as consisting of preliminary preparations followed by sixteen steps. The first twelve of those steps are instructions for entering jhāna, and the final four steps are instructions on what to do when you emerge.

The Preliminaries

A Quiet Place, a Comfortable Seat

First, the Buddha said, go to a quiet place where you will not be disturbed by people, sounds, or things like mosquitoes. Some teachers claim that you can meditate in a marketplace or in your car in busy traffic, but such superficial meditation will not lead to enlightenment. The Buddha consistently recommended that you seek out a quiet place. Tough guys might want to meditate in mosquito-ridden jungles or in the middle of tiger paths, but that is more likely to build only endurance and not the ease of jhāna. The Buddha instead praised pleasant places like orchards or parks, similar to Bodh Gaya where he gained enlightenment.

Next sit down on a comfortable seat. You may sit on a cushion, on a bench, or even on a chair as long as it isn't too comfortable. The comfort required for success in breath meditation is that level where your body can be at ease for long periods of time. Buddhists do not sit on broken glass or beds of nails. Even the Buddha used a cushion of grass under the Bodhi tree. Nor do you need to cross your legs in full lotus and hold your back ramrod straight. I know from experience that you can succeed in meditation in the most unorthodox of postures. The purpose of posture is only to free you from discomfort so that you can let go of the body as soon as possible.

The full sixteen steps of ānāpānasati are best done in a sitting position, just like the Buddha under the Bodhi tree. In walking meditation your attention should rest on the feet and not on the breath. The same goes for standing. Unenlightened meditators who try to watch their breath lying down usually fall asleep. So learn ānāpānasati in the sitting position.

Setting Up Mindfulness

You are now asked to set up mindfulness "in front of you." When the Buddha said "in front of you" he didn't mean putting attention on the tip of your nose, or on your upper lip, or some place in front of your eyes. To put something in front means to make it important. So this preliminary instruction is to establish mindfulness by giving it priority.

This preliminary level of mindfulness is established by following the first two stages of the basic method of meditation in chapter 1—that is, through practicing present-moment awareness and then silent present-moment awareness. From what has been said so far, it should be obvious that when your attention is wandering through the past or into the future, you are not being mindful of what's happening right now. Also, when you are thinking or even just noting, then your attention is on the words, not on the bare experience of now. But when you are silently aware of whatever it is that is happening now (right in front of your mind), then you have established the level of mindfulness required to begin ānāpānasati.

It deserves to be said again that too many meditators go on to the breath too quickly, neglecting the preliminary instruction to establish adequate mindfulness first, and they run into trouble. Either they can't keep the breath in mind at all or, worse, they tenaciously grasp the breath with so much willpower that they end up more stressed out than before they started. The latter type gives Buddhist meditation on the breath a bad reputation.

The Sixteen Steps

The First and Second of the Sixteen Steps

Although the Buddha says to first experience long breaths and then experience short breaths, you do not need to control your breathing to fulfill the instructions. Controlling the breath produces only discomfort. Instead you are meant to simply observe the breath enough to know whether it is long or short. Even though this is not mentioned in the sutta, it is also fulfilling the instructions to observe the breath as neither long nor short, but somewhere close to the middle.

The reason for these instructions is that in the beginning you may find it uninteresting just to watch the feeling of air going in and out of your body, so this instruction gives you more to look at. It makes mindfulness of breathing more interesting. Sometimes I suggest to my students that at this stage they should notice which is longer, the in-breath or the out-breath. Is the gap between the in-breath and the next out-breath as long as the pause between the out-breath and the subsequent in-breath? Are the sensations of inbreathing the same as the sensations of outbreathing? This serves the same function as the Buddha's instructions to experience long breathing and short breathing. It gives mindfulness more details to watch so it won't get bored.

Another method that belongs to this stage is to make a beautiful story around the in and out breathing. I suggest to my students to remember that the oxygen that they are breathing in is being constantly replenished by the plants in the gardens and forests. And that the carbon dioxide they are breathing out is the food of the same plants. So imagine that you are breathing in a precious gift from the flowers and the trees, and that you are breathing out an equally valuable gift to the green nature around you. Your breathing is intimately connecting you with all the vibrant vegetation. Such an uplifting way of perceiving your own breathing makes it more easy to follow.

In the Thai forest tradition, they add a *mantra* to the breathing. As you breathe in you think "Bud" and as you breathe out you think "Dho." These are the two syllables of the Buddha's name (in Pāli nominative singular). Again, it serves to make the breathing easier to follow at this early stage.

The Third Step: Experiencing the Whole of the Breath

The third step is called in Pāli *sabba-kāya-patisamvedī*, experiencing the whole process of breathing. A minority of teachers mistake the Pāli term *kāya* to mean your physical body and so wrongly assume that now you are meant to direct your attention onto all the sensations in the whole of your physical body. This is an error. The Buddha clearly stated in the *Ānāpānasati Sutta* (MN 118,24) that he regarded the process of breathing as "a certain body *(kāya)* among the bodies." Moreover, the direction of the first twelve steps of ānāpānasati is toward simplifying the object of awareness, not making it more complex. Thus, this third step is where your mindfulness increases its agility sufficient to observe every sensation involved in the process of breathing.

You are aware of the in-breath from the very start when it arises out of the stillness. You see the sensations of inbreathing evolve in every moment, reaching its peak and then gradually fading away until it has completely subsided. You have such a degree of clarity that you even see the space, the pause between the in-breath and the next out-breath. Your mind has the attentiveness of a cat waiting for a mouse, as you wait for the next out-breath to begin. Then you observe the first stirrings of the outbreathing. You watch its sensations evolve, changing with every moment, until it too reaches a peak and then enters into its decline before fading into nothingness again. Then you observe the pause, the space between the out-breath and the subsequent in-breath. When the process is repeated breath after breath, you have fulfilled the third step, experiencing the whole breath.

In a classical Indian text, the *Mahābhārata,* there is an illustrative story of a teacher and his three students that I adapt as an explanation for this third step of ānāpānasati. The teacher was training his students in meditation using archery as the means. Having taught his three disciples a long time, he gave them a test to reveal their capabilities. He took a bird, a stuffed doll not a real bird, and carefully secured it to a branch of a tree a long distance from his students. It would take an awesome level of skill to pierce the bird with an arrow from such a distance. But the teacher made it almost impossible when he instructed his students: "I do not want you to hit that bird anywhere on its body. To pass this test, your arrow will have to pierce the left eye of the bird. That is the target."

He gave the bow and a single arrow to the first student and told him that he must meditate first, make his mind one with the target, and only then shoot the arrow. The student was told to take as much time as he liked, but before releasing the arrow he must give a sign to his teacher. Thirty minutes later the first student gave the sign that he was ready to shoot. The teacher told him to wait a few more seconds and asked: "Can you see the bird on the tree?" Without breaking his concentrated gaze the student said, "Yes." At this the teacher pushed the student aside, grabbed the bow and arrow, and said: "You stupid student! Go back and learn how to meditate." He handed the bow and arrow to his second student and gave him the same instructions. This student took a whole hour before giving the teacher the sign that he was ready to shoot. "Can you see the bird on the tree?" asked the teacher. "What tree?" replied the student. The teacher then asked hopefully: "Can you see the bird?"

The student replied, "Oh yes." Then the disappointed teacher shoved the second student aside, snatched the bow and arrow away, and told the second student to go learn how to meditate properly.

Finally he gave the bow and single arrow to his third student with the same instructions. The student took a whole two hours meditating, making his mind one with the target, the left eyeball of the bird. Then he gave the sign that he was ready to shoot. The teacher asked, "Can you see the bird on the tree?" The student replied, "What tree?" The teacher then asked, "Can you see the bird?" The student replied, "What bird?" The teacher started to smile and then continued, "What can you see?" Without averting his gaze the student replied, "Master, all I can see is an eyeball, that's all." "Cool," said the teacher, "Shoot." And of course the arrow went straight through the only thing that remained within the student's awareness.

This story is an accurate simile on how to achieve the third step of ānāpānasati, the experience of the whole breath. Just as the third student focused his whole mind on the target, for him the left eyeball of the bird, so you focus your whole attention on the third step of ānāpānasati, for you the experience of the whole breath. When you have accomplished this third step, if you were to ask yourself, "Can you hear sounds?" you would answer, "What sounds?" "Can you feel the body?"—"What body?" "What can you see?"—"Only the breath happening now." Cool.

The Fourth Step: Calming the Breath

When you are comfortably at one with the breath, it will calm down automatically. There is so little remaining to disturb your progress that you naturally experience the sensations in each moment becoming softer and smoother, like a piece of rough denim changing into fine satin. Or you may assist this process by interrupting the inner silence for a few moments and suggesting to yourself "calm, calm, calm." Then you return to silently experiencing only the breath again. By doing this you are instructing the gatekeeper as was described in chapter 5.

If you jump to the fourth step too soon you will fall prey to sloth and torpor. You must capture a wild horse before you can train it, in the same way you must capture the whole breath, fulfilling step three, before you attempt to calm it down.

Meditators who have achieved step three by using their willpower find it impossible to calm or soften their breath. They have been striving instead of letting go, and now they are blocked. When you are holding a flower you should never grasp it tightly, or you will destroy it. Delicate objects require a delicate touch. To hold the calm breath in the middle of mindfulness for many minutes, you need a very refined mind. Such a refinement of attention is only achieved through gentle and persistent letting go; it is never attained by the brute force of sheer willpower.

When a carpenter begins to saw a piece of wood he can see the whole saw from the handle to the tip of the saw blade. As he concentrates on the cut, the attention focuses closer and closer on the point where the saw touches the wood. The handle and tip of the saw soon disappear from his vision. After a while, all he can see is the one sawtooth that is in contact with the wood, whereas all the teeth to the left and right are beyond his range of perception. He does not know, nor does he need to know, whether that sawtooth is at the beginning, middle, or end of the blade. Such concepts have been transcended. This is the simile of the saw.

In the same way, at this fourth step, you will only know this bit of breath happening now. You simply do not know whether it is an in-breath or out-breath, beginning, middle, or end. As your breath calms down your attention becomes so refined that all you know is this one moment of breath.

The Fifth and Sixth Steps:
Experiencing Joy and Happiness with the Breath

In the fifth step of ānāpānasati you experience joy *(pīti)* along with the breath, and in the sixth step you experience happiness *(sukha)* along with the breath. Because joy and happiness are difficult to separate, and since they usually arrive together anyway, I will treat them as one.

As your unbroken mindfulness watches the breath calming down, joy and happiness naturally arise like the golden light of dawn on an eastern horizon. It will arise gradually but automatically because all your mental energy is now flowing into the knower and not the doer. In fact, you are doing nothing, only watching. The sure sign that you are doing nothing is the tranquillity of your breath. In the early hours of the morning it is only a matter of time until the horizon glows with the first light of day, just as when you remain still with the calm breath it is only a matter of time until joy and happiness appear in your mind. Mental energy flowing into the knower makes mindfulness full of power, and energized mindfulness is experienced as *pīti-sukha,* happiness and joy.

If you reach step four and are continuously mindful of a very calm breath but see no happiness or joy, then my advice is: "Don't panic!" Don't spoil the natural process with your impatience. When you do anything at this stage you just delay, or even prevent, the arrival of happiness and joy. Instead just deepen the experience of the continuous calm breath. Are you fully aware of the peaceful breath, or have interruptions crept in? Perhaps the lack of progress is because you are not continually mindful of only the breath. Has your breath stopped growing calmer? Perhaps the breath isn't peaceful enough yet. If so, give it more time. This is a natural process completely independent of you. When mindfulness rests comfortably on the breath without any interruptions, and the sensation of breath becomes calmer and calmer, then happiness and joy will always arise.

It helps if you are able to spot *pīti-sukha* early. To do this you have to be familiar with what you are looking for. The happiness and joy that are associated with tranquillity can start off as extremely subtle. It is like someone who prefers hard rock attending a performance of classical music by Mahler, and who can't comprehend why the audience pays good money to listen to such stuff. They just don't get it. Or like the person who usually eats at cheap diners going for the first time to a five-star French restaurant and not appreciating the cuisine because their palate is too coarse. As you meditate more and more, you become a connoisseur of tranquil mind states and will naturally apprehend the arrival of joy and happiness at an increasingly early stage.

The fulfillment of these fifth and sixth steps of ānāpānasati is precisely the same as reaching the stage of full sustained awareness of the beautiful breath in my basic method of meditation. The beauty of the breath at this level is my way of describing the experience of joy and happiness. The breath at this stage appears so tranquil and beautiful, more attractive than a garden in springtime or a sunset in summer, and you wonder if you will ever want to look at anything else.

The Seventh Step:
Experiencing the Breath as a Mind Object

As the breath becomes ever more beautiful, as the joy and happiness grow in quiet strength, your breath may appear to completely disappear. In chapter 2, I described this as the breath dropping away from the beautiful breath leaving only the beautiful. I also gave the simile of the grinning Cheshire Cat, who gradually disappeared leaving only the grin, to depict this event. This precisely describes the passage from stage five and six, experiencing joy and happiness with the breath, to stage seven where the breath is known only as a mind object.

To clarify this transition, I invoke the Buddha's analysis of conscious experience into the six sense bases (SN 35)—seeing, hearing, smelling, tasting, touching, and the mind base of knowing. In the early stages of meditation you abandon seeing, hearing, smelling, and tasting to the point where these four sense bases completely shut down for a while. Then you let go of most of the activity of the fifth sense base, touching, by focusing on the touch (physical sensation) of the breath to the exclusion of everything else. The sixth sense base, the mind, is operating throughout. As you pass into this seventh step, the fifth sense base, touching, now shuts down to leave only the sixth sense base, the mind, to know the breath. You are now experiencing the breath through a new sense base.

Imagine an old friend, fuzzy-haired and bearded, who usually goes around in ordinary old clothes. Then he is ordained as a Buddhist monk. When you first see him in the monastery, you probably won't recognize him with his bald head and robes. But it is the same old friend regardless. He appears different in the new setting, that's all. In the same way, your old friend the breath usually goes around dressed in the sensations of touch and is recognized mainly through the fifth sense base. In the seventh step of ānāpānasati, your breath has transcended the world of the five sense bases, in particular the fifth sense base, and is now to be known only through the sixth sense, as a mind object. This is why the Buddha called this step experiencing the *citta-sankhāra,* the mind object.

So if your breath seems to disappear at this stage, be reassured that this is meant to happen, and don't go disturbing the process by searching here and there for the previous perception of breath. Instead, when the breath seems to disappear, ask yourself what is left? If you have followed the instructions carefully, the breath will only seem to disappear after happiness and joy have been established, and so what is left is happiness and joy. Your mindfulness has to be subtle and still to recognize this fine object at first, but with the familiarity born of long experience, the insight will come to you that this subtle happiness and joy is your old friend the breath, only now experienced as a mind object.

If you are unable to remain with this mind object it is because there was insufficient happiness and joy with the breath at steps five and six. You should train in cultivating a *very* beautiful breath with heaps of joy and happiness before you let the fifth sense base shut down. Then you will have a stronger mind object to watch. However, with much practice, you will know what you are looking for at step seven, the mindfulness will be more deft at holding subtle levels of happiness and joy, and you will be able to let go of the fifth sense base earlier and still be able to hold the weaker mental object.

The Eighth Step: Calming the Mental Experience

It can often happen, at this and subsequent stages of the meditation process, that the joy and happiness can become too exciting and therefore disturb the tranquillity. Because of this, the Buddha taught the eighth step of ānāpānasati as calming the mental experience of the breath.

When new meditators, and old ones too sometimes, start to experience some bliss, they carelessly generate the "wow!" response: Wow! At last! Amazing! —and immediately their bliss walks right out of the door. They were too excited.

Alternatively, fear can arise alongside the bliss: This is too much for me! This is scary, I don't deserve this!—and again the bliss departs. The fear destroyed the tranquillity.

So beware of these two enemies, fear and excitement, which can appear at this stage. Remember to keep calming the mental experience of the breath. This bliss is the happiness and joy born of peace, born of silence. Maintain the causes of that bliss. Remain in the stillness, otherwise the bliss will go away.

Ajahn Chah's famous simile of the "still forest pool" helps us understand what's happening here. Others have written about this image, but not in full. This is the way I remember Ajahn Chah explaining it. When he was wandering in the jungles and forests on what we call *tudong* in Thailand, he'd always try and find a stretch of water when late afternoon came. He needed water to bathe. After walking though the jungle, sweating from the heat and the exertion, if you don't bathe in the evening you feel uncomfortably dirty and sticky all night. He also needed water to drink. For these reasons Ajahn Chah searched for a pool, a stream, or a spring somewhere in the forest. When he found one, he'd camp nearby overnight.

Sometimes after drinking and bathing and settling in, Ajahn Chah would sit in meditation a few yards away from the pool. He said that sometimes he used to sit so still with his eyes open that he would see many animals coming out of the jungle. They wanted to bathe and drink as well. He said they would only come out if he sat very, very still, because jungle creatures are timid and far more afraid of human beings than we are of them. When they emerged from the bushes they would look around and sniff to see if it was safe. If they detected him, they would just go away. But if he sat absolutely still, the animals wouldn't be able to hear him. They wouldn't even be able to smell him. Then they would come out and drink. Some would drink and play in the water as if he weren't there, as if he were invisible. He said that sometimes he was so still that, after the ordinary animals came out, some very strange animals emerged, beings whose names he didn't know. He'd never seen such extraordinary creatures before. His parents had never told him about them. These wonderful creatures came out to drink, but only if he was *absolutely still*.

This is a well-drawn simile of what happens in deep meditation. The pool or lake is a symbol for the mind. At this eighth step of ānāpānasati you are just sitting before it and watching. If you give any orders you're not being still. Beautiful creatures—nimittas and jhānas—will approach only if you're absolutely still. If they come out to "sniff around" and you say "wow!" they hurtle back into the forest and don't come out again. If they come out and you look at them, even out of the corners of your eyes, they'll know it and go away. You can't move if you want these beings to come out and play. But if you're absolutely still—no controlling, no doing, no saying, no moving, or anything else—nimittas come out. They look around and sniff the air. If they think no one is there, they come and play right in front of you. But if you move even an eyelid, they go away again. *Only if you're absolutely still do they remain.* The ordinary ones come out first, then the very beautiful ones, and lastly the very strange and wonderful ones. These last are the amazing experiences that you have no names for, the ones you never imagined could exist because they're so strange, so blissful, so pure. These are the jhānas.

This wonderful simile of Ajahn Chah's is a measure of his wisdom, of his profound understanding of the mind. This indeed is how the mind works, and having that wisdom is a tremendous power. The extraordinary jhānas can happen when you arouse joy and happiness in the mind, when you understand that this joy and happiness is not other than the mind experiencing the breath, and when you calm down the whole process of observing.

The Ninth Step: Experiencing the Mind

The ninth step of the *Ānāpānasati Sutta* describes a very important creature that comes to visit the still, silent mind—a nimitta. The step is called *citta-paṭisaṁvedī*, "experiencing the mind." It's only at this stage that you can truly say that you can know the mind. Some people have theories and ideas of what the mind is, and they try to test them out with scientific equipment. They even write entire books about the mind. But this is the only place where you can actually experience the mind.

The way you experience the mind is by a nimitta, which is a reflection of the mind. Remember the mind is that which knows. But is it possible for the knower to know itself? The eye is that which sees, but it can see itself when it looks into a mirror: it sees its reflection. The reflection you see in this stage of meditation, the nimitta, is a true reflection of the mind. You look into a mirror that has been cleaned of all the dust and grime on its surface, and now at last you can see yourself. You can only experience the mind directly through a nimitta or jhāna.

When a nimitta arises it's so very strange that it's next to impossible to describe. Language is built on similes. We describe something as hard like a brick, or soft like the grass. We always use similes from the world of the five senses. But the world of the mind is so different that language fails us. After your first experience of a nimitta you think, "What on earth was that?" You know it's a real experience, but you struggle to find language to describe it. You have to use imperfect similes: it's like a light, like a blissful feeling, sort of like this, sort of like that. You know it's so completely different from any previous experience, but you have to somehow describe it to yourself. That's why I keep on saying that you experience the nimitta sometimes as a light, sometimes as a feeling, sometimes as…a blob of Jell-O, or whatever. They are all exactly the same experience, but we give it different words. For many meditators, however, the mind flashes up very quickly and then disappears again. It's like the animal coming out of the forest. It senses someone becoming excited and flees.

Some meditators have difficulty in seeing nimittas. They reach the stage of calming the beautiful breath and nothing happens. No light appears. They wonder what they are doing wrong. The following analogy may help.

Late one night, I stepped outside from my brightly lit *kuti* (monk's hut) into the dense darkness of the forest. I had no flashlight. It was so black that I could not see anything. I remained still, patient. Slowly, my eyes became accustomed to the darkness. Soon I could make out the shapes of the tree trunks, and then I could look up and see the beautiful stars, the whole Milky Way even, glittering brilliantly in the night sky.

Experiencing nimittas can be like this. In the formless stillness when the breath seems to disappear, at first one can see nothing. Be patient. Do nothing but wait. Soon mindfulness will become accustomed to this "darkness" beyond its usual habitat (the room of the brightly lit five senses) and it begins to see shapes, dimly at first. After a while, the beautiful starlike nimittas may appear, and, if one is still long enough, the best nimittas of all appear, like the brilliant disc of the full moon at night, released from the clouds.

The Tenth Step: Shining the Nimitta

Two flaws of the nimitta may hinder further progress: the nimitta appears too dull, and the nimitta is unstable. To address these two common problems, the Buddha taught the tenth and eleventh steps of ānāpānasati: shining the nimitta and sustaining the nimitta. "Shining" is my expression for the Pāli term *abhippamodayaṁ cittaṁ,* literally, "giving joy to the mind." The more joy there is in the mind, the more brilliant shines the nimitta. To enter jhāna, the nimitta has to be the most brilliant thing that you have ever seen, and of unearthly beauty.

Let's look at why the nimitta can appear dull or even dirty. It is very instructive to recall that the nimitta is just a reflection of your mind. If the nimitta is dull, it means that your mind is dull. If the nimitta is dirty, then it means that your mind is defiled. There is no possibility for dishonesty or denial here, for you are face-to-face with the truth of your mind state.

It is here that the importance of *sīla* (moral conduct) becomes apparent. If the mind is defiled due to impure action, speech, or thought, then the nimitta, if it appears at all, will be dull and stained. If that is your experience, then spend some effort purifying your conduct beyond the meditation cushion. Keep the precepts faultlessly. Check your speech. The Buddha said that without first purifying sīla, it is impossible to purify samādhi (AN VII,61).

Generous, compassionate people with strong faith have what is commonly called a "pure heart." From my experience teaching meditation, it is a general rule that such purehearted meditators are the ones who experience the bright nimittas. So in addition to keeping your precepts spotless, develop what is known as the pure heart.

However, sometimes even good-hearted people experience dull nimittas. Usually this is because their mental energy is low, maybe due to ill health or overwork. A skillful means of avoiding this problem is to spend some meditation periods developing the inspirational meditations, such as the reflections on the Buddha, the Dhamma, and the Sangha. These should be contemplated until the mind becomes suffused with joy. Alternatively, if you are a very charitable sort of person, you could reflect on your past generosity and inspire yourself that way. The Buddha called this *cāga-anussati*. Or you can spend some time on mettā. Once the mental energy is raised to a level of joyful brightness, then you can return to ānāpānasati.

Thus far, I have talked about techniques to shine up the nimitta before you even start ānāpānasati. They are, in fact, the most effective techniques. However, when a nimitta has arisen during meditation but appears dull, there are four ways of proceeding:

Focus on the center of the nimitta. Even in a dull nimitta, the center is brighter than the periphery. By gently suggesting to yourself to look at the center of the nimitta, the central brightness expands. Then focus on the center of that, and that is brighter still. By going to the center, then the center of the center, and so on, the dull nimitta soon becomes incredibly bright and often continues "exploding" in luminosity all the way into jhāna.

Sharpen the attention in the present moment. Even though present-moment awareness was part of the preliminaries to ānāpānasati, it often happens that by this stage the attention is "smeared" around the present moment. Personally, I often find that a gentle reminder to focus more sharply in the present moment brightens the mindfulness and shines up the nimitta, abolishing any dullness.

Smile at the nimitta. Remember that the nimitta is a reflection of your mind. So if the mind smiles, then the nimitta smiles back! It brightens. It may be that a residue of ill will (the second hindrance) is keeping the nimitta dull. Smiling is both gentle and powerful enough to overcome this subtle form of the hindrance. If you do not understand what I mean by smiling at the nimitta, go and look at yourself in a mirror, smile, and then take the mental part of that activity and repeat it in front of the nimitta.

Return to the beautiful breath. Sometimes it is simply too early to go to the nimitta, and it is better to exert a gentle determination to remain with the beautiful breath a bit longer. Even if the nimitta comes up, when it is dull ignore it and return to the mental experience of the breath. Often when I do this, after a short time the nimitta comes up again a little brighter. I ignore it again. It keeps coming up brighter and brighter, but I keep on ignoring it until a really gorgeous nimitta appears. Then I don't ignore it!

So these are the ways to "shine" the nimitta, polishing it, as it were, until it is brilliant, beautiful, and radiant.

The Eleventh Step: Sustaining the Nimitta

The second of the two flaws of the nimitta that hinder a deepening of the meditation experience is instability of the nimitta. It does not stay still but quickly disappears. In order to deal with this problem, the Buddha taught the eleventh step of ānāpānasati, *samādaham cittam,* literally "attentively stilling the mind" and here meaning "sustaining the attention on the nimitta."

It is common that the first few times a nimitta appears, it flashes up for a short time and then disappears, or else it moves around in the mental field of vision. It is unstable. Usually, the bright, powerful nimittas remain longer than the dull, weak ones, which is why the Buddha taught the step of shining the nimitta before the step of sustaining the nimitta. Sometimes shining the nimitta is enough to sustain it—the nimitta becomes so beautifully radiant that it grabs the attention for long periods of time. However, even a brilliant nimitta can be unstable, so there are methods to sustain attention on the nimitta.

The insight that helped me to sustain the nimitta was the realization that the nimitta that I was seeing in my mind was just a reflection of the knower, the one watching. If the knower moved, so did its reflection, the nimitta. Like staring at your image in front of a mirror, if you move then so does the image. So long as you are moving, it is a waste of time trying to keep the image still just by holding the mirror still. It doesn't work. Instead focus on the knower, that one who is experiencing this, and calm that into stillness. Then the image of this knower, the nimitta, will stabilize and appear motionless, gloriously constant.

Once again, it is usually fear or excitement that creates the instability. You are reacting too much rather than passively observing. Experiencing the nimitta for the first time is like meeting a complete stranger. Often, you are on edge because you do not know who they are or how they might behave. After getting to know them, though, you relax in their company. They are good friends, and you are at ease with them. The overreaction disappears. Or it is like when as a child you first learned how to ride a bicycle. For the first few rides, you probably gripped the handlebars so tightly that, like me, your knuckles went white. And because I wasn't relaxed, I kept falling off. I soon discovered, after many cuts and bruises, that the more relaxed I was, the easier it was to keep my balance. In the same way, you soon learn to stop gripping the nimitta. You relax and discover that the more you ease off controlling, the easier it is to sustain the nimitta.

Another skillful means that I developed to stop controlling was to use the image of driving a car. When a bright nimitta comes up, I give it the keys and say, "You drive from here on." I give it full trust, complete confidence. I actually try to visualize my trust and give it over to the bright nimitta. I realize that the last residue of the doer, the control freak, still wants to spoil things. So I use this metaphor to help give up all control. This is the point where I stop. When I stop, the nimitta stops with me.

After sustaining attention on the nimitta a while, it becomes even more brilliant and very powerful. The signs of good nimittas are that they are the most beautiful colors you've ever seen in your life. For example, if you see a blue nimitta, the color is no ordinary blue but the deepest, most beautiful, bluest blue you've ever known. The good, or should I say "useful," nimittas are also very stable, almost motionless. When you are experiencing a beautiful stable nimitta, you are on the edge of the world of jhānas, looking in.

The Twelfth Step: Freeing the Mind

The twelfth step in ānāpānasati is called *vimocayaṁ cittaṁ,* "freeing the mind." Here, you have an experience that you might describe afterward in two different ways, depending upon your perspective. Either you find yourself sinking or diving into the nimitta, or the nimitta with its brilliant light and ecstatic feeling completely envelops you. *You* don't do this. It just happens as the natural result of letting go of all doing.

You enter the jhāna through liberating the mind. The jhānas, the Buddha said, are stages of freedom *(vimokkha)* (DN 15,35). *Vimokkha* is the same word used to describe someone who is released from jail and walks free. You may know it from the Sanskrit *moksha* which has the same meaning. The mind is now free. That is, free from the body and the five senses. I'm not saying the mind is floating somewhere in an out-of-body experience. You are not located in space anymore, because all experiences of space are dependent on the five senses. Here the mind is free from all of that. You're not at all sensitive to what's happening with the body. You're unable to hear anything, unable to say anything. You're blissed out yet fully mindful, still, stable as a rock. These are signs of the mind being freed. This experience becomes one of the most powerful, if not *the* most powerful experience, of your life.

If you get a few of these jhānas, you usually want to become a monk or a nun. The world will have less attraction for you. Relationships, the arts, music and movies, sex, fame, wealth, and so on all seem so unimportant and unattractive when compared to jhānas and the bliss of the freed mind. But there is much more than just the bliss. There is also the philosophical profundity of the experience. When you've spent hours in a jhāna, you can call yourself a mystic, if you like. You've had an experience that in all religious traditions is called a mystical experience—something far from the ordinary. The Buddha called it *uttari-manussa-dhamma* (MN 31,10), something that surpasses ordinary human experience. He called it the mind "gone to greatness" *(mahā-ggata).* He also considered the happiness of jhāna so similar to enlightenment happiness that he named it *sambodhi sukha* (MN 66,21). It's a place where defilements cannot reach. So this is where Māra—the Buddhist devil—cannot reach you. You're awakened and free during this time.

So if you develop these stages, the first twelve steps of ānāpānasati, they will lead you into jhāna.

Emerging from a Jhāna

The last four steps in the *Ānāpānasati Sutta* relate to the meditator who has just emerged from a jhāna. After you emerge from your first experience of jhāna you can't help but think, "Wow, what was that?" So the first thing you should do is review the jhāna. Investigate that experience, though you will struggle to give it words. Ask yourself, How did it arise? What special thing did I do? What did it feel like in jhāna? Why did it feel like that? How do I feel now? Why is it so blissful? All these reflections will give rise to deep insight.

You'll find that the best two words to describe why jhāna happened are "letting go." You've really let go for the first time. Not letting go of what you're attached to, but *letting go of the thing doing the attaching.* You've let go of the doer. You've let go of the self. It's a difficult thing for the self to let go of the self, but through these methodical stages you've actually done it. And it's bliss.

So, having reflected on the experience, you either take up satipaṭṭhāna (the focuses of mindfulness) or just go directly to the last four stages of ānāpānasati.

The Thirteenth Step: Reflecting on Impermanence

The first reflection is on anicca, usually translated as impermanence but meaning much more than this. Its opposite, *nicca,* is the Pāli word used to describe a thing that is regular or constant. For instance, in the Vinaya a regular supply of almsfood, say from a disciple who brings food to a monastery every Tuesday, is called nicca food (Vin II,4,4,6). When that which was once constant stops, that's *anicca.* What's important to reflect upon after the deep experiences of meditation is that there was something that was so constant that you never noticed it—this thing we call a "self." In jhāna, it disappeared! Notice that. Noticing it will convince you of the truth of no-self *(anattā)* so deeply that it's very likely to give rise to the experience of stream winning.

The Fourteenth Step: Reflecting on Fading Away of Things

If reflections on anicca fail to work, there is *virāga,* the fading away of things—sometimes called dispassion. It has this dual meaning, but I usually prefer the meaning "fading away." This is when things just disappear. You've seen many things disappear when you enter jhāna—some of which were so close to you that you assumed that they were an essential part of your identity. They are all gone in jhāna. You're experiencing the fading away of your self.

The Fifteenth Step: Reflecting on Cessation

The third reflection after emerging from a jhāna should be on *nirodha,* or cessation. Something that was once there has now completely disappeared. It has ended, gone, and its place is now empty! Such emptiness can be known only in deep meditation. So much of the universe that you thought was essential has ceased, and you're in a completely different space.

Cessation is also the third noble truth. The end of suffering is called cessation. The cause of that cessation is letting go. You've actually let go. Dukkha, suffering, has ended—most of it anyway, 99 percent. And what's left? What's the opposite of dukkha? Sukha. *The ending of suffering is happiness.* That's why you should reflect that these jhānas are the most blissful experience you've ever felt in your existence. And if you've got a little bit of wisdom or intelligence, you will see that the bliss arises because so much dukkha has ceased.

You experience happiness and you know the cause. Imagine that you had a migraine headache for many, many months and someone gave you a new medicine that had just been invented, saying it works for some but not for everybody. So you take it and find that it works for you. Your migraine has gone! How would you feel? You'd be high as a kite. You'd be blissed out! Sometimes you'd be crying with happiness. The ending of pain is happiness. Why is it that schoolchildren feel so happy when they finish their end-of-year school exams? It is because a lot of suffering has just ended. So often, the happiness in the world is just a measure of how much suffering preceded it. When you finally pay off the mortgage on your house, you feel so happy; all the pain of working for months and years to pay it off is gone.

The Sixteenth Step: Reflecting on Letting Go, Abandoning

The last of the reflections in the *Ānāpānasati Sutta* is on this beautiful word *paṭinissagga,* "letting go, abandoning." In this context *paṭinissagga* is giving away not what's "out there" but what's "in here." Many times people regard Buddhism as being unworldly, giving away what's out there. But paṭinissagga is the letting go of the inner world, the letting go of the doer and even the knower. If you look very carefully, you'll see that what has been happening in jhāna is not only letting go of the external world but also letting go of the internal world, especially letting go of the doer, the will, the controller. This insight gives rise to so much happiness, so much purity, so much freedom, so much bliss. You've found the path to the ending of suffering.

That is how the Buddha described ānāpānasati. It's a complete practice that starts with just sitting down in a quiet place, on a comfortable seat, mindful of what's in front of you and just watching the breath. Step by step—in steps that you know are within your ability—you reach these profound and blissful states called jhāna.

When you emerge from them, you have any one of these four things to contemplate: *anicca,* the impermanence or uncertainty of things; *virāga,* the fading away of things; *nirodha,* cessation of self; and *paṭinissagga,* letting go of all that's "in here." And if you reflect upon those things after the experience of jhāna, then something is going to happen. I often say that jhāna is the gunpowder and reflection is the match. If you put the two together, then there's going to be a bang somewhere. It's only a matter of time.

May you all experience those beautiful bangs called enlightenment!

The Four Focuses
of Mindfulness

8

◆ ◆ ◆

IN THIS CHAPTER I will explain the four focuses of mindfulness, or satipaṭṭhāna, and their bearing on the practice of meditation described thus far.

First of all, the practice of satipaṭṭhāna is not the only way to realize enlightenment, as some overenthusiastic interpreters would claim. According to the Buddha, the only way to realize enlightenment is by means of the noble eightfold path (Dhp 273–74). Satipaṭṭhāna is the seventh factor of the noble eightfold path. Anyone who practices a "onefold path," such as by developing satipaṭṭhāna but neglecting other factors, will not realize enlightenment. Just as anyone who tries to bake a cake using only one ingredient, say, flour, will go hungry.

For the above reason, the explanation of satipaṭṭhāna given here is in the context of the noble eightfold path, demonstrating how the other seven factors of the noble eightfold path are a prerequisite and support for satipaṭṭhāna practice.

Some authors have also claimed that satipaṭṭhāna practice is original to Buddhism, that it is the Buddha's unique discovery that led to his enlightenment and the subsequent enlightenment of his arahant disciples. This, however, is not plausible. Satipaṭṭhāna, as I explain in this chapter, is a focusing of mindfulness on such things as the body, feelings, mind states, and the like. Intelligent and inquisitive people in all races and religions have directed their mindfulness to aspects of nature in order to understand their meaning. Investigation is not unique to Buddhism.

What was original to Buddhism is the practice of jhāna. The realization of a jhāna requires a delicate balance of lifestyle. That balance is called the "Middle Way" (see the *Mahāsaccaka Sutta,* MN 36,31–33). That Middle Way was frowned upon both by ascetics at the time of the Buddha and by people in the world. For example, the Buddha's five ascetic friends left him in disgust when he embarked on the Middle Way. The originality of the Buddha was in using the experience of jhāna to empower investigation, to give mindfulness a huge boost.

Preparing for Satipaṭṭhāna

Satipaṭṭhāna has been commonly translated as "foundations of mindfulness." However, the more accurate and meaningful translation is "focuses of mindfulness." The teaching of satipaṭṭhāna instructs the meditator where to place mindfulness. If we think of mindfulness as like a flashlight beam, then satipaṭṭhāna shows the meditator where to shine that beam to uncover enlightening truths.

In the two versions of the *Satipaṭṭhāna Sutta* that have come down to us (DN 22; MN 10), the Buddha said that "if anyone should develop the satipaṭṭhāna in such a way" (as described in those suttas) for seven days, then they would realize either full enlightenment or the stage of the non-returner. Many Buddhists, monastic and lay, have completed many meditation retreats longer than seven days and remain unenlightened. Please don't blame the Buddha! Instead, look again at the Buddha's promise: "If anyone should develop the satipaṭṭhāna *in such a way...*" The reason why enlightenment doesn't happen is that they do not practice satipaṭṭhāna in the right way. They are like the person who buys an expensive, high-tech household appliance, unpacks it, assembles it, and excitedly plugs it into a power socket. BANG! Something has gone wrong. Only then do they read the instruction manual. Shouldn't we always read the manual first? The reason that Buddhists do not achieve enlightenment is that they do not practice satipaṭṭhāna according to the manual.

The Buddha taught two types of satipaṭṭhāna. The first type is supported by jhāna and leads to enlightenment in a short time. The second type, without jhāna, produces valuable insights, especially ones that enable you to let go and come closer to jhāna, but does not lead to enlightenment. Both types are found in the suttas. In this chapter, I will focus mainly on the first type of satipaṭṭhāna practice.

The Importance of Jhāna for Satipaṭṭhāna

The suttas say that one practices satipaṭṭhāna "having put away covetousness and grief for the world." This is the usual translation of the Pāli *vineyya loke abhijjhā-domanassam,* but it is a wretched rendering. It was first suggested by the well-meaning Professor Rhys Davids over a hundred years ago and has stuck. Not only is the rendering meaningless in practical terms, it is also erroneous. This misleading translation is the main reason why modern Western Buddhists misunderstand the instruction manual and find satipaṭṭhāna not working for them.

As the commentaries explain it, the phrase actually means "having temporarily abandoned the five hindrances." This explanation is consistent with the use of these Pāli words elsewhere in the suttas. That means that a prerequisite for the practice of satipaṭṭhāna is the abandoning of the five hindrances first! This is part of the instruction manual that Buddhists do not apply and that keeps satipaṭṭhāna from delivering the goods.

It is the function of jhāna to abandon, temporarily, the five hindrances. (See the *Naḷakapāna Sutta,* MN 68,6: "not attaining a jhāna, the five hindrances invade one's mind and remain. Attaining a jhāna, the five hindrances do not invade the mind and remain.") Anyone who has experienced a jhāna knows that after emerging, one's mindfulness is so powerful and so easy to sustain. This is the result of the five hindrances being absent.

I remember going out with the girls as a young student at university. At parties the lights were always dimmed. When we went out for dinner, it was by candlelight. When we canoodled on the riverbank, it was under silvery moonlight. I realized that for romance to happen, it had to be dark. So dark, in fact, that I couldn't really see who I was going out with.

Weak mindfulness is like going out at night. You can't see clearly. Maybe all you can see are the silhouettes. Some people like weak mindfulness. They do not want to see the way things truly are, because mindfulness reveals some truths about life that they do not want to face. Many people would rather be infatuated with fantasy, dopey with drugs, or sozzled by spirits. Others run away from being mindful by being busy. Only a few have the courage and honesty to be mindful.

The Power of Mindfulness

If mindfulness is like a light, meditation brightens that light. When I was a young monk at Wat Pa Nanachat in Northeast Thailand, I became quite peaceful by doing walking meditation in the hall. I would walk with my gaze on a spot on the concrete floor some two meters ahead. Then I had to stop. I couldn't believe it, but the dull concrete surface began to open up into a picture of magnificent beauty. The various shades of gray and the texture suddenly appeared as the most beautiful picture I had ever seen. I thought of cutting out that section and sending it to the Tate Gallery in London. It was a work of art. An hour or two later, it was just a boring, ordinary piece of concrete again.

What had happened, and this may have happened to you, is that I had a short experience of "power mindfulness." In power mindfulness, the mind is like a megawatt searchlight, enabling you to see so much deeper into what you are gazing at. Ordinary concrete becomes a masterpiece. A blade of grass literally shimmers with the most delightful and brilliant shades of fluorescent green. A twig metamorphoses into a boundless universe of shape, color, and structure. The petty becomes profound and the humdrum becomes heavenly under the sparkling energy of power mindfulness.

What is happening is that the five hindrances are being abandoned. The five hindrances are said, in the suttas, to "weaken wisdom." When they are gone, the experience is like seeing through a windshield that has been cleaned of grime and dust, or hearing through ears at last unclogged of wax, or reflecting with a mind released from its fog. When you know the difference between power mindfulness and weak mindfulness as a personal experience, not a mere idea, then you will understand the necessity for jhāna prior to satipaṭṭhāna.

Jhāna generates "superpower" mindfulness. If power mindfulness is like a megawatt searchlight, then jhāna-generated superpower mindfulness is like a terawatt sun. If enlightenment is your goal, then the superpower mindfulness is the level that's needed. Anyone who has experienced the states after jhāna would understand why this is so. Consider this simile: weak mindfulness is like digging a hole with a teaspoon; power mindfulness is like digging a hole with a spade; superpower mindfulness is like digging a hole with a huge backhoe that can excavate in one scoop what would take you years to dig out with a spoon.

The Thousand-Petaled Lotus

I want to demonstrate how sustaining mindfulness on a single object uncovers the nature of you: the nature of your mind and body. I will do so by returning to the simile of the thousand-petaled lotus.

Recall that a lotus closes all of its petals during the night. In the morning the first rays of the sun begin to warm the lotus. This is the trigger for the lotus to open its petals. It takes a long time, many minutes, for the warmth to build up enough for the first layer of petals to open. If the day is cloudy or misty then it takes a very long time. Once the outermost petals are opened, the warmth of the sun can shine on the next layer of petals, and after a few minutes of uninterrupted light they too open up. This allows the next layer to receive the warmth, and soon it opens up in turn. Lotuses have many layers of petals and so take a long time to fully open. A thousand-petaled lotus requires a very strong sun, sustained for a very long time, to open every petal and reveal the famed jewel at its heart.

In satipaṭṭhāna, the thousand-petaled lotus is a simile for this body-mind, that is, "you"—or whatever you like to call that which is sitting somewhere right now reading this page. The sun is a simile for mindfulness. You have to sustain power mindfulness for a very long time on this body and mind to allow the innermost petals to open up. If the five hindrances are there, no insight happens, just as when there are clouds or mist, the sun cannot warm the lotus.

If you haven't sustained power mindfulness on this body and mind for long, then your understanding sees only outer petals. But if you generate power mindfulness and sustain it on the body-mind continuously, then you begin to see all this in a completely different light. You thought that you knew what "you" were, but now you realize how deluded you were and how little you knew. Through sustaining power mindfulness on the body and mind, truths start to unfold.

As you meditate in this way, all the old labels disappear. All the old ideas—who you had thought you were, what you were told you were, and what you believed you were—are outer petals. They open up to reveal much deeper truths. Labels and ideas are old conditioning. They are superficial descriptions that hide the truth lying within. As these outer petals are removed, you start to see things that you have never seen before. You experience things for which you cannot find a label, which are beyond every learned perception. Most of our perceptions are merely repetitions of what we were taught in school or at home. "Cow," "dog," "monk," "policeman," all these are examples of inaccurate labels that we are trained to attach to objects in the world. "Thought," "feeling," "consciousness," and "self" are examples of erroneous labels that we have been trained to attach to objects in the mind. They are just so many learned perceptions that hide the truth.

This simile is called the "thousand-petaled lotus" because there are a thousand or so levels of reality to uncover. The practice of meditation takes many hours of sitting, uncovering many deep layers of delusion and wrong ideas about yourself and the world. When the Buddha taught that the root cause of suffering is *avijjā,* or delusion, he did not say that it would be easy to uncover. Avijjā is uncovered, as it were, in layers, like the opening of the lotus petals.

A danger that you should be wary of in your spiritual life, especially in your meditation, is overestimation of your attainment. Sometimes when power mindfulness on the body-mind is sustained, insights appear. Maybe the sun has warmed the lotus so well that forty-nine petals have opened up and you see petal fifty of the thousand-petaled lotus. This fiftieth petal is so beautiful and profound that you think, "Wow! This is it, I've finally understood what's at the heart of this lotus." Sorry, my friend, but you've got another nine hundred and fifty petals to go. So be careful. You're not fully enlightened yet.

When petal number one thousand opens up, so beautiful and unworldly, then you see the famed jewel in the heart of the lotus. Do you know what that jewel is?—a diamond? a ruby? No, it's emptiness. You see the priceless gem of emptiness in the very heart of the body-mind, and this is not what you would ever have expected. That's how you know it is not just another petal. Emptiness is something of a completely different nature to every other petal, to every other thing. Nothing! To reach this far usually requires superpower mindfulness sustained on its focus for a very long time.

The Purpose of Satipaṭṭhāna

Another essential requirement before starting satipaṭṭhāna is to fully comprehend the purpose of satipaṭṭhāna. The purpose of any practice will help explain how it should be done. When you have a clear idea of the goal, then you are more likely to arrive.

So what is the purpose of satipaṭṭhāna? The purpose is to see anattā, that there is no self, no me, nor anything that belongs to a self. As it says in the texts, "Such mindfulness is established enough to discern that there are just the body, feelings, mind, and objects of mind" and that these are not me, nor mine, nor a self (this is how I translate a repeated phrase in the suttas).

When you keep in mind that the purpose of satipaṭṭhāna is to uncover the delusion of me, mine, or a self, to see anattā or the "emptiness in the heart of the lotus," then the way of practice becomes clear. In particular you can appreciate why the Buddha taught just four focuses for mindfulness: body, feelings, mind, and mind objects. He taught these four because these are the major areas where life assumes a "me" or a "mine."

So the satipaṭṭhāna practice sustains superpower mindfulness on each of the four objects in order to unravel the illusion of a self. You have been deluded for too long, identifying with the physical body, regarding your feelings as yours (and therefore subject to your control), assuming the mind (the process of knowing) to be your self, and attaching to the objects of mind as matters of concern to you.

Summary of the Preliminaries

These then are the preparations for successful satipaṭṭhāna practice. In tabular form they are:

1. *vineyya loke abhijjhā domanassam*—first abandon the five hindrances through an experience of jhāna.
2. *satimā*—be possessed of superpower mindfulness resulting from jhāna.
3. *atāpi*—diligently sustain that superpower mindfulness on the focus.
4. *sampajāno*—keep in mind the purpose of satipaṭṭhāna: to realize no-self.

Now I will describe the practice of satipaṭṭhāna on each of the four focuses in turn.

Body Contemplation

In the *Satipaṭṭhāna Sutta*s there are fourteen areas for focusing mindfulness involving the body. They are grouped as follows: (1) breath, (2) bodily posture, (3) bodily activity, (4) composition of the body, (5) the body seen as four elements, and (6) the nine corpse contemplations. Here, I will discuss briefly all but the fifth.

Breath

In Indian philosophy, the breath (*prāṇa* in Sanskrit) is sometimes considered to be the vital essence of a human being. Indeed, the Pāli word for "animal" is the same as the word for "breath," *pāṇa*. Similarly, the English word *animal* is derived from the Latin *animalis*, meaning "having breath." Certainly, in ancient times the breath was considered to be such an important part of life that it was thought to be almost identical to a self or soul.

By focusing superpower mindfulness on the breath, it is possible to experience the breath as an empty process, completely subject to conditioning, with no being in here doing the breathing. Moreover, in deep jhāna, we can experience the breath disappearing altogether (in the fourth jhāna) with no danger to life.

During my teacher Ajahn Chah's long sickness, he would often stop breathing. On one such occasion the new nurse on duty became alarmed. He knew that Ajahn Chah must die one day, but he didn't want it to happen on his shift! The attendant monks on duty that night reassured him that Ajahn Chah had done the same many times before and that it was just a sign of deep meditation. The nurse was still worried and so took blood samples every few minutes during the hours without breathing to ensure that the blood was still well oxygenated. After all, as long as there is enough oxygen available in the blood there will be no harm to the body. The nurse discovered that even though Ajahn Chah was not breathing for a long time, the oxygen level in the blood remained constant. In jhāna, the metabolism is so slowed down that you are using almost zero energy. You don't need to breathe.

Why is it that ordinary people gasp when they are excited, or struggle for breath just before they die? Perhaps their attachment to their breath is deeper than they realized. Remember, satipaṭṭhāna uncovers attachments that are completely unexpected. When you experience the cessation of breath, then it is obvious that it is not yours at all. From that insight, attachment to breath unravels.

Bodily Postures and Bodily Activities

There are two ways to understand something: by contemplating what it is made of and by contemplating what it does. Here we are analyzing this body by contemplating what it does. It is an illusion to think that *I* am walking, standing, lying down, sitting, stretching my arm, and so on. The truth is that there is a body doing this, not an *I*.

Many high achievers in sports, the arts, or even meditation, describe a state of selflessness called entering the "zone." When a famous classical Indian dancer I knew was asked how she could perform to such a high standard, she replied that she practices and practices, but when the performance begins, she deliberately forgets everything she has been taught. She "gets herself out of the way" and allows the dance to take over. This is a classic description of entering the zone. When the athlete is in the zone, she can move effortlessly, gracefully, and faultlessly. When the meditator is in the zone, he can watch samādhi deepen beautifully, seamlessly, and wordlessly. You clearly experience all this as mere process, with no being driving the process. It is anattā, no-self.

You observe bodily postures and activities with superpower mindfulness and quickly enter a zone where all bodily postures and activities are seen to be mere cause-driven processes, not self-driven ones. You become less of a control freak concerning this body. You detach and live at ease.

Some teachers mistakenly think that mindfulness must always be focused on activities in the present moment. In fact the Pāli word for mindfulness, *sati,* also means remembering. Superpower mindfulness can focus on an object many moments old, bore into it without the object fading, and uncover its truth.

For example, in the *Satipaṭṭhāna Sutta* one is asked to practice mindfulness focused on sleeping. Even arahants are not aware when they're asleep, so what does this mean? Some translators have attempted to solve this question by changing the meaning of the exercise to mindfulness on falling asleep. However, the Pāli word used in the *Satipaṭṭhāna Sutta* means "in sleep," and there is a different phrase for falling asleep, *niddaṃ okkamati.* The practice of mindfulness focused on sleeping means one uses a previous experience of having been asleep as the focus of superpower mindfulness in the present. It is mindfulness that takes an old experience as its object. This may seem pedantic to you now, but it becomes crucially important, as you will see, when I explain the focus of mindfulness on the citta (mind consciousness).

Composition of the Body

I remember when I was about eleven years old watching a television program on my parents' black-and-white set that showed in gory detail major surgical operations common at that time. My parents and my brother had to leave the room, but they let me watch after I argued that the program was educational. I found it fascinating to see the innards of a body.

Many years later as a Buddhist monk I was eager to observe autopsies in Thailand and Australia. What fascinates me now is why some persons are repelled by the very thought of watching an autopsy, and often faint when they attend one. Even though we have all been taught biology at school, most of us are still in denial about the nature of our bodies. Why else would we faint or groan when seeing guts exposed?

We have a huge amount of attachment to this body, a delusion that causes us much suffering. By focusing superpower mindfulness on the composition of your body, you can penetrate the barrier of denial and fear and see the body as it truly is. It is just a body. Bits and pieces strung together and falling apart, neither beautiful nor ugly, neither strong nor weak. It is simply a thing of nature, not something of yours. Can you keep it fit and healthy forever? Can you stop it from dying? So who owns your body? Surely it must be obvious that nature owns your body, not you.

The sign that you have penetrated the truth of the body is the complete lack of fear about your own death. Another test of your insight is your response when a loved relative or close friend dies. If you receive a phone call telling you they have just been killed in a road accident and you reply, "Yes, that's to be expected," then you are free of attachment to the body.

The Corpse Meditations

Meditation on a corpse combines the contemplations of what a body is and what a body does. It produces revulsion at the beginning, insight in the middle, and liberation in the end. It's powerful and effective.

A corpse from a road accident is quickly covered and sent to a funeral home, where it is embalmed and made up with cosmetics. The embalmer's skill makes Uncle George look like he is happily sleeping rather than stone dead. We do not want to see a corpse as it truly is. We are more content to have the fantasy. Unfortunately, delusion demands a heavy price. The longer we delay understanding death, the more we will have to suffer from it.

When superpower mindfulness is focused on a corpse or on the clear memory of one, the dead body opens up like a thousand-petaled lotus and reveals the truth hidden deep beneath the surface. The corpse is teaching you that this is what your body does—it gets old, falls apart, and dies. This is the destiny of your body and all others. Such insight produces dispassion with regard to this body and disinterest in getting another body. Seeing a corpse disintegrate and return to its natural state proves once again who the real owner is—nature. No longer will you be attached to your body, take delight in your partner's body, or fear death. And if the insight reaches to the core, then you will never again come to birth in another body.

Feeling Contemplation

The second focus of mindfulness is feeling *(vedanā)*. This term needs explanation because "feeling" is not quite accurate as a translation. In English "feeling" has a wide range of meanings. It can mean both emotional states and physical sensations in the body. The Pāli word *vedanā* means that quality of every conscious experience—whether through sight, sound, smell, taste, touch, or mind—that is pleasant, unpleasant, or somewhere in between.

In English we use different words to convey pleasantness or unpleasantness in each of the six senses. If we're relating to a sight, we call vedanā "beautiful," "ugly," or "average." If we are talking about sound, vedanā is "sonorous," "grating," or "uninteresting." If we're describing bodily sensations, vedanā is "pain," "pleasure," or "dullness." That agreeable quality which is common to beauty, melody, and physical pleasure is called *sukha vedanā,* or "pleasant feeling." That disagreeable quality common to ugliness, discordance, and physical pain is called *dukkha vedanā,* or "unpleasant feeling." That which is neither agreeable nor disagreeable is called "neutral feeling."

It is to be remembered that the qualities that we perceive as beautiful, ugly, sonorous, pleasurable, and so on do not reside in the object. Otherwise we would all agree on what was beautiful or pleasurable. The agreeable, disagreeable, and neutral qualities are values that we add to reality through our conditioned mind. Again, *vedanā* means that quality accompanying every conscious experience that you feel as pleasant, unpleasant, or somewhere in between.

When mindfulness is strong and stable, you can investigate vedanā, present and past, without complicating the matter with desire and aversion. When the mind is weak in samādhi and the five hindrances are present, the mind reacts to unpleasant vedanā with aversion and responds to agreeable vedanā with desire. Such reactions stir the mind and distort the truth, in much the same way that winds stir up waves on a lake and distort the images of fish swimming below the surface. This demonstrates yet again the importance of jhāna experience prior to satipaṭṭhāna in order to suppress the five hindrances, especially desire and ill will, in order to have the capability to view the vedanā with complete dispassion.

The Rise and Fall of Vedanā

When the mind is still and free from both desire and aversion, it sees that sukha vedanā (pleasant feeling) is no more than a pause between two moments of dukkha vedanā (unpleasant feeling). Indeed, you can also discern that the intensity of the pleasure in sukha vedanā is directly proportional to the degree of unpleasantness that went just before, and the intensity of the pain in dukkha vedanā is measured by the amount of happiness that you have just lost.

In a chilling book describing imprisonment and torture as a political prisoner in Argentina during the 1970s, an author relates that his most painful experience was not the beatings or the sessions on "Susan" (the name the guards gave to the electric shock torture machine).[5] The worst moment, after endless months of imprisonment, was when his persecutors handed him a letter from his wife. He had blotted out from his mind all memory of the happy years before prison in order to cope with the terror and hopelessness of the present. That letter brought up many warm memories of his wife and family, and made the darkness and agony of his situation even more unbearable. He cursed his wife for sending that letter and screamed deep inside, louder than he ever had under electric shock. As this story graphically illustrates, the intensity of your pain or discontent is proportional to the degree of the happiness that you recall has now vanished.

Vedanā Does Not Belong to You

Vedanā is thus clearly seen to be conditioned, in the same way that night conditions day and day conditions night. It is merely the dualistic play of nature. Vedanā is beyond your control and beyond anyone's control. It is understood to be not mine, not me, not a self. Understanding vedanā in this way through superpower mindfulness, as just vedanā and beyond anyone's control, gives rise to dispassion toward pleasure and pain. You realize with certainty that there can be neither permanent pleasure nor permanent pain. A perfect heavenly world is seen as a sensory impossibility, merely wishful thinking, and an eternal hell is similarly implausible.

Thus the purpose of this second focus of mindfulness is to gain the insight that vedanā is not mine, that pleasure and pain twirl around each other, two inseparable partners on the dance floor of saṃsāra. Craving becomes pointless. And when craving is finally abandoned, there is freedom from pain (and from happiness too).

Mind Contemplation

This third focus of mindfulness, observing the citta or mind consciousness, is one of the most difficult to practice. Most people's meditation is not developed sufficiently to even see mind consciousness. Mind consciousness is like an emperor covered from head to toe in five thick garments: his boots go up to his knees; his trousers go from his waist to his calves; a tunic stretches from his neck to his thighs and along his arms to his wrists; gloves cover his hands and forearms; and a helmet covers all of his head. Being so completely covered, the emperor cannot be seen. In the same way, mind consciousness is so completely clothed by the five senses of sight, hearing, smell, taste, and touch that you cannot see it underneath.

To see the emperor, you have to remove his clothes. In the same way, to see the citta, you have to remove the five external senses. It is the task of the jhāna to remove the five senses and reveal the citta. Thus you cannot even start to practice this third focus of mindfulness until you have experienced a jhāna. For how can you contemplate citta when you haven't really experienced it? It would be like contemplating the emperor when all you can see are his (or *her?*) clothes.

Investigating the nature of citta is also like investigating the nature of gold. Before chemists even begin to test the material, they must ensure that the sample of gold is purified from all other elements and that what they have is 100 percent pure gold. Similarly, before you begin to investigate the nature of citta you have to ensure that this mind consciousness is purified from all other types of consciousness, i.e., that the five external sense-consciousnesses have been abandoned. Again, this can be done only after emerging from a jhāna. Then superpower mindfulness takes the jhāna experience just past, a sustained experience of the citta set apart from the five senses, as its object of investigation. Only in this way will the truth be seen that the citta is anattā, that mind consciousness is subject to arising and passing, that it is neither "me" nor "mine" nor a self, that it is neither God nor cosmic consciousness—that it is just citta, a flame burning because of fuel.

Where the Citta Goes after Enlightenment

A flame depends on fuel. The word for "fuel" in Pāli is *upādāna*. A candle flame depends on heat, wax, and a wick. If any one of those three "fuels" disappears, then the flame ceases. If a wind takes away the heat, the flame ceases. If the wick burns out, the flame ceases. And if the wax is used up, the flame ceases. Once the flame ceases, it doesn't go anywhere. There is no heaven where all good flames go happily to flicker for eternity. Nor does the flame merge with a cosmic, transcendent Flame. It just ceases, that's all. In Pāli the word for a flame "going out" is nibbāna.

The citta too depends on fuel. The suttas say that the citta depends on *nāma-rūpa* (body and objects of mind) and when *nāma-rūpa* ceases, the citta completely ceases (SN 47,42). It goes out. It "nibbānas." It doesn't go anywhere; it just ceases to exist. Interestingly, the two famous bhikkhunīs Kisāgotamī and Paṭācārā became fully enlightened when they saw the flame of a lamp go out (Dhp 275; Thig 116).

The Nature of Citta

When you sustain superpower mindfulness on the pure citta, the nature of all types of consciousness reveals itself. You see consciousness not as a smoothly flowing process but as a series of discrete, isolated events.

Consciousness may be compared to a stretch of sand on a beach. Superficially the sand looks continuous over several hundred meters. But after you investigate it closely, you discover that it is made up of discrete, isolated particles of silicate. There are empty spaces between each particle of sand, with no essential sandiness flowing in the gap between any two particles. In the same way, that which we take to be the flow of consciousness is clearly seen to be a series of discrete events, with nothing flowing in between.

Another analogy is the fruit salad analogy. Suppose on a plate there is an apple. You clearly see this apple completely disappear and in its place appears a coconut. Then the coconut vanishes and in its place appears another apple. Then the second apple vanishes and another coconut is there. That vanishes and a banana appears, only to vanish when another coconut manifests on the plate, then another banana, coconut, apple, coconut, mango, coconut, lemon, coconut, and so on. As soon as one fruit vanishes, then a moment later a completely new fruit appears. They are all fruits but completely different varieties, with no two fruits the same. Moreover, no connecting fruit-essence flows from one fruit to the next. In this analogy, the apple stands for an event of eye consciousness, the banana for an incident of nose consciousness, the mango for taste consciousness, the lemon for body consciousness, and the coconut for mind consciousness. Each moment of consciousness is discrete, with nothing flowing from one moment to the next.

Mind consciousness, the "coconut," appears after every other species of consciousness and thereby gives the illusion of sameness to every conscious experience. To the average person, there is a quality in seeing that is also found in hearing, smelling, tasting, and touching. We can call that quality "knowing." However, with superpower mindfulness, you will discern that this knowing is not part of seeing, hearing, and so on, but arises a moment after each type of sense consciousness. Moreover, this knowing has vanished when, for example, eye consciousness is occurring. And eye consciousness has vanished when knowing (mind consciousness) is occurring. In the simile of the fruit salad, there can't be an apple and a coconut on the plate at the same time.

That Which Knows Is Not Self

Contemplating consciousness in this way—seeing it as a series of discrete, isolated events with no thing continuing from one moment to the next—undermines the illusion that there is a knower, constantly present, which is always there to receive the experience of the world. You are unraveling the last refuge of the illusion of a self. Previously it may have seemed so obvious to you that "I am the one who knows." But what seems obvious is often wrong. Now you see it as just a "knowing," as mind consciousness, like the coconut that is sometimes there and sometimes not. Citta is just a natural phenomenon, subject to ceasing. It cannot be me, mine, or a self. That which knows, citta, is finally understood as anattā.

Satipaṭṭhāna, as noted above, is practiced for the purpose of realizing anattā—no-self. The two last resorts of the illusion of a self or soul are the knower and the doer. If you identify with anything as the essential "you," it will be one or both of these. You assume that you are that which does or that which knows. These two deep-seated, long-held delusions are what stand between you and enlightenment. See through these illusions once, and you are a stream winner. See through these illusions every time, and you are an arahant.

Mind Object Contemplation

Objects of the mind are the last of the four focuses of mindfulness. The mind objects listed in the *Satipaṭṭhāna Sutta* are the five hindrances, the five aggregates, the six senses, the seven enlightenment factors, and the four noble truths. I understand this list to represent examples of mind objects, and therefore other mind objects not mentioned in the *Satipaṭṭhāna Sutta,* such as thought and emotions, may also be included.

Contemplating the Five Hindrances

As I've explained regarding contemplation of feeling *(vedanā),* the five hindrances must be abandoned before you can effectively contemplate anything. But how can you contemplate the five hindrances after you have abandoned them? As I stated above, mindfulness can take as its object an experience that has already passed. Mindfulness includes memory. So superpower mindfulness can take up, for example, a previous experience of sloth and torpor and hold that past experience still in its strong light long enough to see into its true nature. What you apprehend with superpower mindfulness is that these five hindrances are mere instances of images on the screen, that they are not yours or anything to do with you, as the following simile demonstrates.

An old school friend visited Jamaica many years ago. He went to see a movie in a drive-in theater in a remote town well known for its violence. He was surprised to see that the screen was a two-foot thick reinforced concrete wall. It must have cost a fortune. People of that town, it turns out, were very fond of Westerns. However, whenever the story came to the inevitable gunfight, many members of the audience took out their own guns and joined in the action! If they didn't like the sheriff, they shot at his image on the screen, or they blasted away at the Indians or at whomever else upset them. The owner of the theater could not stop them from joining in the gunfights, and he had replaced so many bullet-riddled canvas screens that he built this indestructible concrete screen. Then his audience could join in the gunfights without ruin.

If, like these moviegoers, you identify images on the screen as real, you will want to shoot them. With mindfulness, however, you will see them as having nothing to do with you. When you see the hindrances merely as images on the screen of consciousness, they will not bother you ever again. You will be free.

Contemplating Thought

Thought, the inner conversation, is an object of the mind that can generate immense suffering. It can manifest as restlessness, remorse, doubt, desire, or ill will. As such, thought is at the heart of the five hindrances. Persistent pessimistic thoughts lead to depression, even suicide. Obsessive fearful thoughts lead to paranoia. It should be obvious that there are great benefits to be won through contemplating thought according to this fourth satipaṭṭhāna.

Again, only superpower mindfulness can see through the con game that is thought. With ordinary mindfulness you tend to believe in the thinking, get caught up in it, even worship it as more truthful than reality. A hungry man goes to dine at an expensive restaurant and is handed the menu. He eats the menu, pays, and leaves. He is still hungry. The menu is not the food any more than thoughts are reality.

Superpower mindfulness sees that thought, at best, is one step removed from reality, and at worst it is completely removed. Ill will bends thought into anger, sensory desire inflates thoughts into lust, and restlessness twists thoughts into frustration. When seen clearly, thoughts can't be trusted. Not even this one!

When satipaṭṭhāna sees thinking for what it truly is, a makeshift approximation, then we experience dispassion with regard to our thinking. The sign of such dispassion and wisdom is that you can let go of thoughts at any time. The proof of such insight is your ability to be silent. In the suttas, a term for an enlightened one is *santamuni,* "silent sage."

Contemplating Will

Another important mind object that I wish to discuss here is "will" *(cetanā),* which comes under the contemplation of the five aggregates *(khandha)* in this fourth satipaṭṭhāna. Will is "that which does," or the doer. As I mentioned above, the will is one of the two last resorts of the illusion of self, along with the knower *(citta).* Contemplating the will, the doer, and seeing it as anattā is therefore crucial to the experience of enlightenment.

Years ago I was an active member of the Psychic Research Society at Cambridge University. Every year we would invite a professional hypnotist to demonstrate his craft, often to the great amusement of us students. Once the hypnotist put a receptive volunteer student into a deep state of hypnosis. In front of all the students, the hypnotist told him that later in the evening when the hypnotist touched his left ear, the student was to stand up and sing the British national anthem. And later after coming out from the hypnotic trance, when the hypnotist touched his ear the poor student arose and sang "God Save the Queen"! He sang alone, accompanied by great laughter. The most fascinating part of this demonstration was that, when questioned, the student was of the firm opinion that he had freely decided to sing the national anthem and gave some convoluted reason for it. It showed that even brainwashing appears to the brainwashed as free will.

You are deluded to assume that you are reading this of your own free will. My friend, you had no choice but to read this! Will is not the action of a being; it is the end product of a process.

When superpower mindfulness takes a recent experience of jhāna as its object, it sees that will, the "doer," has completely ceased within that state. It has vanished for long periods of time. Contemplating a fully mindful state that is free of will allows you to see that "will," "choice," and the "doer" are not me or mine, not a self. Whatever you do is just a result of complex programming.

When I talk like this, people get frightened. Such fear is a symptom that something you are so attached to, your will, is about to be taken away. We in the West are so attached to the delusion of free will, in fact, that we enshrine the illusion in our constitutions and declarations of human rights. You may raise the objection that if there is no free will, why bother to generate the great effort needed for enlightenment? The answer should be obvious. You put forth great effort because you have no choice!

It is only superpower mindfulness that has the strength to penetrate the barrier of fear erected by attachment and observe the process of will as it truly is. Like the thousand-petaled lotus, when the layer of petals that represent "the doer" fully opens up, you see the unexpected, that there is no one in here doing all this. The will is anattā. Craving begins to unravel at this point.

Contemplating Emotions

The last of the mind objects that I want to discuss here is emotion. Emotion is that texture of mind categorized as depressed or inspired, guilty or forgiving, worried or serene, angry or compassionate, and so on. Emotions toss us around, and this often hurts. Emotions are mind objects, things that appear on the screen of consciousness, and are part of this fourth satipaṭṭhāna.

When I was already a young Buddhist I went to see the movie *West Side Story*. There is a heartbreaking scene at the end when the hero, Tony, runs to his lover, Maria, under a New York City streetlight, is shot, and dies in Maria's arms. As their doomed relationship is tragically rent, they sing, "There's a place for us. Somewhere a place for us." Many in the audience began sobbing uncontrollably. Why did they cry? It was only a movie after all, just the play of light on a cloth screen.

When you are deluded by emotions, you take them to be important, real, "mine." You can get so sucked in that you seek even unpleasant emotions like sadness repeatedly. Why is it that many people go to a movie with a box of tissues knowing, from the reviews, that it is a tear-jerker? It is because they are attached to emotions, delight in them, and identify with them. They don't want to be free.

Superpower mindfulness focused on emotions uncovers the reality of whether you want to be free or not. It pushes aside your preferences. You recognize that the emotions are seductive sirens beckoning you to their treacherous rocks. But in their essence they are but mind objects, causally conditioned, like weather fronts passing overhead, having nothing to do with you. When you see the truth, you are detached from emotions and free from their tyranny.

Whatever is an object of the mind, whatever appears on the screen of consciousness—whether it be the five hindrances, thought, will, or emotions—can be put under the unremitting and penetrating beam of superpower mindfulness. There you will realize the completely unexpected. You will see what the Buddha saw under the Bodhi tree. The realization will dawn that all these events on the screen of consciousness are just the play of nature, not the play of God, not the play of a soul. There is nothing here. There is "nobody at home." These mind objects are empty. They are no-self *(anattā)*. The illusion has been seen through. You are now free, unaffected by any mind object.

The Buddha promised that anyone who practices the four satipaṭṭhānas diligently will reach the state of either the nonreturner or full enlightenment in seven days. Perhaps you now understand why many meditators have been disappointed that after many more than seven days they're still not enlightened. As I said earlier, the reason is that they have not been practicing satipaṭṭhāna following the Buddha's instructions. Try it and see. Develop superpower mindfulness generated by jhāna so you know for yourself how impotent ordinary mindfulness is. Put the citta (the knower) or cetanā (the will) under the spotlight of superpower mindfulness, courageously going beyond the comfort of your views. Await the unexpected. Don't second-guess truth. Wait with patience until the thousandth petal of the lotus fully opens to reveal the heart. That will be the end of delusion, the end of saṃsāra, and the end of satipaṭṭhāna.

Part 2
To Bliss and Beyond

The Jhānas I: Bliss

9

◆ ◆ ◆ ─────────────────────────────

I N THE ORIGINAL Buddhist scriptures there is only one word for "meditation" and that is *jhāna*. According to the fully enlightened Ven. Ānanda in the *Gopaka-Moggallāna Sutta* (MN 108,27) the only kind of meditation that the Buddha recommended was jhāna. Thus jhāna designates Buddhist meditation proper, where the meditator's mind is stilled of all thought, secluded from all five-sense activity, and is radiant with otherworldly bliss. Put bluntly, if it isn't jhāna then it isn't true Buddhist meditation! Perhaps this is why the culminating factor of the Buddha's noble eightfold path, the one that defines *right* meditation, is nothing less than the four jhānas.

The Buddha's Discovery

The ancient Buddhist texts state that the Buddha discovered jhāna (SN 2,7; AN IX,42). Not once in the original texts does it say that the Buddha discovered *vipassanā*. These authoritative texts also state that the four jhānas only arise with the appearance of a buddha (SN 45,14–17). The fact that the Buddha discovered jhāna should not be overlooked, for the discovery was a central act in the drama of enlightenment.

When it is said by no less an authority than the arahant Ānanda that the Buddha discovered jhāna, it is not to be understood that no one had ever experienced jhāna before. For instance, in the era of the previous buddha, Kassapa, countless men and women achieved jhāna and subsequently realized enlightenment. But in the India of twenty-six centuries ago, all knowledge of jhāna had disappeared. For example, the famous leader of the Jains and contemporary of the Buddha, Mahāvīra, publicly dismissed jhānas as an impossibility after hearing them described (SN 41,8). Either the most prominent (according to many scholars) religious leader of that time was unbelievably ignorant of common spiritual practices, or else jhāna was indeed an original discovery of the Buddha. The latter is far more plausible, and it is further supported by the observation that there is no mention at all of jhāna in any religious text before the time of the Buddha.

Some might raise the objection that the Buddha's earlier teachers, Alāra Kalāma and Udaka Rāmaputta, taught jhāna because the texts say that they instructed the Bodhisatta (the Buddha-to-be) in the attainment of the state of nothingness and in the attainment of the state of neither perception nor nonperception (MN 26). Although these two attainments are never called jhāna in the early texts (the term *arupa-jhāna* first appears in the much later commentarial literature), it is implicit that they can only be accessed by first proceeding through each of the four jhānas step by step. So did these two early leaders know the four jhānas and teach them to the Bodhisatta?

If they did, then why did the Buddha state that their methods did not lead to nibbāna (MN 26,16) but that jhāna did lead to nibbāna (MN 36,31; 52,4–7; 64,9–12)? And why, when the Bodhisatta abandoned asceticism and asked, "Could there be another path to enlightenment?" (MN 36,30), did he recall the more distant memory of first jhāna as a boy under the rose-apple tree instead of a more recent and intense experience of jhāna under his two early teachers? These questions need to be satisfactorily answered by anyone who still maintains that Alāra Kalāma and Udaka Rāmaputta taught jhāna.

An answer to the question of what these two early teachers taught, one that maintains the Buddha's consistency in rejecting the efficacy of their teachings while praising the efficacy of jhāna (MN 108,27), is that Udaka Rāmaputta and Alāra Kalāma never taught jhāna, and that the two formless attainments that they espoused were not the real thing, most likely diluted versions of the original from the time of the previous Buddha Kassapa. Just as today some teachers present a level of meditation and call it "jhāna" when it is clearly less than the real thing, or some colleges will, for a fee, send a university degree by return mail when the degree is not the real thing, so the attainments taught by Alāra Kalāma and Udaka Rāmaputta could not have been the real thing. The "real thing," the attainment of the sphere of nothingness, *does* lead to enlightenment (MN 52,14), but the different experience of the same name taught by Alāra Kalāma did not.

Another reason why jhāna was unknown before the arising of the Buddha was that the cause of jhāna, the practice of the Middle Way, was also unknown then. Ancient texts such as the *Dhammacakka-ppavat-tana Sutta* (the first sermon, SN 56,11) state that the Buddha discovered the Middle Way and that the Middle Way is synonymous with the noble eightfold path. Another sutta states that the Buddha discovered the noble eightfold path, like a long-lost path to an ancient city (SN 12,65). It should also be noted that the noble eightfold path, the Middle Way, is a gradual path that culminates in jhāna (AN X,103). Thus if one accepts that the Buddha discovered the Middle Way, the noble eightfold path, one must also accept that the Buddha discovered the final stage of the way, the end portion of the path, which is jhāna.

The *Arana-vibhanga Sutta* (MN 139) equates the Middle Way with the pursuit of jhāna. The sutta explains in detail that one should not pursue asceticism nor pleasure of the five senses, but instead one should pursue the Middle Way. If one does not pursue suffering in any of the six senses (asceticism) and one does not pursue pleasure in the five senses *(kāma-sukha)*, then the only pursuit remaining is for the happiness of the sixth sense (mind), and this must be the Middle Way. This sutta continues with the Buddha encouraging the pursuit of internal happiness, obviously the Middle Way, only here he defines it as the pursuit of the four jhānas. Conclusion: the Middle Way is the pursuit of jhāna.

In the story of the Buddha's awakening, once the Bodhisatta realized that jhāna was the way to enlightenment (MN 36,31), he immediately recognized that it was impractical to attain jhāna with an emaciated body and so began eating well. Seeing this, his first five disciples left him in disgust, thinking he had given up striving (MN 36,32). This indicates that the gentle practices that lead to tranquillity of the body and then on to jhāna were not recognized before the arising of the Buddha as a valid path by learned seekers such as these five disciples. When the path to jhāna was not widely recognized as worthwhile, it is no wonder that the path was not pursued and jhāna was not achieved. It should also now be clear why the first part of the first sermon of the newly awakened Buddha was the teaching of the Middle Way, the noble eightfold path, that opens the way to jhāna and the enlightenment beyond.

I have written at length on this point, citing many original texts, because it is a new idea to the West. What is groundbreaking is bound to be controversial. I ask all sincere readers to put aside their existing views for a while, since the Buddha said that attachment to views can be an obstacle to insight, and fairly consider the evidence presented here. After all, the *Pancālacando Sutta* (SN 2,7) is certainly an original sutta, because it is referred to elsewhere in the canon (AN IX,42) and was thus confirmed as authentic Dhamma by the five hundred arahants at the First Council—and it states that the Buddha discovered jhāna.

Can One Be Attached to Jhāna?

When the Bodhisatta had the insight that jhāna was the way to enlightenment, he then thought, "Why am I afraid of that pleasure which has nothing to do with the five senses nor with unwholesome things? I will not be afraid of that pleasure [of jhāna]!" (MN 36,32). Even today, some meditators mistakenly believe that something as intensely pleasurable as jhāna cannot be conducive to the end of all suffering, and they remain afraid of jhāna. However, in the suttas the Buddha repeatedly stated that the pleasure of the jhāna "is to be followed, is to be developed, and is to be encouraged. It is not to be feared" (MN 66,21).

In spite of this clear advice from the Buddha himself, some students of meditation are misled by those who discourage jhāna on the grounds that one can become so attached to jhāna that one never becomes enlightened. It should be pointed out that the Buddha's word for attachment, *upādāna,* refers only to attachment to the comfort and pleasure of the five-sense world or to attachment to various forms of wrong view (such as a view of a self). It never means attachment to wholesome things like jhāna.[6]

Simply put, jhāna states are stages of letting go. One cannot be attached to letting go, just as one cannot be imprisoned by freedom. One can indulge in jhāna, in the bliss of letting go, and this is what some people are misled into fearing. But in the *Pāsādika Sutta* (DN 29,25), the Buddha said that one who indulges in the pleasure of jhāna may expect only one of four consequences: stream winning, once-returning, nonreturning, or full enlightenment! In other words, indulging in jhāna leads only to the four stages of enlightenment. Thus, in the words of the Buddha, "One should not fear jhāna."

For some meditators, the jhānas seem far from their experience and thus irrelevant. This is not so. Discussing such sublime states can create inspiration, as well as map out the territory ahead. More crucially, discussion informs one about what to do when one draws close to any of these profound states of freedom. Finally, it gives a deeper understanding of the Dhamma, especially into the third noble truth, the cessation of all suffering. This is because the rapture and bliss of jhāna is directly related to the amount of saṃsāra that is abandoned, albeit temporarily. Thus, discussing the jhānas is well worthwhile, even if they may seem distant.

Some readers may have already gotten close enough to be able to understand this discussion from their own experience, and it may help them make that last leap into the jhānas. Furthermore, when meditators experience a profound state of meditation, they want to find out exactly what it was, to recognize the state in terms of the Buddha's descriptions. So it is important to be able to correctly identify the levels of depth in meditation.

It is also important to generate some inspiration in one's achievement. Such a positive emotion will encourage further letting go. It is my intention to show you how wonderful and profound these states of jhāna are, and to illustrate how crucial their experience is to the event of enlightenment.

Eventually, the seeds that are planted in you through reading a discussion on jhāna will someday bear fruit. At the right time, the mind will know automatically what it must do. For example, when nimittas arise, the mind will spontaneously know how to respond. Then sometime later you might reflect, "Where did that response come from?" The answer is that it came from reading discussions such as this. Sometimes it comes from what one has learned in a past life!

So please do not think that just because you have not yet reached the jhānas this discussion is of no use to you. In fact it will be very useful. You will realize this when, having achieved one of the jhānas, you recognize that such instructions as given here came to your help just at the right time.

The Beautiful Breath: The Beginning of the Journey into Jhānas

Having discussed the jhānas from a historical and theoretical point of view, I will now explain the jhānas in terms of their practice. It is best to begin the description of the journey into jhāna from the starting point of the beautiful breath. Before this stage is accomplished, the mind has insufficient contentment, awareness, or stability to launch itself into the higher states of consciousness. But when you are able to maintain an effortless awareness on the breath without a break for long periods of time, when the mind has settled into such a rich awareness that the breath appears delightful, then you are ready to set off on the journey into jhāna.

Do not fear delight in meditation. Happiness in meditation is important! Moreover, you deserve to bliss out. Blissing out on the breath is an essential part of the path. So when delight does arise alongside the breath, cherish and guard it like a valuable treasure.

The delight that arises at the stage of the beautiful breath is the glue that holds the mind's attention onto the breath. It results in the mindfulness staying with the breath without effort. One stays with full attention on the breath because the mind enjoys watching the breath and doesn't want to go anywhere else. It remains with the breath automatically, and all wandering ceases.

Without the experience of delight, there will be some discontent.

And discontent is the source of the wandering mind. Before one reaches the stage of the beautiful breath, discontent pushes mindfulness away from the breath. Then the only way to keep mindfulness upon the breath is through an effort of will, through control. But when the stage of the beautiful breath is achieved, when delight generates long-lasting contentment, then the mind will not wander. Control can be relaxed, effort relieved, and the mind remains motionless, naturally.

Just as gasoline is the fuel that propels a car, so discontent is the fuel that moves the mind. When a car runs out of gas, it gently rolls to a stop. One doesn't need to use the brake. In the same way, when the mind runs out of discontent, through the arising of the beautiful breath, it gently comes to a stop. One doesn't need to use the brake of willpower. The mind comes to a state of stillness quite naturally.

Pīti-sukha—Joy and Happiness

In Pāli, the compound word *pīti-sukha* means the combination of joy with happiness. One can use those words for many kinds of experiences, even worldly ones. But in meditation, pīti-sukha refers only to that joy and happiness that is generated through letting go.

Just as various types of fire can be distinguished by their fuel, such as a wood fire, oil fire, or bushfire, so can the various types of happiness be differentiated by their cause. The joy and happiness that arises with the beautiful breath is fueled by the letting go of the burdens of past and future, internal commentary, and diversity of consciousness. Because it is a delight born of letting go, it cannot produce attachment. One cannot be attached and let go at the same time. The delight that arises with the beautiful breath is, in fact, a clear sign that some detachment has taken place.

Pīti-sukha may arise from sensual excitement, from personal achievement, or from letting go. These three types of happiness differ in their nature. The happiness generated by sensual excitement is hot and stimulating but also agitated and therefore tiring. Repetition makes it fade. The happiness caused by personal achievement is warm and fulfilling but also fades quickly, leaving a vacant hole. But the happiness born of letting go is cool and long-lasting. It is associated with the sense of real freedom.

Moreover, the happiness generated by sensual excitement produces ever-stronger desires, making the happiness unstable and tyrannical. The happiness caused by personal achievement produces more investment in being a control freak and encourages the illusion of personal power. The controller then kills any happiness. The happiness born of letting go inspires more letting go and less interference. Because it encourages one to leave things alone, it is stable and effortless. It is the happiness most independent of causes and closest to the unconditioned, the uncaused.

It is important for success in meditation to recognize the different types of happiness. If the happiness that arises with awareness of the breath is of the sensual excitement type—for example, waves of physical pleasure coursing through your body—it will soon disappear when effort is relaxed, leaving you heavy and tired. If the happiness is associated with the sense of achievement—"Wow! At last I'm getting somewhere in my meditation"—it will often disintegrate, destroyed by the arousal of the controller, ruined by the interfering ego. But if the happiness that arises with the beautiful breath is that born of letting go, then you feel that you don't need to say anything or do anything. It becomes the happiness whose brother is freedom and whose sister is peace. It will grow all by itself in magnificent intensity, blossoming like a flower in the garden of jhāna.

In addition to the beautiful breath, there are many other objects of meditation: loving-kindness *(mettā)*, parts of the body *(kāyagatāsati)*, simple visualizations *(kasiṇa)*, and others. However, in all meditation that develops into jhāna there must come a stage where the pīti-sukha born of letting go arises. For example, loving-kindness meditation opens into a wonderful, gorgeous, unconditional love for the whole cosmos, filling the meditator with delicious joy. Pīti-sukha born of letting go has arisen, and one is at the stage of "beautiful mettā." Some meditators focus on parts of the human body, often a skull. As the meditation deepens, as mindfulness rests on the inner image of a skull, an amazing process unfolds. The image of the skull in one's mind starts to whiten, then deepen in color, until it appears to glow with intense luminosity as the "beautiful skull." Again, pīti-sukha born of letting go has appeared, filling the whole experience with joy and happiness. Even some monks who practice *asubha* (loathsomeness) meditation, on a decaying corpse, for instance, can experience the initially repugnant cadaver suddenly changing into one of the most beautiful images of all. Letting go has aroused so much happiness that it overwhelms the natural disgust and floods the image with pīti-sukha. One has realized the stage of the "beautiful corpse."

In meditation on the breath, the Lord Buddha taught the arousing of pīti-sukha along with the experience of one's breath as the fifth and sixth steps of the sixteen-step ānāpānasati method. I dealt with this crucial stage of meditation at length above.[7]

When pīti-sukha doesn't arise, it must be because there is not enough contentment, that is, *one is still trying too hard.* One should reflect on the first two of the five hindrances. The first hindrance, sensory desire, draws the attention toward the object of desire and thus away from the breath. The second hindrance, ill will, finds fault with the experience of breath, and the dissatisfaction repels the attention from the breath. Contentment is the "middle way" between desire and ill will. It keeps one's mindfulness with the breath long enough for pīti-sukha to arise.

The Way into Stillness

Stillness means lack of movement. Since will causes the mind to move, to experience stillness one must remove all will, all doing, all control. If you grasp a leaf on a tree and try your hardest to hold it still, no matter how hard you try, you will never succeed. There will always be some vibration caused by slight tremors in your muscles. However, if you don't touch the leaf and just protect it from the breeze, then the leaf comes to a natural state of stillness. In exactly the same way, you cannot achieve stillness by holding the mind in the grip of the will. But if you remove the cause of movement in the mind, the will, the mind soon becomes still.

Thus one cannot *will* the mind to be still. The way into stillness is through the pīti-sukha born of letting go. Once the delight that comes with the beautiful breath appears, then the will becomes redundant. It becomes unnecessary since mindfulness stays with the breath all by itself, effortlessly. Mindfulness enjoys being with the beautiful breath, and so does not need to be forced.

When stillness appears it enriches the pīti-sukha. The deepening of pīti-sukha, in turn, creates even less opportunity for effort, and so stillness grows stronger. A self-reinforcing feedback process ensues. Stillness deepens pīti-sukha, and pīti-sukha increases the stillness. This process continues, when not interrupted, all the way into jhāna, where stillness is profound and pīti-sukha ecstatic.

In this chapter I have explored some of the issues often raised about the jhānas. The next chapter, on the nimitta, takes us farther down the road to the deep absorptions.

The Jhānas II: Bliss upon Bliss 10

+ + +

The Nimitta: The Home Stretch into Jhāna

WHEN THE BREATH DISAPPEARS and delight fills the mind, the nimitta usually appears. I briefly discussed nimittas and their characteristics in chapter 2; here I discuss them in greater depth. *Nimitta,* in this context, refers to beautiful "lights" that appear in the mind. I would point out, though, that the nimittas are not visual objects, in that they are not seen through the sense of sight. At this stage of the meditation, the sense of sight is not operating. The nimittas are pure mental objects, known by the mind sense. However, they are commonly perceived as lights.

What is happening here is that perception struggles to interpret such a pure mental phenomenon. Perception is that function of mind that interprets experience in terms we can understand. Perception relies crucially on comparison, interpreting new experience as similar to previous experience. However, pure mental phenomena are so rarely visited that perception has great difficulty finding anything at all comparable to these new experiences. This is why nimittas appear strange, like nothing one has ever experienced before. But the phenomena in the catalogue of one's past experiences that come closest to these nimittas are simple visual lights, such as a car headlight, a flashlight in the dark, or a full moon in the night sky. Perception adopts this close but imperfect comparison and interprets the nimittas as lights.

It was for me a fascinating discovery to realize that everyone who experiences these nimittas experiences exactly the same thing! It is only that meditators interpret the experience in many different ways. Some see the nimitta as a pure white light, others see it as golden, some as deep blue. Some see it as a circle, others as an oblong; some see it as sharp edged, others as fuzzy edged. There is indeed no end to the features of nimittas that meditators describe. The important thing to know is that color, shape, and so on are irrelevant. Perception colors the nimitta and gives it shape just so one can make sense of it.

When the Nimitta Comes Too Early

Sometimes a "light" can appear in the mind at a very early stage of the meditation. For all except accomplished meditators, however, such intruders are highly unstable. If one focuses one's attention on them, one will not get anywhere. It is not the right time for nimitta. It is best to regard them as distractions and go back to the main task of the early stage out of which they came.

There is more uncertainty what to do when a nimitta appears at the stage of the beautiful breath when the breath has yet to be calmed close to disappearance. Again, the nimitta appears intrusive. It interferes with the main task of sustaining one's awareness on the beautiful breath. If one deliberately turns from the breath to the nimitta, it usually doesn't remain long. The mind is not sufficiently refined to hold a subtle nimitta. One needs additional practice on the breath. So the best thing to do is to ignore the nimitta and train all one's attention on the beautiful breath.

Often, after one has followed this advice, the nimitta comes back, stronger and brighter. Ignore it again. When it returns a third time, even more powerful and radiant, go back to the breath. Practicing this way, eventually a very powerful and brilliant nimitta will break into your awareness. You can go with that one. Actually, it is almost impossible to ignore. That one usually takes you into jhāna.

The above can be compared to a visitor knocking on your door. It could be just a salesman, so you ignore his knocking and go on with your own business. Often, that's the end of the matter. Sometimes, though, the visitor knocks again, louder and longer. You ignore him a second time. Then after a few moments' silence, he bangs even louder and more vigorously. This persistence suggests that that the visitor must be a good friend of yours, so you open the door, let him in, and have a great time together.

Another method of dealing with an early nimitta that arises at the stage of the beautiful breath is to incorporate the nimitta into the middle of the breath. One trains to visualize the situation as similar to a jewel being held in the center of lotus petals. The shimmering jewel is the nimitta, the lotus petals represent the beautiful breath. If the mind isn't quite ready to stay with the nimitta, it still has the breath to anchor it. Sometimes, the mind is so unprepared that the breath appears to close in on the nimitta, and as a result the nimitta disappears leaving only the beautiful breath. This step backward does not disturb the meditation. At other times, the mind is well prepared for the nimitta, and the nimitta strengthens and expands, pushing out the breath, which disappears beyond the edges of one's awareness, leaving only the nimitta. This method is skillful because it doesn't involve moving the mind from one thing to another—a coarse movement that disturbs the meditation significantly. Instead, one just passively observes the transition from the beautiful breath to the nimitta, and maybe back again, allowing the process to develop or recede according to nature, not according to one's desire.

Although the following advice is for accomplished meditators only, by which I mean those with plentiful experience of jhāna already, it is included here for the sake of completeness. When one is skillful in entering into jhāna and one has experienced a jhāna recently, the mind is so still and powerful, even before one begins to meditate, that one may skip many stages. So much so that one may arouse the nimitta almost immediately after starting. The mind, being so used to nimittas and so favorably disposed toward them, literally leaps onto the nimitta and the nimitta stays. Soon jhāna is reached. For such accomplished meditators, the earlier the nimitta arises, the better.

When the Nimitta Does Not Appear

For some, when the breath disappears, the nimitta doesn't happen. No lights appear in their mind. Instead, they are left with a deep feeling of peace, of emptiness, of nothing. This can be a very beneficial state and should not be belittled, but it is not jhāna. Moreover, it lacks the power to proceed any further. It is a cul-de-sac, and a refined one at that, but it is incapable of being developed further. There are a number of methods to bypass this state, generate the causes for nimitta, and go deeper into the jhānas.

The state above arises because one did not cultivate sufficient pīti-sukha along with the breath. There was not enough delight when the breath disappeared, so mindfulness had no clear mental object of beauty on which to settle. Understanding this, one needs to put more value on developing delight when one is watching the breath, and cultivating that delight until it becomes a strong sense of beauty. For example, you may regard the breath as an old and well-loved friend with whom you have shared such wonderful times. Remembering those happy moments brings you joy, and that joy lets you look on the breath as beautiful. Whatever skillful means one employs, by paying careful attention to the beauty alongside the breath, the beauty will blossom. What one pays attention to usually grows.

In the previous chapter, one was cautioned not to be afraid to delight in meditation. I regard this exhortation as so important that I repeat it here almost word for word: Do not be afraid to delight in meditation. Too many meditators dismiss happiness, thinking it unimportant or believing that they don't deserve such delight. Happiness in meditation is important, and you deserve to bliss out! Blissing out on the meditation object is an essential part of the path. So when delight does arise along-side the breath, you should cherish it and guard it accordingly.

Another reason for the nimitta not arising is that one hasn't invested enough energy into the knower. As explained in the previous chapter, delight is generated by letting energy flow into the knower. Usually, most of our mental energy gets lost in the doing, that is, in planning and remembering, controlling and thinking. If one would only redi-rect one's energy away from the doer and give it all to the knower, to attentiveness, then one's mind would become brightened and energized with delight. When there is lots of delight, strong pīti-sukha, then after the breath disappears the nimitta appears. So maybe the reason why a nimitta doesn't appear is that one has devoted too much energy to controlling and not enough to knowing.

However, if the breath has disappeared but still no nimitta arises, then one must be careful not to fall into discontent. Discontent will wither any pīti-sukha already there and will urge the mind into restlessness. Thus discontent will make the arising of a nimitta even more unlikely. So one must be patient and seek the remedy in becoming aware of contentment and letting it consolidate. Just through paying attention to contentment, it usually deepens. As contentment grows stronger, delight will arise. As delight grows in power, the nimitta appears.

Another useful method to arouse the nimitta when the breath disappears is to focus more sharply in the present moment. Present-moment awareness is the very first stage of this method of meditation. It should have been established at the beginning. But in practice, as the meditation progresses and one pays attention to other things, the present-moment awareness can become a little sloppy. It may be that one's mindfulness has become smeared around the present moment instead of being precisely focused. By noticing this as a problem, it is very easy to adjust the focus of mindfulness to be knife-edged in the center of now. Like adjusting the lens of a telescope, the slightly blurred image becomes very sharp. When the attention is sharply focused in the present moment, it experiences more power. Pīti-sukha comes with the sharpening of focus, and the nimitta soon follows as well.

Suitable Nimitta and Useless Nimitta

It is very helpful to cultivate nimittas of the sort perceived as a light. These "light nimittas" are the best vehicle for transporting the meditator into the jhānas. However, it is just possible, but rarely done, to enter a jhāna by using "feeling nimittas" instead. By this I mean that one sees no light in the mind but instead experiences a feeling of bliss in the mind. It is important to note that the sense of touch (the last of the five senses) has been transcended and such a feeling of bliss is experienced completely by the mind sense. It is a pure mental object again, but perceived as relating closely to a physical feeling of bliss. This is a bona fide nimitta. But it is much more difficult to work with such a nimitta to gain access into jhāna, though it is not impossible. For these reasons, it is recommended to cultivate the light nimitta if one aspires for the jhāna.

There are some visual nimittas that are of no use on the path into jhāna. It is helpful to identify these "useless" nimittas so that one will waste no time with them.

Sometimes whole scenes can appear clearly in the mind. There might be landscapes, buildings, and people, familiar or strange. Such visions might be fascinating to watch, but they are of little use. Moreover, they are meaningless, and one should certainly not mistake them as some revelation of truth. Experience shows that visions arising at this stage are notoriously deceptive and completely untrustworthy. If one likes to waste time, one can linger on them a while. But the recommended thing to do is to remove all interest and go back to the beautiful breath. Such complex nimittas are merely a reflection of an overcomplicated mind. The mind should have been calmed into simplicity much more effectively before letting go of the breath. When one sustains the attention on the beautiful breath, uninterrupted for long periods of time, then one is training in simplicity. Then when the breath disappears, a simple unified nimitta arises, one that is suitable for progress.

A less elaborate nimitta, which is still overcomplicated, can be called the "firework nimitta." As the name suggests, this consists of many bursts of light coming and going, never lasting very long and exhibiting much movement. There may be several bursts of light at the same time, even of different colors. Again, this firework nimitta is a sign that the mind is still too complicated and very unstable. If one wants, one can enjoy the sideshow for a short time, but one should not waste too much time there. One should ignore all its razzle-dazzle, return to the breath, and develop more one-pointedness and calm.

The next type of nimitta can be called the "shy nimitta," a single pure light that flashes up quickly and then disappears. After a few moments, it flashes up again. Each time, it lasts only a second or two. Such a nimitta is much more encouraging. Its simplicity shows that the mind is one-pointed. Its power is a sign that pīti-sukha is strong. But its inability to remain after breaking through into consciousness shows that the level of calm is not quite enough. In such a situation, one need not return immediately to the beautiful breath. Instead, one patiently waits, developing more calm, allowing the mind to become more receptive to the very shy nimitta. As will be explained later at greater length, this nimitta disappears because the mind overreacts to its arrival, usually with excitement or fear. By establishing a solid calm and having the confidence to not react at all, the shy nimitta returns and stays longer each time. Soon such a nimitta loses its shyness and, feeling accepted within the mind's calmness, remains a long time. One should attempt this approach first. But if the nimitta continues being shy and shows no sign of remaining longer, then one should return to the beautiful breath and ignore it. When one has built more tranquillity of mind with the beautiful breath, then one can return to the shy nimitta to see if it will establish itself this time.

Another type of nimitta is the "point nimitta," a simple and powerful light but ever so small, which persists many seconds. This nimitta can be very useful. It shows that one-pointedness is excellent, calm is sufficient, but pīti-sukha is still a bit lacking. All one needs to do is gently look deeper into the point nimitta, letting mindfulness zero in. Then it appears as if one's awareness comes closer to this nimitta and its size starts to increase. As it expands a little, one should keep one's focus on the center, not on the edges or beyond the edges. By maintaining the mind's focus sharply on the center of the point nimitta, it increases in power and grows in pīti-sukha. Soon the point nimitta unfolds into the best nimitta of all.

The best nimitta, the one most suitable for jhāna, begins by resembling the full moon at midnight in a sky free of clouds. It rises unhurried when the beautiful breath softly disappears. It takes three or four seconds to establish its presence and settle down, remaining still and very beautiful before the mind's eye. As it remains without effort it grows brighter, more luminous. Soon it appears brighter than the sun at midday, radiating bliss. It becomes by far the most beautiful thing one has ever seen. Its beauty and power will often feel unbearable. One wonders whether one can take so much bliss of such extreme power. But one can. There's no limit to the bliss one can feel. Then the nimitta explodes, drowning one in even more bliss, or one dives into the center of the radiating ecstasy. If one remains there, it is jhāna.

Shining Up the Nimitta

In chapter 7, I first introduced the simile of the mirror. It is a far-reaching insight to realize that this nimitta is actually an image of one's mind. Just as one sees an image of one's face when one looks in a mirror, one sees an image of one's mind in the profound stillness of this meditation stage.

So when the nimitta appears dull, or even dirty, it means that one's mind is dull, even dirty! Usually, this is because one has been lacking in virtue recently; possibly one was angry, or maybe self-centered. At this stage of meditation, one is looking directly at one's mind and there is no opportunity for deceit. One always sees the mind as it truly is. So, if one's nimitta appears dull and stained, then one should clean up one's act in daily life. One should take moral precepts, speak only kindly, practice more generosity, and be selfless in service. This stage of meditation when nimittas appear makes it abundantly clear that virtue is an essential ingredient for success in meditation.

Having taught many meditation retreats over the years, I have noticed that the meditators who have the easiest progress and most sensational results are those who we would call purehearted. They are the people who are joyously generous, whose nature would never allow them to harm another being, who are soft-spoken, gentle, and very happy. Their beautiful lifestyle gives them a beautiful mind. And their beautiful mind supports their virtuous lifestyle. Then, when they reach this stage of the meditation and their mind is revealed in the image of a nimitta, it is so brilliant and pure that it leads them easily to jhāna. It demonstrates that one cannot lead a heedless and self-indulgent lifestyle and have easy success in one's meditation. On the other hand, purifying one's conduct and developing compassion prepare the mind for meditation. The best remedy, then, for shining up a dull or dirty nimitta is to purify one's conduct outside the meditation.

That being said, if one's conduct in daily life isn't too outrageous, one can shine up the dirty nimitta in the meditation itself. This is achieved by focusing the attention on the center of the nimitta. Most areas of the nimitta may appear dull, but the very center of the nimitta is always the brightest and purest part. It is the soft center of an otherwise stiff and unworkable nimitta. As one focuses on the center, it expands like a balloon to produce a second nimitta, purer and brighter. One looks into the very center of this second nimitta, the spot where it is the brightest of all, and that balloons into a third nimitta, even purer and brighter. Gazing into the center effectively shines up the nimitta. One continues in this way until the nimitta is beautifully brilliant.

When, in life, one has developed a strong fault-finding mind, obsessively picking out what's wrong in this and that, then one will find it almost impossible to pick out the beautiful center of a dull nimitta and focus attention thereon. One has become so conditioned to pick out the blemishes in things that it goes against the grain to ignore all the dull and dirty areas of a nimitta to focus exclusively on the beautiful center. This demonstrates once again how unskillful attitudes in life can prevent success in deep meditation. When one develops a more forgiving attitude to life, when one becomes more embracing of the duality of good and bad—not being a negative obsessive nor a positive excessive but a balanced acceptive—then not only can one see the beauty in mistakes, but one can also see the beautiful center in a dull and dirty nimitta.

It is essential to have a bright and luminous nimitta to take one through to jhāna. A dull and dirty one is like an old, beat-up car that will break down on the journey. The dull nimitta, when not made to shine, usually vanishes after some time. So if one is unable to shine up the nimitta, then go back to the beautiful breath and build up more energy there. Generate greater pīti-sukha, huge happiness and joy, along with the breath. Then, next time the breath disappears and a nimitta arises, it will be not dull but beautiful and luminous. In effect, one has shined up the nimitta in the stage of the beautiful breath.

Stabilizing the Nimitta

When the nimitta is very bright, it is also very beautiful. It usually appears unearthly in the depth of its beauty and more wonderful than anything one has ever experienced before. Whatever the color of the nimitta, it is a thousand times richer than anything that can be seen with one's own eyes. Such awesome beauty will captivate one's attention, making the nimitta remain. The more beautiful the nimitta, the more likely it is that the nimitta will become stable and not jump about. Thus one of the best methods to stabilize the nimitta, so that it persists a long time, is to shine the nimitta into brilliance, as explained above.

However, some brilliant nimittas still don't last long. They burst into the mental field of awareness with strong pīti-sukha, but they persist not much longer than a glorious shooting star in a clear night sky. These nimittas have power but lack sufficient stability. In order to stabilize such a nimitta, it is important to know that the two enemies that disperse the nimitta are fear and excitement.

Of the two enemies, fear is more common. These nimittas appear so immense in their sheer power and beauty that one often becomes very afraid. Fear is a natural response to the recognition of something much more powerful than oneself. Moreover, the experience is so unfamiliar that one's personal security looks seriously threatened. It seems as if one might lose all control. And one will—blissfully so—if one could only let go of the "self" and trust in the nimitta! Then one would experience desire and control overwhelmed by supramundane bliss, and, in consequence, much of what one took to be one's self would vanish, leaving a real sense of freedom. It is the fear of losing part of one's ego that is the root cause of alarm when a powerful nimitta appears.

Those who have understood something of the Buddha's teaching of anattā, that there is no self, will have an easier time transcending this fear and accepting the nimitta. They realize that they have nothing to protect and so can let go of control, trust in the emptiness, and selflessly enjoy the beauty and power. Thus the nimitta settles. Even an intellectual understanding that there is no one in here will help overcome the terror of letting go of the innermost controller. However, those who have no appreciation of the truth of no-self may overcome this fear by substituting the more powerful perception of bliss.

The simile of a child in a swimming pool illustrates this last point.

When children who have just learned to walk see a swimming pool for the first time, they are likely to be scared. The unfamiliar environment threatens their security, and they are deeply concerned whether their little bodies can manage in such an unsolid material. They are afraid of losing control. So they put one toe into the water and quickly pull it out. That felt all right. So they place three toes into the water for just a little bit longer. That was okay too. Next they dip a whole foot in, then a whole leg. As the confidence increases and the swimming pool promises to be fun, the anticipation of joy overpowers the fear. The child jumps into the water and immerses itself fully. Then they have such a great time that their parents can hardly get them to leave!

Similarly, when fear arises with the powerful nimitta, it is all one can do to stay there just for an instant. One then reflects how that felt. To say it felt wonderful is an understatement. So the next time one stays longer, and it feels even better. By this gradual method, confidence soon becomes strong and the expectation of joy so dominant that when the awesome nimitta arises, one jumps right in and immerses oneself fully. Moreover, one has such a great time that it is only with great difficulty that anyone can make you come out.

Another skillful means for overcoming fear at this stage, especially when fear is not too strong, is to perform a little mental ceremony of handing over trust. It is as if one has been the driver of one's meditation until now, but this is the moment to hand over control to the nimitta. As I suggested in chapter 7, one may imagine handing over a set of keys to the powerful nimitta, the way one allows a trusted friend to take over driving one's car. With an imaginary gesture of handing over the keys, one transfers control and places full trust in the nimitta. Such a transfer of faith usually leads to a greater stability of the nimitta and its subsequent deepening.

Here again one is placing faith in the knower and withdrawing it from the doer. This is the theme underlying the whole of the meditation path. One trains from the very beginning in passive awareness, that is, the ability to be clearly aware without interfering at all with the object of awareness. Energy, coupled with faith, flows into the mindfulness and away from activity. When one learns to watch an ordinary object like the breath without meddling, then one's passive awareness will be challenged by a more seductive object like the beautiful breath. If one passes this test, then the most challenging object of all, the nimitta, will be presented to you as the ultimate test of passive awareness. For if one gets involved with the nimitta and tries to control it however slightly, then one fails the final examination and gets sent back to the beautiful breath for remedial training. The more one meditates, the more one learns to be powerfully mindful while letting go of all doing. When this skill is fully perfected, it is easy to pass the final test and stabilize the nimitta with flawless passive awareness.

Again, the simile of the mirror is applicable here. When you look at your reflection in a mirror and the image is moving around, it is because you are not still. It is futile to try to stabilize the image by holding the mirror still. In fact, if you try this, the reflection is apt to move even more. The image in the mirror is moving because the watcher is moving, not the mirror. Only when the watcher is still will the image be still.

The nimitta is in reality a reflection of the mind, an image of that which knows. When this reflection, this nimitta, moves back and forth, it is futile trying to stabilize the nimitta by holding the nimitta still. The nimitta is moving because that which is watching the nimitta is moving. When this is understood, one focuses on that which knows, letting it come to stillness. When that which knows doesn't move, then neither does the nimitta.

The other enemy of the nimitta's stability is excitement or exhilaration, what I have called the "wow!" response. When there is success in the meditation and amazing things happen, then the meditator can get very excited, especially when a wonderful nimitta first appears, more radiant than the sun and more beautiful than exquisite flowers! On such occasions it is common for the mind to say "wow!" Unfortunately, the nimitta immediately withdraws and may be reluctant to return for a very long time, even months. In order to avoid such a calamity, one should bear in mind Ajahn Chah's famous simile of the still forest pool, which I described in detail in chapter 7.

In this simile the forest pool represents the mind, and the forest monk sitting near its edge stands for mindfulness. When mindfulness is still, then animals like the beautiful breath and pīti-sukha come out from their jungle to play by the mind's edge. Mindfulness must remain still. If it does, then, after the beautiful breath and pīti-sukha have finished their business in the mind, the beautiful, shy nimitta will cautiously emerge to play in the mind. If the nimitta senses the knower thinking "wow!" it will bashfully run back into the jungle, not to reemerge for a very long time.

So when the powerful and beautiful nimittas appear, watch with the stillness of an Ajahn Chah, sitting absolutely motionless by the remote forest lake. Then one will watch this strange and wonderful nimitta make merry in the mind for a very long time, until it is ready to take one into jhāna.

Entering the Jhāna

When the nimitta is stable and radiant, then one is at the entrance to jhāna. One must train oneself to wait patiently here, maintaining the stillness and nondoing until the causes or conditions are ready for the transition into jhāna. At this stage, however, some meditators make the mistake of disturbing the process by peeking at the edge of the nimitta.

Once the nimitta is stable and bright, one might become interested in its shape or size. Is it circular or oblong? Are the edges precise or ill defined? Is it small or is it big? When one looks at the edge, mindfulness loses its one-pointedness. The edge is the place of duality, of inside and outside. And duality is the opposite of one-pointedness. If one looks at the edge, the nimitta will become unsettled and may even disappear. One should keep mindfulness on the very center of the nimitta, away from the edge, until any perception of edge vanishes into the nonduality of one-pointedness. Similarly, if one attempts to expand or contract the nimitta, then one will also be sacrificing the essential one-pointedness. Expansion and contraction involve the perception of size, and that involves awareness of the edge of the nimitta and the space that lies beyond. Again one is falling back into the trap of duality and loss of one-pointedness through this unprofitable expanding and contracting.

So when the nimitta is stable and bright, you must be patient. Don't move. One is building up the jhāna factors of pīti-sukha and one-pointedness. When they are built to sufficient power, they will unfold into jhāna by themselves.

An oft-quoted passage from the suttas, often erroneously translated to imply the existence of an original mind, is relevant here. The passage is from the Aṅguttara Nikāya.[8]

This mind, O monks, is luminous, but it is defiled by adventitious defilements. The uninstructed worldling does not understand this as it really is; therefore for him there is no mental development.

This mind, O monks, is luminous, and it is freed from adventitious defilements. The instructed noble disciple understands this as it really is; therefore for him there is mental development. (AN I,6,1–2)

At the stage of the beautiful and stable nimitta, it is the nimitta that is radiant and incredibly luminous. And the nimitta, as already explained, is an image of the mind. When one experiences such a nimitta, one recognizes it as the luminous (or radiant) mind of the Aṅguttara passage above. This nimitta is radiant because the mind has been freed from the "adventitious defilements," which mean the five hindrances. Then one understands that this nimitta—this luminous mind freed of the five hindrances—is the doorway into jhāna, then one truly understands what is meant by "mental development."

When the nimitta is radiant and stable, then its energy builds up moment by moment. It is like adding peace upon peace upon peace, until the peace becomes huge! As the peace becomes huge, the pīti-sukha becomes huge, and the nimitta grows in luminosity. If one can maintain the one-pointedness here by keeping one's focus on the very center of the nimitta, the power will reach a critical level. One will feel as if the knower is being drawn into the nimitta, that one is falling into the most glorious bliss. Alternatively, one may feel that the nimitta approaches until it envelops the knower, swallowing one up in cosmic ecstasy. One is entering jhāna.

Yo-Yo Jhāna

It sometimes happens that when inexperienced meditators fall into a nimitta, they immediately bounce back to where they began. I call this a "yo-yo jhāna," after the children's toy. It isn't a real jhāna because it doesn't last long enough, but it is so close. It is the enemy I identified above, excitement, that causes mindfulness to bounce back from jhāna. Such a reaction is quite understandable since the bliss that one experiences when falling into the nimitta is greater joy than one can ever imagine. One may have thought that the best sexual orgasm was something nice, but now one discovers that it is trivial compared to the bliss of these jhānas. Even after a yo-yo jhāna, one often bursts into tears of happiness, crying at the most wonderful experience by far of one's whole life. So it is understandable that novice meditators first experience yo-yo jhānas. After all, it takes a lot of training to be able to handle such immensely strong bliss. And it takes a lot of wisdom to let go of excitement when one of the great prizes of spiritual life is theirs for the taking.

For those who are old enough to remember the game of snakes and ladders, the simple children's board game played with dice, they will remember the most dangerous square to land on is the square just before the goal. The ninety-ninth square holds the head of the longest of snakes. If you land on the hundredth square you win. But if you land on the ninety-ninth square, you fall down the snake to its tail, right back at the beginning. A yo-yo jhāna is like landing on the ninety-ninth square. You are very close to winning the game and entering a jhāna, but you fall just a little short, land on the snake head of excitement, and slide, or rather bounce, right back to the start.

Even so, yo-yo jhānas are so close to the real thing that they are not to be sneered at. In the yo-yo jhāna one experiences incredible bliss and transports of joy. It makes one feel as high as a weather balloon for hours, without a care in the world and with so much energy that one can hardly sleep. The experience is the greatest in one's life. It will change you.

Through a little more training and wise reflection on one's experiences, you will be able to fall into the nimitta, or be enveloped by it, without bouncing out. Then you have entered the amazing world of jhāna.

The Jhānas III: Bliss upon Bliss upon Bliss 11

The Landmarks of All Jhānas

FROM THE MOMENT of entering a jhāna, one will have no control. One will be unable to give orders as one normally does. When the will that is controlling vanishes, then the "I will" that fashions one's concept of future also disappears. Since the concept of time ceases in jhāna, the very question "What should I do next?" cannot arise. One cannot even decide when to come out. It is this absolute absence of will, and of its offspring, time, that gives the jhānas their timeless stability and allows them to last sometimes for many blissful hours.

Because of the perfect one-pointedness and fixed attention, one loses the faculty of perspective within jhāna. Comprehension relies on comparison—relating this to that, here to there, now with then. In jhāna, all that is perceived is an unmoving, enveloping, nondual bliss that allows no space for the arising of perspective. It is like that puzzle where one is shown a photograph of a well-known object from an unusual angle, and one has to guess what it is. It is very difficult to identify some objects without looking at them from different angles. When perspective is removed, so is comprehension. Thus in jhāna not only is there no sense of time but also there is no comprehension of what is going on. At the time, one will not even know which jhāna one is in. All one knows is great bliss, unmoving, unchanging, for unknown lengths of time.

Even though there is no comprehension within any jhāna, one is certainly not in a trance. One's mindfulness is greatly increased to a level of sharpness that is truly incredible. One is immensely aware. Only mindfulness doesn't move. It is frozen. And the stillness of the superpower mindfulness, the perfect one-pointedness of awareness, makes the jhāna experience completely different from anything one has known before. This is not unconsciousness. It is nondual consciousness. All it can know is one thing, and that is timeless bliss that doesn't move.

Afterward, when one has emerged from the jhāna, such consummate one-pointedness of consciousness falls apart. With the weakening of one-pointedness, perspective reemerges, and the mind has the ability to move again. The mind has regained the space needed to compare and comprehend. Ordinary consciousness has returned.

Having just emerged from a jhāna, it is the usual practice to look back at what has happened and review the jhāna experience. The jhānas are such powerful events that they leave an indelible record in one's memory store. In fact, one will never forget them as long as one lives. They are easy to recall with perfect retention. One comprehends the details of what happened in the jhāna, and one knows which of the jhānas it was. Moreover, *data obtained from reviewing a jhāna form the basis of the insight that leads to enlightenment.*

Another strange quality that distinguishes jhāna from all other experience is that within jhāna, all the five senses are totally shut down. One cannot see, hear, smell, taste, or feel touch. One cannot hear a crow cawing or a person coughing. Even if there were a thunderclap nearby, it wouldn't be heard in a jhāna. If someone tapped you on the shoulder, or picked you up and let you down, in jhāna you cannot know this. The mind in jhāna is so completely cut off from these five senses that they cannot break in.[9]

A lay disciple once told me how, completely by chance, he had fallen into a deep jhāna while meditating at home. His wife thought he had died and sent for an ambulance. He was rushed to hospital in a loud wail of sirens. In the emergency room, no heartbeat registered on the ECG, and no brain activity was seen by the EEG. So the doctor on duty put defibrillators on his chest to reactivate his heart. Even though he was being bounced up and down on the hospital bed through the force of the electric shocks, he didn't feel a thing. When he emerged from the jhāna in the emergency room, perfectly all right, he had no knowledge of how he had got there, nothing of ambulances and sirens, nothing of body-jerking defibrillators. All that long time that he was in jhāna, he was fully aware, but only of bliss. This is an example of what is meant by the five senses shutting down within the experience of jhāna.

Summary of the Landmarks of All Jhānas

It is helpful to know, then, that within a jhāna:

1. There is no possibility of thought;
2. No decision-making process is available;
3. There is no perception of time;
4. Consciousness is nondual, making comprehension inaccessible;
5. Yet one is very, very aware, but only of bliss that doesn't move;
6. The five senses are fully shut off, and only the sixth sense, mind, is in operation.

These are the features of jhāna. So during a deep meditation, if one wonders whether it is jhāna or not, one can be certain it is not! No such thinking can exist within the stillness of jhāna. These features will only be recognized upon emergence from a jhāna, using reviewing mindfulness once the mind can move again.

The First Jhāna

The Wobble (Vitakka and Vicāra)

All jhānas are states of unmoving bliss, almost. However, in the first jhāna, there is some movement discernible. I call this movement the "wobble" of first jhāna. One is aware of great bliss, so powerful it has subdued completely the part of the ego that wills and does. In jhāna, one is on automatic pilot, as it were, with no sense of being in control. However, the bliss is so delicious that it can generate a small residue of attachment. The mind instinctively grasps at the bliss. Because the bliss of the first jhāna is fueled by letting go, such involuntary grasping weakens the bliss. Seeing the bliss weaken, the mind automatically lets go of its grasping, and the bliss increases in power again. The mind then grasps again, then lets go again. Such subtle involuntary movement gives rise to the wobble of the first jhāna.

This process can be perceived in another way. As the bliss weakens because of the involuntary grasping, it seems as if mindfulness moves a small distance away from the bliss. Then the mindfulness gets pulled back into the bliss as the mind automatically lets go. This back-and-forth movement is a second way of describing the wobble.

This wobble is, in fact, the pair of first jhāna factors called *vitakka* and *vicāra*. Vitakka is the automatic movement back into the bliss; vicāra is the involuntary grasping of the bliss. Some commentators explain vitakka and vicāra as "initial thought" and "sustained thought." While in other contexts this pair can refer to thought, in jhāna they certainly mean something else. It is impossible that such a gross activity as thinking can exist in such a refined state as jhāna. In fact, thinking ceases a long time prior to jhāna. In jhāna, vitakka and vicāra are both subverbal and so do not qualify as thought. Vitakka is the subverbal movement of mind back into the bliss. Vicāra is the subverbal movement of mind that holds on to the bliss. Outside of jhāna, such movements of mind will often generate thought, and sometimes speech. But in jhāna, vitakka and vicāra are too subtle to create any thought. All they are capable of doing is moving mindfulness back into the bliss and holding mindfulness there.

One-Pointedness (Ekaggatā)

The third factor of the first jhāna is one-pointedness, *ekaggatā*. One-pointedness is mindfulness that is sharply focused on a minute area of existence. It is one-pointed in space because it sees only the point-source of bliss, together with a small area surrounding the bliss caused by the first jhāna wobble. It is one-pointed in time because it perceives only the present moment, so exclusively and precisely that all notion of time completely disappears. And it is one-pointed in phenomena because it knows only one object—the mental object of pīti-sukha—and is totally oblivious to the world of the five senses and one's physical body.

Such one-pointedness in space produces the peculiar experience, only found in jhāna, of nondual consciousness, where one is fully aware but only of one thing, and from one angle, for timeless periods. Consciousness is so focused on the one thing that the faculty of comprehension is suspended a while. Only after the one-pointedness has dissipated, and one has emerged from the jhāna, will one be able to recognize these features of the first jhāna and comprehend them all.

The one-pointedness in time produces the extraordinary stability of the first jhāna, allowing it to last effortlessly for such a long period of time. The concept of time relies on measuring intervals: from past to present or from present to future or from past to future. When all that is perceived within the first jhāna is the precise moment of now, then there is no room for measuring time. All intervals have closed. It is replaced with the perception of timelessness, unmoving.

One-pointedness of phenomena produces the exceptional occurrence of bliss upon bliss, unchanging throughout the duration of the jhāna. This makes the first jhāna such a restful abode.

In academic terms, *ekaggatā* is a Pāli compound meaning "one-peakness." The middle term *agga* (Sanskrit *agra*) refers to the peak of a mountain, the summit of an experience, or even the capital of a country (as in Agra, the old Moghul capital of India). Thus ekaggatā is not just any old one-pointedness; it is a singleness of focus on something soaring and sublime. The single exalted summit that is the focus of ekaggatā in the first jhāna is the supreme bliss of pīti-sukha.

Joy-Happiness (Pīti-sukha)

Indeed, the last two factors of the first jhāna are pīti and sukha, which I will discuss together since they are such a close-knit pair. In fact, they only separate out in the third jhāna, where pīti ceases and leaves sukha "widowed." Therefore, only after the third jhāna can one know from experience what sukha is and what pīti was. Here, it is sufficient to explain the pair as one thing.

These two factors of the first jhāna refer to the bliss that is the focus of mindfulness, and which forms the central experience of the first jhāna. Bliss is the dominant feature of the first jhāna, so much so that it is the first thing that one recognizes when reviewing after emerging from the jhāna. Indeed, mystic traditions more recent than Buddhism have been so overwhelmed by the sheer immensity, egolessness, stillness, ecstasy, ultimateness, and pure otherworldliness of the first jhāna that they have understood the experience as "union with God." However, the Buddha explained that this is but one form of supramundane bliss and there are other forms that are superior. In the Buddhist experience of jhāna, one comes to know many levels of supramundane bliss. The first jhāna is the first level. Even though after emerging from the first jhāna, one cannot conceive of an experience more blissful, there is much more!

Each level of bliss has a different "taste," a quality that sets it apart. These different qualities can be explained by the diverse causes of the bliss. Just as heat generated by sunlight has a different quality than heat caused by a wood fire, which in turn is different from heat generated by a furnace, so bliss fueled by different causes exhibits distinguishing features.

The distinguishing feature of the bliss of first jhāna is that it is fueled by the complete absence of all five sense activities. When the five senses have shut down, including all echoes of the five senses manifesting as thoughts, then one has left the world of the body and material things *(kāmaloka)* and has entered the world of pure mind *(rūpaloka)*. It is as if a huge burden has dropped away. Or, as Ajahn Chah used to describe it, it is as if you have had a rope tied tightly around your neck for as long as you can remember. So long, in fact, that you have become used to it and no longer recognize the pain. Then somehow the tension is suddenly released and the rope is removed. The bliss you then feel is the result of that noose disappearing. In much the same way, the bliss of the first jhāna is caused by the complete fading away of a heavy burden, of all that you took to be the world. Such insight into the cause of the bliss of the first jhāna is fundamental to understanding the Buddha's four noble truths about suffering.

Summary of the First Jhāna

In summary then, the first jhāna is distinguished by the five factors, here compressed into three:

    1 + 2. *vitakka-vicāra:* experienced as the "wobble," being the fine, subtle movement in and out of the bliss;

3. *ekaggatā:* experienced as nonduality, timelessness, and stillness;

4 + 5. *pīti-sukha:* experienced as a bliss surpassing anything in the material world, and fueled by the complete transcendence of the world of the five senses.

The Second Jhāna

Subsiding of the Wobble

As the first jhāna deepens, the wobble lessens and the bliss consolidates. One comes to a state where vicāra is still holding on to the bliss with the most subtle of grasping, but this is not enough to cause any instability in the bliss. The bliss doesn't decrease as a result of vicāra, nor does mindfulness seem to move away from the source. The bliss is so strong that vicāra cannot disturb it. Although vicāra is still active, there is no longer any vitakka, no movement of mind back to the source of bliss. The wobble has gone. This is a jhāna state described in the suttas as without vitakka but with a small measure of vicāra (MN 128,31; AN VIII,63). It is so close to the second jhāna that it is usually included within that jhāna.

As the bliss strengthens into immutable stability, there is no purpose for vicāra to hold on anymore. At this point, the mind becomes fully confident, enough to let go absolutely. With this final letting go, born of inner confidence in the stability of the bliss, vicāra disappears and one enters the second jhāna proper.

The first feature, then, of the second jhāna described in the suttas is *avitakka* and *avicāra*, meaning "without vitakka and vicāra." In experience, this means that there is no more wobble in the mind. The second feature is *ajjhattaṁ sampasādanaṁ*, meaning "internal confidence." In experience, this describes the full confidence in the stability of the bliss, which is the cause for vicāra to cease.

Perfect One-Pointedness of Mind

The third and most recognizable feature of the second jhāna is *cetaso eko-dibhāvaṁ*, or perfect one-pointedness of mind. When there is no longer any wobble, then the mind is like an unwavering rock, more immovable than a mountain and harder than a diamond. Such perfection in unyielding stillness is incredible. The mind stays in the bliss without the slightest vibration. This is later recognized as the perfection of the quality called *samādhi*.

Samādhi is the faculty of attentive stillness, and in the second jhāna this attention is sustained on the object without any movement at all. There is not even the finest oscillation. One is fixed, frozen solid, stuck with "super-glue," unable even to tremble. All stirrings of mind are gone. There is no greater stillness of mind than this. It is called perfect samādhi, and it remains as a feature not only of this second jhāna but of the higher jhānas as well.

The Bliss Born of Samādhi and the End of All Doing

It is this perfection of samādhi that gives the bliss of the second jhāna its unique taste. The burden that affected the first jhāna, the affliction of movement, has been abandoned. Everything stands perfectly still, even the knower. Such absolute stillness transcends the mental pain born of the mind moving, and it reveals the great bliss fueled by pure samādhi. In the suttas, the bliss of the second jhāna is called the *pīti-sukha born of samādhi (samādhija pīti-sukha)* (DN 9,11). Such bliss is even more pleasurable, hugely so, than the bliss resulting from transcending the world of the five senses. One could not have anticipated such bliss. It is of a totally separate order. After experiencing this second jhāna, having realized two rare "species" of supramundane bliss that are extreme, one ponders what other levels of bliss may lie ahead.

Another salient feature of the second jhāna is that all doing has totally ceased, even the involuntary activity that caused the wobbling has completely vanished. The doer has died. Only when one has experience of the second jhāna can one fully appreciate what is meant by this term "doer"—just as a tadpole can fully appreciate what is meant by the term "water" only when water disappears during the frog's first experience on dry land. Not only is the doer gone, it seems as if this apparently essential part of one's eternal identity has been deleted from existence. What was seemingly obvious turns out to be a mirage, a delusion. One penetrates the illusion of free will using the data from raw experience. The philosopher (Sartre) who proposed "to be is to do" could not have known the second jhāna, where "being" is without any "doing." These jhānas are weird, and they defy normal experience. But they are real, more real than the world.

Summary of the Second Jhāna

Thus the second jhāna is distinguished by another four collections of factors:

1 + 2. *Avitakka-avicāra, ajjhattaṁ sampasādanaṁ:* experienced as the subsiding of the "wobble" from the first jhāna due to internal confidence in the stability of the bliss;

3. *Cetaso ekodibhāvaṁ:* perfect one-pointedness of mind due to full confidence in the bliss. This is usually experienced as rocklike stillness, or the perfection of samādhi;

4. *Samādhija pīti-sukha:* being the focus of this jhāna, the supramundane bliss generated by the end of all movement of the mind;

5. *The end of all doing:* seen as the first time that the "doer" has completely gone.

The Third Jhāna

As the stillness of the knower continues, the stillness of the known grows ever more profound. Remember that in jhāna, what is known is the image of the mind, and the mind is the knower. First the knower becomes still, then its image, the known, gradually becomes still.

In the first two jhānas, this image of the mind is recognized as a bliss that up until now has been called pīti-sukha. In the third jhāna, the image of the mind has gone to the next level of stillness, to a very different kind of bliss.

Pīti Has Vanished

Prior to the third jhāna all bliss had something in common, although it differed in its taste due to the distinguishing causes. That something in common was the combination of pīti plus sukha. Because they were always together, as inseparable as Siamese twins, it was not only pointless but even impossible to tell them apart. It was this combination that, up to now, gave all bliss a common quality. Now in the third jhāna pīti vanishes to leave only sukha, which produces a very different species of bliss altogether.

It is only after the experience of the third jhāna that one can know what sukha is, and by inference what pīti was. The pīti of the second jhāna seemed more euphoric than anything else. Yet it is now seen as the lesser part of the bliss. Sukha is the more refined part.

Great Mindfulness, Clear Knowing, and Equanimity

With all jhānas, the experiences are next to impossible to describe. The higher the jhāna, however, the more profound the experience and the more difficult it becomes to describe. These states and their language are remote from the world. At a stretch, one may say that the bliss of the third jhāna, the sukha, has a greater sense of ease, is quieter, and is more serene. In the suttas, it is accompanied by the features of mindfulness *(sati),* clear knowing *(sampajañña),* and equanimity *(upekkhā),* although these qualities are said in the *Anupada Sutta* (MN 111) to be present in all jhānas. Perhaps these features are emphasized as qualities of the third jhāna in order to point out that in this very deep jhāna one is exceptionally mindful, very clear in the knowing, and so still that one looks on without moving, which is the root meaning of equanimity *(upekkhā).*

The Same Rocklike Stillness and Absence of a Doer

The third jhāna retains the perfect samādhi, the rocklike stillness, the absence of a doer, and the inaccessibility from the world of the five senses. It is distinguished from the second jhāna by the nature of the bliss, which has soared up to another level and appears as another species of bliss altogether. So much so that the suttas quote the enlightened one's description of the third jhāna as "abiding in bliss, mindful, just looking on" (DN 9,12).

Summary of the Third Jhāna

Thus the third jhāna has the following features:

1. The bliss has separated, losing the coarse part that was pīti;
2. The bliss that remains, sukha, exhibits the qualities of great mindfulness, clear knowing, and the sense of just looking on;
3. The same absolute rocklike stillness, and absence of a doer, as in the second jhāna.

The Fourth Jhāna

As the stillness of the knower calms that which is known, the bliss that was the central feature of the first three jhānas changes again when one enters the fourth jhāna. Only this time it changes more radically. Sukha completely disappears. What remains is an absolute still knower seeing absolute stillness.

From the perspective of the fourth jhāna, the bliss of the previous jhānas is seen as a residual movement of the mental object, and an affliction obscuring something much greater. When the bliss subsides, all that is left is the profound peace that is the hallmark of the fourth jhāna. Nothing moves in here, nothing glows. Nothing experiences happiness or discomfort. One feels perfect balance in the very center of the mind. As in the center of a cyclone, nothing stirs in the center of the mind's eye. There is a sense of perfection here, a perfection of stillness and of awareness. The Buddha described it as the purification of mindfulness, just looking on *(upekkhā sati pārisuddhi)* (DN 9,13).

The peace of the fourth jhāna is like no other peace to be found in the world. It can only be known having passed though the experience of the previous three jhānas. That passage is the only way of later confirming that the unmoving peace that one felt was indeed that of fourth jhāna. Furthermore, the state of fourth jhāna is so very still that one remains on its plateau for many hours. It seems impossible that one could experience the fourth jhāna for any less time.

Though pīti and sukha have both ceased in the fourth jhāna and all that is left is the perfection of peace, such an experience is later recognized, upon reviewing, as supremely delightful. The perfect peace of the fourth jhāna is seen as the best bliss so far. It is the bliss of no more bliss! This is not playing with words, trying to sound clever and mystical. This is how it is.

Summary of the Fourth Jhāna

Thus the fourth jhāna has the following features:

1. The disappearance of sukha;
2. An extremely long-lasting, and unchanging, perception of the perfection of peace, reached only through the lower three jhānas;
3. The same absolute rocklike stillness, and absence of a doer, as in the second and third jhāna;
4. The complete inaccessibility from the world of the five senses and one's body.

The Buddha's Similes for the Four Jhānas

The Buddha would often describe the experience within the four jhānas by evocative similes (e.g., MN 39,15–18; 77,25–28). Before explaining these similes, it is helpful to pause and clarify the meaning of *kāya,* a key Pāli word used in all the similes. *Kāya* has the same range of meanings as the English word "body." Just as "body" can mean things other than the body of a person, such as a "body of evidence," for example, so too *kāya* can mean things other than a physical body, such as a body of mental factors, *nāma-kāya* (DN 15,20). In the jhānas the five senses do not operate, which means that there is no experience of a physical body. The body has been transcended. Therefore, when the Buddha states in these four similes, "so that there is no part of his whole kāya unpervaded (by bliss and so on)," this can be taken to mean "so that there is no part of his *whole mental body of experience* unpervaded" (MN 39,16). This point is frequently misunderstood.

The Buddha's simile for the first jhāna is a ball of clay (used as soap) with just the right amount of moisture, neither too dry nor too wet. The ball of clay stands for the unified mind, wherein mindfulness has been restricted to the very small area created by the "wobble." The moisture stands for the bliss caused by total seclusion from the world of the five senses. The moisture that completely pervades the clay ball indicates the bliss that thoroughly pervades the space and duration of the mental experience. This is later recognized as bliss followed by bliss, and then more bliss, without interruption. That the moisture is not in excess, and so does not leak out, describes how the bliss is always contained in the space generated by the wobble, never leaking out of this area of mind-space into the world of the five senses, as long as the jhāna persists.

The second jhāna is likened to a lake with no external entry for water but with an internal spring that replenishes it with cool water. The lake represents the mind. The complete absence of any way that water from outside can enter the lake describes the inaccessibility of the mind by any influence from outside. Not even the doer can enter such a mind in this jhāna. Such hermetic inaccessibility is the cause of the rock-like stillness of the second jhāna. The internal spring that supplies the cool water represents *ajjhattam sampasādanam,* the internal confidence in the bliss of second jhāna. This internal confidence causes complete letting go, cooling the mind into stillness and freeing it from all movement. The coolness stands for the bliss itself, born of samādhi or stillness, which pervades the whole mental experience, unchanging throughout the duration of the jhāna.

The third jhāna is described by the metaphor of a lotus flower that thrives immersed in the cool water of a lake. The lotus represents the mind in the third jhāna. Water can cool the petals and leaves of a lotus but can never penetrate the lotus, since all water rolls off. The coolness stands for sukha, and the wetness stands for pīti. So like the lotus immersed in water, the mind in the third jhāna is cooled by sukha but is not penetrated by pīti. The mind in the third jhāna experiences only sukha. In the third jhāna, the mind continues to experience a rocklike stillness, never moving outside, just as the lotus in the simile always remains immersed within the water. Just as the cool water causes the lotus to thrive, so the bliss of the third jhāna sustains the mind therein. Once again, just as the cool waters in the simile pervade the lotus with coolness from its roots to its tips, so the unique bliss of the third jhāna pervades the whole mental experience from beginning to end.

The fourth jhāna is likened to a man draped from head to toe in a clean white cloth. The man represents the mind, while the cloth represents the perfect purity of equanimity and mindfulness that is the hallmark of the fourth jhāna. The mind in the fourth jhāna is stainless, spotless as a clean cloth, perfectly still and just looking on, purely and simply. This absolute purity of peacefulness pervades the whole body of mental experience, from the start to the end, just as the white cloth completely covers the man's body from head to toe.

Such is the meaning of the four similes for jhāna, as I understand them.

Moving from Jhāna to Jhāna

As I've indicated before, in a jhāna one cannot make any move. One cannot formulate any decision to proceed from this jhāna to that. One cannot even make a decision to come out. All such control has been abandoned within the jhāna. Furthermore, the profound stillness of mindfulness in jhāna freezes the mental activity of comprehension to the extent that, while in jhāna, one can hardly make sense of one's experience. The landmarks of jhāna are only recognized later, after emerging and reviewing. Thus, within any jhāna not only can one not move, but also one cannot know where one is nor where to move to! So how then does movement from jhāna to jhāna occur?

Imagine a four-room house with only one entrance door. Going through that door, one enters the first room. One must walk through the first room to enter the second, through the second room to enter the third, and through the third to enter the fourth. When leaving the house, one exits the fourth room and goes back to the third room, then to the second, then to the first. So one leaves the house by the same door through which one entered. Now suppose that the floors in all the rooms are so slippery that one cannot apply any additional momentum. Thus, if one enters the house with only a little momentum, one slides to a halt in the first room. With a greater amount of entry momentum, one may come to a stop in the second, the third, or the fourth room.

Such a simile describes how moving from jhāna to jhāna actually occurs. Within a jhāna one has no control. If one enters into jhānas with little momentum, one stops in the first jhāna. With greater momentum, one reaches the second or third jhānas. And with yet more entry momentum, one may reach the fourth jhāna. The entry momentum can only be generated outside of jhāna, when control is possible.

The momentum referred to here is that of letting go. One cultivates letting go *before* entering jhāna, to the point where it becomes an involuntary inclination of the mind, a strong natural tendency. If one enters the doorway into the jhānas with a modicum of letting-go momentum, one will stop in the first jhāna. With a stronger automatic tendency to let go, one reaches the second or third jhānas. With a very strong inclination to let go, one attains to the fourth jhāna. But one cannot increase the strength of letting-go momentum while inside the jhānas.

One can cultivate this momentum of letting go outside of jhāna by reviewing the experiences of bliss and by recognizing the obstacles called attachments. When the mind recognizes the great happiness of letting go, the inclination to let go grows. Sometimes I have taught my stubborn mind by thinking, "See, mind! See! See how much more bliss there is in the states of letting go. See, mind! Don't forget, mind, okay?" The mind then leans ever more strongly to letting go. Or the mind can recognize the obstacles to deeper bliss, which are the various levels of attachment. When the mind learns, through reviewing, to recognize the enemies to its own happiness—the attachments—then its inclination to let go becomes empowered by wisdom.

For another way to understand how one moves from jhāna to jhāna, recall the simile of the thousand-petaled lotus that opens in the sun. The first jhāna can be compared to a rare and delicate row of petals very near the center. Just as the petals of this row, now being warmed by the sun, conceal an even more fragrant row of petals underneath, so the rare and delicate first jhāna, now being warmed by still mindfulness, opens to reveal an even more blissful second jhāna. Thus the second jhāna lies within the first jhāna, the third within the second, and the fourth within the third, like the inner rows of lotus petals, one within the other.

When one has had much experience of jhāna, one can move from jhāna to jhāna using the power of *adhiṭṭhāna*. In this context, the word *adhiṭṭhāna* refers to the Buddhist way of programming the mind. At the beginning of one's meditation, one can program the mind to enter a specified jhāna for a predetermined length of time. Of course, this works only for an accomplished meditator who is familiar with the destination and is well acquainted with the route. It is like setting the automatic pilot shortly after takeoff. Even accomplished meditators, however, must traverse the usual path to reach a specified jhāna. For example, if one programs the mind to enter the third jhāna, then one must pass through the first and second jhānas first, although one may do so quickly.

The Immaterial Attainments

In the simile of the thousand-petaled lotus, four of the innermost rows of petals represent the jhānas. The eighth innermost row is the first jhāna; the seventh innermost, the second jhāna; the sixth innermost, the third jhāna; and the fifth innermost, the fourth jhāna. You now are probably wondering what the last four rows of petals represent. Beyond the four jhānas lie the four immaterial attainments. It is noteworthy that the Buddha never calls these attainments "jhānas" in the suttas. Only the commentaries, compiled a thousand years later, call them that. The four immaterial attainments are as follows:

the mind-base of unlimited space
the mind-base of unlimited consciousness
the mind-base of nothingness
the mind-base of neither perception nor nonperception

Just as the fourth jhāna lies within the third jhāna, so the first immaterial attainment lies within the fourth jhāna, the second immaterial attainment within the first immaterial attainment, and so on like the rows of petals in a lotus. Thus, of necessity, all four immaterial attainments possess the following features carried over from the jhāna:

✦ The mind remains inaccessible to the world of the five senses and all knowledge of the body;

✦ The mind persists in rocklike stillness, incapable of forming any thought or making any plan, for long periods of time;

✦ Comprehension is so frozen that one can hardly make sense, at the time, of one's experience. Comprehension is achieved after emerging;

✦ The pure equanimity and mindfulness of the fourth jhāna remains as a foundation for each immaterial attainment.

Just as the first three jhānas take different forms of bliss as their object, and the fourth jhāna takes a sublime state of pure peace as its object, so each of the immaterial attainments takes a pure mental object. The perceptions of these objects I call *mind-bases,* since they are the mental platforms on which the immaterial attainments rest. These unmoving mind-bases become ever more refined, and empty, the higher the immaterial attainment.

Back in the fourth jhāna, mindfulness is powerful and still, just looking on at the perfection of peace well beyond the world of the five senses and precisely one-pointed. In states of precise one-pointedness, ordinary concepts derived from the world are squeezed out, and other unworldly perceptions replace them.

For example, when a meditator in the early stages becomes perfectly focused in the present moment, which means one-pointed in time, ordinary concepts of time are squeezed out, and unworldly perceptions of time replace them. When one is fully centered within the present moment, on the one hand it feels timeless and, on the other hand, it feels as if one has all the time in the world. Within the point of absolute now, time is without edges, undefined, empty, and immeasurable. It is infinite and nothing at the same time. It is unlimited *(anantā).* The experience of one-pointedness in time, seen early in the meditation, can be the key to understanding the simultaneous sense of infinity and emptiness in the immaterial attainments.

The Mind-Base of Unlimited Space

From the fourth jhāna, the mind can look into the perfect peace to perceive absolute one-pointedness in space. This is one of the features of the fourth jhāna always available for inspection, as it were, and it is the doorway into the immaterial attainments. In this absolute one-pointedness, space is perceived as both infinite and empty, a sort of no-space. Because it is perceived as empty of that which usually limits space, that is, material form *(rūpa)*, this attainment and those following are called immaterial *(arūpa)* attainments.

The first immaterial attainment, then, is the mind-base of unlimited space, perceived as both infinite and empty, immeasurable and undefined. This is the perception that fills the mind thoroughly and persists without blinking for the long duration of the attainment. Mindfulness, powerful, still, and purified, looks on at this perception with utter contentment.

The Mind-Base of Unlimited Consciousness

Within the perception of unlimited space lies the perception of no-space, of space losing its meaning. When the mind attends to this feature within the first immaterial attainment, space disappears and is replaced by the perception of absolute one-pointedness of consciousness. In this state, consciousness simultaneously feels infinite and empty, immeasurable and undefined. One has entered the second immaterial attainment of the mind-base of unlimited consciousness. This perception fills the mind completely and persists without wavering for even longer periods of time.

The Mind-Base of Nothingness

Within the perception of unlimited consciousness lies the perception of no-consciousness, of consciousness now losing its meaning as well. When the mind focuses on this feature within the second immaterial attainment, all perceptions of consciousness disappear. Perceptions of material form and space have already disappeared, so all that is left is the one-pointedness of nothingness. One has entered the third immaterial attainment of the mind-base of nothingness. This concept fills the mind totally, persisting unchangingly for yet longer periods of time.

The Mind-Base of Neither Perception nor Nonperception

Within the perception of nothingness lies the perception of not even nothing! If the mind is subtle enough to see this feature, then the perception of nothingness disappears and is replaced by the perception of neither perception nor nonperception. All that one can say about this fourth immaterial attainment is that it is, in fact, a perception (AN IX, 42). In the simile of the thousand-petaled lotus, this state is represented by the last row of petals, still closed, with all the other petals fully open. This last row of petals is almost not like petals at all, being the most subtle and sublime, for it clasps within its gossamer fabric the famous "jewel in the heart of the lotus," nibbāna.

Nibbāna, the Cessation of All Perception

Within the perception of neither perception nor nonperception lies the end of all perception, the cessation of all that is felt or perceived, nibbāna. If the mind attends to this, the mind stops. When the mind starts again, one gains the attainment of arahant or anāgāmī. These are the only possibilities.

Gradual Cessation

Another way of viewing the jhānas and the four immaterial attainments is by placing them in the sequence of gradual cessation. The process that leads into the first jhāna is the cessation of the world of the five senses together with the body and all doing. The path from the first to the fourth jhāna is the cessation of that part of the mind that recognizes pleasure and displeasure. The road from the fourth jhāna to the fourth immaterial attainment is the cessation, almost, of the remaining activity of mind called "knowing." And the last step is the cessation of the last vestige of knowing. Through jhānas and the immaterial attainments, first one lets go of the body and the world of the five senses. Then one lets go of the doer. Then one lets go of pleasure and displeasure. Then one lets go of space and consciousness. Then one lets go of all knowing. When one lets go of an object, the object disappears, ceases. If it remains, one hasn't let go. Through letting go of all that can be known, the knower ceases. This is the cessation of everything, including the mind. This is the place where consciousness no longer manifests, where earth, water, fire, and air find no footing, where name–and–form are wholly destroyed (DN 11,85). Emptiness. Cessation. Nibbāna, the jewel in the heart of the lotus.

In this chapter on the jhānas, I have led you on a journey from theory to practice, up to the high mountain ranges where lie the great summits that are the jhānas, and up higher to the rarefied peaks that are the immaterial attainments. Though the tour may seem way beyond you today, tomorrow you may find yourself well advanced along the route. So it is helpful even today to have this road map before you.

Moreover, these jhānas are like immensely rich gold mines, but carrying the most precious of insights rather than a precious metal. They supply the raw material, the unexpected data, which build those special insights that open one's eyes to nibbāna. The jhānas are jewels that adorn the face of Buddhism. They are essential to the experience of enlightenment, and they are possible today.

I conclude this chapter with the words of the Lord Buddha:

There is no jhāna without wisdom;
There is no wisdom without jhāna;
But for one with both jhāna and wisdom,
They are in the presence of nibbāna.

(Dhp 372)

The Nature of Deep Insight 12

♦ ♦ ♦

INSIGHT IS COMMON; deep insight is rare. Insight is comforting; deep insight is challenging, sometimes terrifying. Insight makes little impression on one's character; deep insight changes one's life.

For example, two monks were arguing over a flag in the wind. One said that the flag moved. The other said that the wind moved. They went to see a Zen master who told them that they were both wrong. The mind moved. Then a Theravāda forest monk came along and said that all three of them had missed the point. The problem was that their mouths moved! That's insight.

A monk I know told me that as a layman he had once had a powerful meditation experience of deep prolonged bliss, better than sexual orgasm, wherein the body had vanished and everything was still. That unusual experience challenged his previous understanding of happiness; it overturned it and changed his whole life. He became a monk for the rest of his life. That was a *deep* insight.

The Tenfold Path

In the collection of suttas called the Aṅguttara Nikāya, the Buddha's sermons are arranged according to the number of items mentioned in the text. For example, the four right efforts, the four roads to power, and many other fourfold groups are collected in the chapter titled "Fours." When I first read the "Eights" chapter in this collection, I expected to find the most famous of the eights, the eightfold path. It wasn't there, and I was stunned. You see, in the Aṅguttara Nikāya, the famous eightfold path is found in the "Tens" chapter, because two extra factors are added by the Buddha (AN X,103). The two additional factors of this tenfold path are right (or perfect) wisdom *(sammā-ñāṇaṁ)* and right liberation *(sammā-vimutti).*

It can be concluded that the eightfold path refers to the practice, to what one does, whereas the extra two factors, perfect wisdom and perfect liberation, refer to the goal, to the result of the practice. Thus the tenfold path teaches the way together with the destination.

Deep insight refers to perfect wisdom, sammā-ñāṇaṁ. As the Aṅguttara texts make plain, deep insight/perfect wisdom is not possible without jhāna, perfect samādhi (AN X,103). Furthermore, the inevitable consequence of deep insight is perfect liberation, in other words, enlightenment.

Perfect Wisdom— Seeing Things as They Truly Are

In the suttas perfect wisdom or deep insight is often called "seeing things as they truly are" *(yathā bhūta ñāṇadassana).* Many people claim insight and assert that they see things as they truly are. However, they seldom agree. Thus it is that we have so many religions and so many sects within each religion, each claiming that it sees things as they truly are but that others do not! Even those holding no religion are the same, since they believe that only no-religion sees things as they truly are. Why is "insight" so conducive to arguments?

The problem is that there are few indeed who see things as they truly are. The vast majority see things as they appear to be, and then take that to be insight, to be truth. Be warned! Even when one is mindful, what appears to the senses has already been filtered, washed, and dressed to please you.

A fellow monk, a veteran of the Vietnam War, had received a bullet to the back of his head, and the injury had destroyed a small part of his brain. The doctors thought he would be blind, but they were wrong. His sight appeared perfect. Many weeks later, while playing baseball with some friends, the batsman slugged the ball high in the air in his direction. As he moved to make the easy catch, following the trajectory with his eyes, the ball suddenly vanished. It disappeared from the universe! A few seconds later, it reappeared again further along its trajectory. It was the first time that he realized that he had a blind spot. The problem with blind spots is that one cannot see them. There is, indeed, a hole in one's visual field, but the mind fills in that hole with what it assumes to be there, and one cannot see the mind doing this! Our experiences, even when they are mindfully observed, are not always the way things truly are.

Temporary blind spots, which we don't know are there, arise whenever we are seduced by lust or burned by anger. When one is in love one is blind to the faults in one's partner. As one man said to his new son-in-law, "That you regard my daughter as perfect is quite natural since you are in love. But in one or two years' time, when you begin to see her defects, always remember this: if my daughter didn't have those faults to begin with, she would have been able to marry someone much better than you!" Because of desire or wishful thinking, we bend reality to meet with our liking.

Similarly, when one is angry, one can only see the faults in the world, in one's partner, and even in the dog. So we kick the dog! The way things truly are, as it seems in states of anger, is that one's suffering is the fault of others, including the poor dog. In Buddhism, anger is called temporary insanity. It is a dangerous illness wherein we think we see things as they truly are, but in fact our views are distorted.

Pride is, perhaps, the most invisible and insidious of forces that corrupt our wisdom. We build our identity out of our views. So much so, that to change one's view, to admit that one is wrong, often threatens one's very idea of oneself. It becomes easier and more comfortable to deny the evidence and nurture more blind spots in one's mind. That way, what enters our conscious awareness is only what we want to know. Indeed, it takes much courage to see things the way they truly are, because one has to let go of so many precious views. And to see the Dhamma is terrifying, because one has to let go of the most precious idea of all, the view of a self.

So how can one be sure that one is seeing things as they truly are? How does one recognize the difference between deep insight and delusion? The answer is, only when the five hindrances are suppressed can one be certain that one is seeing things as they truly are.

The Five Hindrances and Deep Insight

The five hindrances block one seeing things the way they truly are. As a reminder, the five hindrances are

> sensory desire
>
> ill will
>
> sloth and torpor
>
> restlessness and remorse
>
> doubt

Sensory desire bends the truth to suit our liking. For example, when I drank my first glass of beer in my early teens, I could not believe how disgusting it tasted. However, the male society in which I lived almost worshipped beer and held it up as an essential part of all celebrations. So, after a short time, I began to enjoy the taste of beer. It wasn't that the taste of beer had changed but that my perception of the taste had changed to fit what I wanted. The truth had been bent by desire. Sex is similar. The socially conditioned hormonal hunger for copulation twists raw experience to make sex appear as pleasure. Is sexual pleasure the way things truly are, or just the way desire makes it seem? Venerable Ānanda said to Venerable Vaṅgīsa that lust is but an inversion of perception (SN 8,4)!

Ill will, the second hindrance, is the force behind denial. We are so averse to old age, sickness, and death that we are in denial, thinking it will not happen to us. We refuse to see the reality of this body as it truly is and instead maintain a lie. We hate the idea of separation from our loved ones and so live in the fantasy that they'll be there for us always. We detest being proved wrong so much that we manipulate the facts to deceive ourselves. In summary, the truth is often not to our liking, and we simply block it all out, subconsciously. Ill will is a major hindrance blocking us from seeing the way things truly are.

Sloth and torpor is lethargy of body and dullness of mind. It is experienced as if walking in the dark when nothing is clear. Again, it is at nighttime, when one cannot see clearly, that one's girlfriend looks like a supermodel or one's boyfriend looks like a football-star hunk. Not many would fall in love if they went courting during the day, when they could clearly see each other's pimples. The night bends the truth of things. Just as the dim light of sloth and torpor distorts the way things truly are.

Restlessness and remorse don't allow one time to fully see things as they truly are. When the mind is moving fast, the information arriving at awareness is incomplete. For example, my monastery is situated on the top of a hill, just over two kilometers from the highway. After going up and down that hill for several years only in a car, I decided one day to walk up the steep road. While walking, I was surprised that the hillside and valley, which I had assumed I knew well, appeared different from anything I had seen before. Not only did it seem more beautiful, but the scenery was also more rich in detail and color. Then I stood still and it all changed again. Not moving, I saw the view become ever more glorious, noticing exquisite features that I had missed before. It was all so clear, so full, and so delightful. When one looks through the window of a moving car, one's eyes can only receive a fraction of what is going on beyond the window. The light that falls on one's retina does not have enough time to form a complete picture before the next image takes its place. When one is walking, sight has more time to pick up the features. And then when one stands still, seeing has full opportunity to know all the rich beauty of that wonderful valley. Only when I stopped moving could I see the full truth that lay in the hillside. Similarly, only when the mind stands still can one see the full truth of the way things really are.

Doubt was compared by the Buddha to being lost in a desert (MN 39,14), with no signpost or map to find the way. Doubt blocks seeing the way things truly are simply because one does not know where to look, nor how to look. The Buddha gave a map called the Dhamma, recorded for posterity in the suttas, to point out the way. Books such as this one play their part in reinforcing the message of the suttas by adding more signposts in the desert.

In summary, the five hindrances are delusion's spin doctors. They block one from seeing things as they truly are, and instead present to one's awareness what is socially acceptable, pleasing, and unchallenging. Moreover, the work of these five hindrances is done behind the scenes. One is mostly unaware of their manipulations. That is why it's called delusion. So when these five hindrances have been operating, one cannot be sure that the object of one's mindfulness is the way things truly are. The only time of certainty, when insight can be trusted, is when the five hindrances have been suppressed for some time.

Thus the prerequisite for all meaningful insight, especially deep insight, is that the five hindrances are abandoned for long periods of time.

Upacāra Samādhi— the Immediate Neighbor of Jhāna

The five hindrances are abandoned through jhāna. It is true that one cannot gain deep insight while experiencing jhāna. This is because the jhāna states are too still for the mental activity of contemplation to occur. Nevertheless, the jhāna experience serves the purpose of firmly suppressing the five hindrances for long periods of time after emerging from a jhāna, and it is then that deep insight is possible.

The state of meditation immediately after emerging from a jhāna is called *upacāra samādhi,* which means "the immediate neighbor of jhāna." In this state, the five hindrances are totally inactive for several hours or more. Mindfulness is superpowerful, easily focused, and fearless. This is because the disabling five hindrances are suppressed. It is here that, in the Buddha's own words, "the mind is purified, bright, unblemished, rid of imperfection, malleable, wieldy, steady, and attained to imperturbability" (MN 4,27), so that deep insight can happen.

The period just before entering the first jhāna is also upacāra samādhi. During this period one is also in the immediate neighborhood of the first jhāna. This is usually experienced as the ability to remain effortlessly for a long time with a very beautiful and still nimitta. Here the five hindrances are also suppressed. However, the upacāra samādhi prior to jhāna is notoriously unstable when compared with that occurring post-jhāna. At this time the five hindrances can easily sneak back in, because they have been only recently and lightly suppressed. Should one attempt to contemplate Dhamma at this time, the upacāra samādhi will be lost and the five hindrances will return. This is why the Buddha stated in the suttas (AN III,100) that contemplating the Dhamma at this time is an obstacle and should not be done.

Thus, as the Buddha said in the *Naḷakapāna Sutta* (MN 68,6), so long as one has not yet attained the first jhāna or a higher jhāna, the five hindrances together with discontent and weariness will invade one's mind and remain. But when one does attain at least the first jhāna, then the five hindrances, discontent, and weariness do not invade one's mind nor remain. Since the suppressing of the five hindrances is necessary for deep insight, so also is jhāna necessary.

The Story of the Two Messengers

To emphasize that jhāna is essential for deep insight, the Buddha taught the simile of the two messengers. The main elements of the simile are found in the *Kiṃsuka Sutta* (SN 35,245)[10] and told in detail in the commentary. Here, I will paraphrase the simile.

An emperor was preparing his son in the skills of governing. To give the young prince direct experience, he appointed him viceroy over a small state just within the borders of the empire. He granted his son all the powers of a king and sent him off to learn how to rule.

Some months later, a delegation of leading citizens from that state came to complain to the emperor that the prince was failing to fulfill his duties. The prince was partying every day, which was understandable, perhaps, since it was the young man's first time away from home.

The emperor summoned his wisest minister and asked him to go to that state and instruct his son on the responsibilities of a ruler. But the wise minister foresaw that the arrogant young prince would not listen to him if he went alone. So he asked that the most powerful of the generals in the imperial army accompany him on the mission. The emperor concurred, and thus the two messengers—the wise minister and the powerful general—went together to instruct the young prince.

When they eventually arrived at the prince's palace, they could hear the merriment of a party in full swing inside the living quarters, but they were prevented from entering by the prince's five friends. When the wise minister announced who they were and who had sent them, the prince's five companions simply laughed in ridicule and told them to go back from where they had come. "This is our prince's territory," they asserted, "and he will do as he likes here!"

The wise minister was unable to talk any sense into the prince's five friends, so the powerful general took out his sword and approached the five friends. In a moment, the prince's five companions completely disappeared from sight.

Then the pair entered unhindered into the palace, stopped the party, and stood before the prince. Once again, the wise minister announced who they were and where they were from. The prince, like his five friends, told the pair to get lost, since this was his principality and he would do as he liked. He stubbornly refused to listen to his father's wisest counselor. So the powerful general took out his sword once again, grabbed the prince by his hair, and held the sharp edge of the sword against the throat of the prince.

"Listen, prince, to your father's minister!" ordered the general.

"I'm listening! I'm listening!" squeaked the prince, feeling the blade against his skin.

Thus it was, with the powerful general holding the prince absolutely still, with the prince giving his fullest attention, and with the emperor's wise minister instructing the young man, that the prince understood all about the duties and rewards of a ruler. From that time on, he was a changed man. He ruled his state wisely, and in due course the whole empire, to the happiness of all.

In this simile, the emperor was the Buddha and the prince one of his disciples. The wise minister stands for insight and the powerful general stands for jhāna. It is jhāna, not insight that dispels the five hindrances, represented by the prince's five friends. And it is the upacāra samādhi following jhāna that holds the mind still long enough for insight to occur and instruct the mind in Dhamma.

The Gong Bonger

As the above simile of the two messengers shows, the mind needs to be held still to see deeply into the nature of things. I often demonstrate this point in public with the "gong bonger exercise."

I hold up the stick that is used to strike the gong by my seat and ask my audience, "What is this?"

"A stick," someone says.

"What else?" I reply.

"Cylindrical," another offers.

"Anything else?" I continue.

"Black one half, white the other." "Cloth on the white half." "Six inches long," "Used to strike the gong."

"Is that all this thing is?" I encourage.

"Shiny." "Rounded ends." "Worn where you grip it."

When the descriptions dry up and my audience is still looking, they realize that they haven't finished understanding what the gong bonger is yet. The longer they look, the more they see. And that which they begin to see now hasn't got words to describe it. They realize that the labels were superficial. It is much, much more than a "stick," "cylindrical," "half black, half white," and so on. The labels are what we are taught as children in school. They are what the Buddha called "conventional reality." They obstruct understanding when we mistake the label for the thing. When my audience said "It's a stick" and thought that they had captured its meaning, they stopped investigating further. I had to cajole them into continuing their discovery until all the labels were exhausted, until they began to see the thing beyond all the labels, to see with a silent, still mind.

The Most Beautiful Clump of Bamboo in the World

On my first meditation retreat, while still a student at Cambridge, we were all allowed to go for a walk for an hour each morning to exercise the body. On the first morning, having experienced some quiet meditation already, I decided to go to the botanical gardens nearby. When I entered the gardens my mind was struck by the beauty of a clump of bamboo just inside the entrance gate. It was the most exquisite plant that I had seen in my life. The shape and texture of the long stems were bewitching, the colors shone brilliantly in the morning light, the proportions of trunk to tapering branch to slender leaf were perfection, and the way the whole ensemble swayed so gracefully in the breeze entranced me. I stood still for I don't know how many minutes just gazing in awe at that wondrous bamboo. Then I sat down on a bench close by and continued to explore the beauty of the bamboo until the hour was up. I had to force myself back to the meditation retreat.

The following day I returned and the wonder of the bamboo grabbed me again. Once more, I spent the hour for physical exercise sitting still on the bench staring at the same small clump of bamboo. For eight of the nine mornings of that retreat (for one day I walked along the river Granta in need of real exercise), I spent my hour gazing in pleasure at a simple stand of bamboo at the entrance to the Cambridge botanical gardens, and I never had enough!

A week or so after the retreat had concluded, when I had a free hour one morning, I rode my bicycle to revisit my old friend, the most beautiful clump of bamboo in the world. When I arrived I was confused and disappointed. The same bamboo was there, but it looked so ordinary, spindly, drab, and uninspiring. It appeared such a scruffy little bush!

The change made me investigate what had altered that clump of bamboo, so gorgeous a few days before. I soon understood that it was my mind that had changed, not the bamboo. After the retreat, and after riding my bicycle through Cambridge city traffic, my mind was far from the stillness it had known on retreat. Now it could only see the surface of things, the labels, and the faults. It was unable to hold the bamboo long enough in stillness to dive deep into its beautiful and inexhaustible depths. Just like the prince in the simile of the two messengers above, it cannot see the truth until it has been held still by samādhi.

During that first meditation retreat, I had my first experiences of deep meditation. My mind was extraordinarily still when I walked into those gardens. So when my eyes turned to that bamboo, my mind stayed there, played there, dived into the heart of the matter, and enjoyed itself greatly. When one's mind is that still, even the gong bonger becomes amazingly intricate and charming. And so much is seen going on in the gong bonger, that one can watch it happily for hours, never finishing with all it has to teach.

The Flashlight Plus the Map

It is exciting and enormous spiritual fun to see a drab clump of bamboo transform into the most beautiful bush in the world, but it doesn't change one's life. Delusion is much harder to penetrate than the hardest bamboo. Nevertheless, such experiences serve to show how much deeper the mind can see when it has been empowered by samādhi. The more peaceful the samādhi, the more still and fearless is the mind, and the more penetrating is the mindfulness. This is why the mind after jhāna is the usual place where deep insights occur.

After jhāna, deep insight can fail to occur when one does not know where to look. A clump of bamboo is an example of the wrong place to look! To continue the simile from chapter 8, the mind after jhāna can be compared to a very powerful flashlight that illuminates all before it. But when one does not know where to point that flashlight, one is unlikely to discover the hiding place of deep insight. Thus, as well as a powerful flashlight, one also needs an accurate map. The teaching of the Buddha, the Dhamma, is that map.

When one has only a map but no flashlight, or only a very weak one, then again one will not find deep insight. This is like the scholar who has studied the suttas, discussed them with highly attained meditators, and thus has a good grasp of the theory—but who has no personal experience of jhāna. Deep insight cannot occur because the flashlight is too weak.

But for one who has the map, who has listened to experienced teachers, asking questions and studying, and who also has the powerful flashlight, the jhāna-empowered mind—such a person is close to deep insight. As the Buddha once said, "Those with jhāna [the flashlight] and wisdom [the map] are in the presence of enlightenment." (Dhp 372)

The Deep Insight That Liberates 13

+ + +

Remembering Past Lives

ACCORDING TO THE ACCEPTED ACCOUNT of the Buddha's enlightenment under the Bodhi tree, having empowered his mind by entering the jhānas, the very first area of deep insight to which he applied his mind was the question of past lives. Thus, according to the "map" found in the suttas, this is a valid place to begin in order to gain deep insight.

Much discussion is heard in modern Buddhist circles regarding the validity of past lives. Unfortunately, many of these views are misinformed, mistaken, or devoid of any deep insight. An investigation into the earliest Buddhist suttas clearly shows that rebirth is not simply a "cultural addition," as some would have us believe, but instead that rebirth forms a central pillar of the Buddha's deep insight. For instance, the standard definition by the Buddha for one who has wrong view is one who does not believe in kamma and rebirth (MN 117,5). More emphatically, the Buddha said in the *Apaṇṇaka Sutta* ("The Incontrovertible Teaching"; MN 60,8), "Since there actually is another world [rebirth], one who holds the view 'there is no rebirth' has wrong view."[11]

Skeptics rightly demand to know how one can verify for oneself, here and now, that rebirth is a truth. I will explain how verification is done, that is, how one penetrates to one of the life-changing deep insights: that which sees one's past lives.

One evening, while emerging from a very peaceful meditation, I gave a simple, clear instruction to my mind: What is my earliest memory? Then I returned to inner silence, not expecting a thing, alert to the content of the present moment.

A few moments later, a familiar smell came to my nose. I was not imagining the smell; I was reexperiencing it clearly in the present moment. Along with the smell came the eerie but certain recollection that this was the smell of my pram when I was a baby. Immediately it was as if I was back in my pram, reexperiencing the world of a newly born infant in all its details. I couldn't help smiling at seeing with my inner eye one of my favorite toys of that time, a cute blue toy pig my mother called Porky, which rattled when she walked it for me. With extraordinary precision and ease, I was remembering details of the life of a newly born infant, while sitting in the body of a forty-plus-year-old monk. The whole event was accompanied by an extraordinary sense of certainty that there was not the slightest doubt that this baby was me over forty years ago. It totally surprised me and changed the way I understood memory. As a matter of interest, I later found out from a medical doctor that the first sense that develops in a newborn child is the sense of smell. A baby recognizes its mother and other familiar things, like its own pram, by their smell. I can confirm this from my own direct experience.

When one understands the method to access early memories, one can continue by suggesting clearly to one's mind, "Earlier, please." Then one returns to inner stillness with no expectations, quietly attending to the present moment. If the previous state of samādhi was deep enough, another memory will come. If it comes, it comes quickly, effortlessly, and if it is a genuine early memory, it is always accompanied by the extraordinary sense of certainty, that this was from an earlier time. If there is the slightest of doubt, the memory can't be trusted and is probably wishful thinking.

Some of my students have reexperienced themselves within their mother's womb, floating in the waters, warm and contained. Some reexperience even stranger memories, being a person much older than they are now, in another body at another place in a time long ago. The realization is shocking but unavoidable, that this was them in a previous life.

These recollections generated by jhāna are substantially clearer than what we normally call memory, and they are totally different from what we call fantasy. They occur only in states of heightened awareness, where one's clarity of perception is greatly enhanced, both of which produce the unique feature of certain recognition of the identity involved.

Moreover, often these early memories are so disturbing that they cannot be the products of wishful thinking. One student, remembering her first weeks as a newborn infant, looked up at the woman who was lovingly cradling her and was alarmed to see the features of a woman so different from those of the person she knew as her mother. Had she been adopted? Was there something her mother hadn't told her? At the first opportunity she confronted the person that she had called her mom for as long as she knew, and asked her bluntly if she really was her biological mother. Her mother, taken aback, first inquired why she was asking this question. When the mother was told of the meditation-induced memory, she asked my student to describe the woman that she had seen in her meditation. With ease, and in great detail, my student described that woman's features. Her mother smiled as she recognized the description immediately. For that woman was the nanny that her mother had hired in the first weeks of her life. The mother was amazed that her daughter could remember this woman so accurately. And the daughter was relieved that her mom was her mom.

Some memories are even more disturbing, for they recall one's own death in a past life. Some students have found this so unpleasant that they have recoiled from the memory after only a few seconds. It is to be noted that one's previous death is the past-life event closest in time to our present existence, and the commonly intense experience leaves an indelible scar. It takes the fearlessness generated by samādhi to watch this harrowing event and then go beyond, back to earlier times. It takes a commitment to truth. Its unpleasantness proves beyond doubt that these are not wishful fantasies but accurate and shocking recollections of real events from one's past life.

These recollections of past lives qualify as deep insight for four reasons. First, the Buddha called them the first of the "threefold knowledges" *(tevijjā)* (MN 91,33) leading to enlightenment. And in the *Sekha Sutta* (MN 53,20), the Buddha likened the recollection of one's past lives to the first breaking out of a hen's chicks from their eggs. Second, they arise only after an experience of jhāna, just as the seeing of things as they truly are *(yathā bhūta ñāṇadassana)* happens only after jhāna (AN VII,61). Third, the recollection of past lives is based on personal experience here and now, and not on beliefs, traditions, or inferences. Fourth, these recollections change one's whole life. One experiences a great paradigm shift. For instance, the fear of one's own death and grief over other people's deaths are immensely diminished. The present life is now viewed from another perspective. One has the "big picture," as they say, the whole jigsaw puzzle rather than one tiny piece called the years of this life. Most important, only now has one received the raw data from one's own widened experience to truly appreciate what the Buddha means by *dukkha,* or suffering. One will understand why the Buddha's wisest disciple, Sāriputta, said: "Getting reborn again is the meaning of dukkha, ending rebirth is the meaning of happiness!" (AN X,65).

Deep Insight into Dukkha

The four noble truths are the central teaching of the Buddha. The first of these truths is the truth of dukkha. The Buddha then stated that the main reason why beings are not enlightened is that they do not *fully* understand dukkha (DN 16,2,1).

One reason why beings do not understand dukkha fully is that they see only this present life, and often only a portion of this life. Already in denial about their inevitable sickness and death, they deny their past and future lives even more strongly! When one does not seek out the full picture, one will never reach full understanding. Thus those who commit themselves to truth, and aspire to the freedom that truth brings, must challenge this profound denial of rebirth with the deep insight born of jhāna.

For when one does gain the deep insight of many lives, based on jhāna and consequently without any doubt, then deep insight can arise into the full meaning of dukkha. One can now understand the sayings of the Buddha like the following:

The stream of tears that you have shed through countless lives in saṃsāra, through meeting misfortune, is more than all the waters in the oceans. (SN 15,3)

The dead bones that you have left behind through countless deaths, if heaped together would be taller than any mountain. (SN 15,10)

For such a long time have your bones filled the cemeteries, long enough to experience revulsion to life, to become dispassionate to life and liberated from life. (SN 15,1)

Full understanding sees that whenever there is birth, there will be consequent suffering. Deep insight, based on the direct knowledge of the almost unimaginable breadth of saṃsāra, sees this in one's guts, not in the intellect. It sees the crucial first link of dependent origination *(paṭiccasamuppāda),* "birth is the cause of dukkha" *(jātipaccayā dukkha).* From this life-changing insight, craving and attachments begin their unraveling. There's nothing worth clinging to anymore.

The experience of a jhāna opens up a second avenue to the full understanding of dukkha: deep insight into happiness! One of the major features of a jhāna is the prolonged experience of a bliss that one never knew before. The bliss of jhāna, as I have said, is far more pleasurable and lasting than sexual orgasm. It is unforgettable. It overturns one's conception of happiness. Even falling in love is not as enjoyable as this. It is unavoidable that one will inquire what is this bliss and where did it come from.

The Rope That Strangles

Ajahn Chah's vivid simile of the rope that strangles, mentioned in chapter 11, helps to explain such happiness. Imagine a man born with a rope around his neck, continually pulled tight by two strong and invisible demons. He grows up like this, and knowing no different becomes accustomed to the difficulty to the point that he doesn't even notice it. Even when he practices mindfulness he cannot discern the tight rope.

It is always there, it is considered normal, and so it is excluded from his field of attention. Then one day the two demons, called "Five Senses" and "Doing," disappear for a while and let go of the rope. For the very first time in his life the man experiences freedom from constriction, freedom from the burden of the five senses and doing. He experiences incredible bliss, unlike anything he has ever known. Only then can he comprehend what happiness is, and how much suffering was the tight rope and the two deceptive demons. He also realizes that happiness is the ending of suffering.

Similarly, one is born with a body "tied" tightly around one's mind, with the demons of one's five senses and the doing (will, choice, control, etc.) keeping a firm grip. One has grown up with this, gotten used to it, and so considers it normal. Some even begin to enjoy their five-sense world and get off on doing things, even mentally doing things called thinking. People actually consider this as happiness. Incredible! Even when one practices mindfulness of the five senses, or of will *(cetanā)*, one cannot discern their essential suffering nature. How can one, since it has always seemed that "this is the way it is"? Then one day, for the very first time, one enters into a jhāna. The five senses together with the movement of mind called "doing" completely disappear for a while. With their vanishing the body also disappears, and for the first time in this life the mind is free from all doing, all five-sense activity, and free from the burdensome body like a tight rope strangling the beautiful mind. One experiences the bliss of a jhāna, greater than any happiness one has ever known. Only now can one understand what happiness is and what dukkha is. Only now does one realize that the body *is* suffering, that seeing or hearing or smelling or tasting or feelings are each and every time dukkha, and that doing is dukkha through and through. Deep insight into the pervasiveness of dukkha has occurred. And one realizes that the bliss of the jhāna was the result of this immense suffering disappearing for the duration of the jhāna.

Unless one has experience of jhāna, where all five senses have vanished, one will be unable to comprehend that to see a dew-speckled rose in the early morning sunlight is suffering, or to listen to Beethoven's imperious Fifth Symphony is dukkha, or to experience great sex is as painful as being burned. One will deem such statements as madness. But when one knows jhāna from personal experience, one will recognize these statements as being so true. As the Buddha said in the suttas, "What ordinary folk call happiness, the enlightened ones call dukkha" (SN 35,136). Deep insight sees what is inaccessible to ordinary folk, what is incomprehensible to them, and what is often shocking. To see the birth of one's first child might appear as the most wonderful moment of one's life, but only if one knows of nothing better. Jhāna is that something better, and it can change your whole understanding of what is happiness. And, in consequence, it unveils the meaning of dukkha. It literally blows your mind.

The Prison Simile

Another simile, to emphasize the same point, is that of the man who was born and raised in a prison and who has never set foot outside. All he knows is prison life. He would have no conception of the freedom that is beyond his world. And he would not understand that prison is suffering. If anybody suggested that his world was dukkha, he would disagree, for prison is the limit of his experience. But one day he might find the escape tunnel dug long ago that leads beyond the prison walls to the unimaginable and expansive world of real freedom. Only when he has entered that tunnel and escaped from his prison does he realize how much suffering prison actually was, and the end of that suffering, escaping from jail, is happiness.

In this simile the prison is the body, the high prison walls are the five senses, and the relentlessly demanding prison guard is one's own will, the doer. The tunnel dug long ago, through which one escapes, is called jhāna (as at AN IX,42). Only when one has experienced jhāna does one realize that the five-sense world, even at its best, is really a five-walled prison, some parts of it a little more comfortable but still a jail with everyone on death row! Only after deep samādhi does one realize that "will" was the torturer, masquerading as freedom, but preventing one ever resting happily at peace. Only outside of prison can one gain the data that produces the deep insight that discovers the truth about dukkha.

In summary, without experience of jhāna, one's knowledge of the world is too limited to fully understand dukkha, as required by the first noble truth, and proceed to enlightenment.

Deep Insight into Anicca

Insight into the impermanent nature of all things seems so easy. It is obvious that nothing lasts. One doesn't even need to be a meditator to understand this. So if one can be fully enlightened by seeing anicca, why aren't more people enlightened?

It is because one has profoundly invisible blindspots, as in the story of the Vietnam veteran monk. One is blind to phenomena that have always been present without apparent change. Some things are so stable that one doesn't even notice them. These are the blind spots that constitute delusion *(avijjā)*. The following similes may help.

The TV Simile

Imagine one is sitting at home watching TV. One can contemplate impermanence watching the box. Scenes come and go, programs come and go, channels come and go. One can even observe the "emptiness channel" when the TV is turned off and one is left with a blank screen. But any insight into impermanence that arises here is superficial. It does not shatter your attachment to the tube.

Similarly, one may contemplate relationships coming and going, days turning into night, flowers fading, bodies aging. But though one sees the impermanence of all these, still one's cravings are not quelled. Even when one contemplates death, when life has been switched off and all that remains is the inert body, like a dark TV, that too will not explode one's attachments. Doctors in the morgue and funeral directors see death every workday, but they aren't enlightened. Such contemplations are helpful, but they are still superficial.

Let us return to the TV and imagine one is sitting at home, watching TV, and contemplating impermanence when, suddenly, not only does the program stop but the whole TV set disappears as well! It completely vanishes in a instant. Television sets are not supposed to do that. It isn't covered by the warranty. It is absolutely unexpected, shocking, and life changing. This is the stuff of deep insight.

There are some phenomena that one is blind to, whose solid stability one relies on, whose impermanence one just can't imagine. For example, one's will, the potential to do things. Even when one suppresses the will, holds it in check in some focused activity, still one knows that the ability to do something, the potential to do, is ever present. One is always in control to some degree.

In deep meditation the will, the potential to do, suddenly vanishes. It is as unexpected, shocking, and weird as seeing one's television set vanish before one's very eyes. In jhāna, especially in the second jhāna and beyond, the will ceases but consciousness continues, brighter and clearer than ever. Even the potential to do is gone. One is mindfully frozen. The mind is harder and much more brilliant than a diamond. It is unshakable as emptiness. These are weird experiences but real, exceptionally real. And their message is plain to see, as obvious as a huge neon sign on a moonless dark night; that something one took to be ever present—the potential to do, one's will—has completely ceased, disappeared into the void. This is what is meant by a deep insight into impermanence. Something unimaginable and upsetting is seen to be true. The "I," the doer, the will, is subject to stopping, while consciousness continues. After such a deep insight, you will never assume again that you are in charge of you.

The Vanishing Ocean

Imagine watching the waves on the ocean rising and falling, coming and going. It is just like watching pleasant feelings *(vedanā)* and unpleasant feelings rise and fall, come and go. One is contemplating impermanence, true, but only superficially.

Now imagine that one day, as one is contemplating the rise and fall of the waves, suddenly the whole ocean vanishes, taking with it all the land mass that contains the ocean. The whole lot disappears—all gone. Now *that* is deep insight, unimaginable, astonishing, and very upsetting. Oceans aren't meant to suddenly disappear out of existence.

That is what happens in jhāna. One was contemplating the pleasant and unpleasant waves, rising and falling on the ocean of the five senses, and then the whole sea of the five senses completely disappears, taking with it the body that contains the five senses. One has literally gone out of this world, out of this *kāmaloka,* and entered the jhāna realms, *rūpaloka.* One has another level of understanding into the real meaning of anicca and how far it extends. One has deep insight into the cessation of the five sense consciousnesses. Never again will one assume that *I* am the one who sees, who hears, who smells or tastes or touches.

The Eyeball and the Telescope

Imagine looking through a telescope at the stars. Then someone fixes a flat mirror to the end of the instrument, so instead of seeing the heavens, one sees what is doing the looking. Whenever one does this, all one sees is one's own eyeball, always the same. It is so difficult to gain even superficial insight into the impermanence of the one who knows.

Now imagine that when looking at the one doing the looking using the mirrored telescope, suddenly the image of the eyeball completely disappears, taking everything with it, leaving not even emptiness. One soon realizes, after the event has passed by, that if all that is known vanishes, then that which does the knowing must also have vanished. The deep insight arises that the one who knows is impermanent, and that the knower is not me.

This is precisely what happens as one proceeds through the jhānas and the immaterial attainments. The five sense consciousnesses have already disappeared on entering the first jhāna. Now the remaining consciousness, mind consciousness, is peeled away layer by layer. Just before attaining the last of the eight freedoms *(atthavimokha),* the attainment of the cessation of all that is felt or perceived, the last remnant of mind disappears. The "eyeball of the mind," the citta, ceases, and all is gone. Deep insight has discovered that the "one who knows"—the mind, the citta, the ground of all being, *ātman,* whatever each culture calls it—is impermanent, subject to a final ending, which is called *parinibbāna.*

Thus the deep insights into anicca go so much deeper than most meditators expect. When one uses the data of jhāna experiences, one sees the dissolution of the once-solid ground on which so many assumptions of oneself had survived for so long. Whole clusters of self-views topple and crumble. Deep insight soon realizes that there is nothing stable anywhere, anytime, on which a self can stand. Which is no problem anymore, because it is realized that there's no one left to do the standing.

Deep Insight into Anattā

There are three bombshells set off by deep insight, any one of which can demolish the foundations of delusion. They are *dukkha, anicca,* and *anattā,* meaning suffering, impermanence, and no-self. Together, they are called by the Buddha, "the three characteristics of existence." I have shown how deep insight into dukkha and anicca leave one nothing at all to cling to and nowhere to stand. Now I will light the fuse of the third bombshell of insight, the truth of no-self, which has the potential to blow one away literally!

Once again, deep insight into no-self can only occur using the data provided uniquely by jhāna and with a mind empowered by jhāna. One simply cannot close in on these truths employing only rational thinking based on incomplete experience. For instance, some traditions aspire to reach deep insight through a method of reasoned investigation into the question "Who am I?" In the *Sabbāsava Sutta,* the Buddha specifically called such an inquiry "attending unwisely" (MN 2,7). Actually, the relevant Pāli phrase is *"ayoniso manasikāra,"* which literally means "work of the mind that does not go back to the source." The question "Who am I?" does not penetrate deep enough, because it carries with it a mistaken assumption. The inquiry "Who am I?" assumes that a being called "I" exists and, on that questionable premise, only seeks to discover the "who" that being is. Even when one investigates "Who is asking this question?" again one misses the point. It would be more productive to ask, "What is it that I take to be me?" or "What is asking this question?"

In medieval Buddhist India, a famous public debate on no-self occurred between a learned monk and Mahādeva, which went something like this:

LEARNED MONK: Good morning. Who are you?

MAHĀDEVA: Mahādeva.

L.M.: Who is "Mahādeva"?

M.: Me.

L.M.: Who is "me"?

M.: A dog.

L.M.: Who is "a dog"?

M.: You are!

L.M.: Who is "you"?

M.: Mahādeva.

L.M.: Who is "Mahādeva"?

M.: Me.

L.M.: Who is "me"?

M.: A dog.

L.M.: Who is a "dog"?

M.: You are!

...and so the debate went round and round until the laughter of the audience gave the learned monk an insight. He realized he had allowed himself to be called a dog many times by the clever Mahādeva. This amusing historic dialogue demonstrates how language contains implicit assumptions. The assumptions underlying the words of the two monks were very different. It shows that if you do not frame the question well, you will not receive an adequate answer.

A more productive line of inquiry is to investigate not who but *what* one takes oneself to be, and then ask, does this fit the facts of experience? I might take myself to be a monk, British–Australian, white (or rather patchy pink), fifty-four years of age, healthy, and so on. However, superficial insight can see all these identities as merely temporary, and therefore not the essential "me." As one ages, it becomes increasingly clear that one cannot take oneself to be identical with the disintegrating body. Nor can one take oneself to be a by-product of the brain.

The Mind Surviving the Death of the Brain

Recent medical research backs up my assertion that the mind is not merely a by-product of the brain. According to researchers,

> Recent studies in cardiac arrest survivors have indicated that although the majority of cardiac arrest survivors have no memory recall from the event, nevertheless, approximately 10% develop memories that are consistent with typical near death experiences [NDE]. These include an ability to "see" and recall specific detailed descriptions of the resuscitation, as verified by the resuscitation staff. Many studies in humans and animals have indicated that brain function ceases during cardiac arrest, thus raising the question how such lucid, well-structured thought processes with reasoning and memory formation can occur at such a time.[12]

> Sabom mentions a young American woman who had complications during brain surgery for a cerebral aneurysm. The EEG of her cortex and brain stem had become totally flat. After the operation, which was eventually successful, this patient proved to have had a very deep NDE, including an out-of-body experience, with subsequently verified observations during the period of the flat EEG.[13]

These two quotes come from separate studies that show the persistence of consciousness after clinical death. The first study was conducted by a team of doctors at Southampton General Hospital in England in 2000, and the second study by a team of doctors in the Netherlands in 2001. The latter study was published in one of the most prestigious medical journals in the world, *The Lancet*. They rigorously researched the occurrence of NDE in those with cardiac arrest. As the authors concluded, "Our results show that medical factors cannot account for the occurrence of NDE…all patients had been clinically dead."[14]

In lay language, these two broad studies uncovered a significant number of cases where the mind was shown to survive the death of the brain. If the mind was only a by-product of the brain, then this would not occur. The fact that consciousness has been found to exist when the brain is no longer functioning is convincing evidence that the mind can be independent of the brain. Another study says:

> The data suggests that in this cardiac arrest model, the NDE arises during unconsciousness. This is a surprising conclusion, because when the brain is so dysfunctional that the patient is deeply coma-tose, the cerebral structures which underpin subjective experience and memory must be severely impaired. Complex experiences such as are reported in the NDE should not arise or be retained in the memory. Such patients would be expected to have no sub-jective experience (as was the case in 88.8 percent of patients in this study) or at best a confusional state if some brain function is retained. Even if the unconscious brain is flooded with neu-rotransmitters this should not produce clear, lucid remembered experiences, as those cerebral modules which generate conscious experience and underpin memory are impaired by cerebral anoxia [lack of oxygen]. The fact that in cardiac arrest loss of cortical function precedes the rapid loss of brain stem activity lends further support to this view.[15]

Having dismissed the "usual suspects," we get to two final candidates for what one takes oneself to be.

The Final Citadel of the Illusion of Self

The last two candidates for selfhood are the doer and the knower. Underneath all the temporary identities, these two lurk as the last strong-hold against truth, the final citadel of self-illusion. The unenlightened person, when pressed hard by reason and insight, will eventually fall back on defending their self-existence as either "the one who does" or "the one who knows," if not both. It takes powerful, deep insight based on jhāna to storm this last citadel and see beyond the illusion.

It seems so obvious that one's self is in control. One takes it for granted that it is one's self that chooses to listen to music, watch TV, or read something. It appears true to experience that one's self generates one's will. Unfortunately, what seems obvious is often untrue.

The neuroscientist Benjamin Libet of the University of California in San Francisco asked volunteers to extend one of their arms and, whenever they felt like it, out of their own free will, to flex their wrist. A clock allowed the subjects to note exactly when they decided to act, and by fitting electrodes to their wrists, the start of the action could be timed. More electrodes on the volunteers' scalps recorded a particular brain wave pattern called the "readiness potential," which occurs just before any complex action and is associated with the brain planning its next move. It was found that the conscious decision to act came *after* the readiness potential![16] The inescapable conclusion of this experiment is that what we can observe as "the decision to act," what we take to be our own free will, occurs only after the process of action has begun. "Will" does not initiate the action but is a by-product of the process.

Such hard evidence is hard to accept. It goes against one's basic assumptions of life. It even evokes fear in some persons when they imagine the possibility that they are not in charge of either their body or their mind. Even strong scientific evidence is not powerful enough to destroy the illusion of will. One needs jhāna to see directly that it is not a self that generates the will but an empty process of cause and effect.

Meditation can well be summarized as going into the center of things. One goes first to the center of time, called the "now." Then into the center of the now that is free of all thought. Then into the center of the body with one's breath. Then into the center of the breath, which is the beautiful breath. Then into the center of the beautiful breath, where one experiences the nimitta. Then into the center of the nimitta to enter the first jhāna. Then into the center of the first jhāna, which is the second jhāna, and so on. This is *yoniso manasikāra,* "work of the mind that goes to the source." As one goes deeper into the source of body and mind, one comes to the source of will, the seat of the doer, the citadel in which potential doing abides. And one sees it all empty of a self.

The Simile of the Driverless Bus

If one's life is compared to a bus journey, with the bus representing our body and mind, the bus driver our will, and the view from the window our experience of pleasure and suffering, then most would agree that we're in a bus with a pretty bad driver. For sometimes our bus goes through some very pleasant scenery, and our hopeless driver doesn't even stop but even accelerates faster. Just as life's happy times never seem to last as long as we want them to. Then at other times our bus goes through some ghastly territory, and our incompetent driver doesn't speed out as fast as possible but slows down and even stalls. Just as life's very unhappy moments seem to last longer than they should. There comes a point when we need to find this inept driver, our will, and train it to travel only to happy lands, lingering slowly there, and avoid or race out of the toxic-waste dumps of life. It takes a long spiritual inner journey to find the bus driver's seat, the source of one's will. It is found in the jhāna. However, when one gets there, one has the shock of one's life. The driver's seat is empty. Life, my friend, is a driverless bus!

The result of seeing that there is no one driving the bus is to go back to one's seat, sit down quietly, and stop complaining. There is no one to complain to anymore. Beautiful experiences come and go, painful experiences come and go, and one just sits there with equanimity. Complaining, otherwise known as discontent, a.k.a. craving for happiness, has finally ceased.

Craving is like an arm with two ends, which reaches out to grab things or push them away. Too often, meditators only observe the objects of craving—loved ones or possessions or chocolate and so on. They are looking at the wrong end of the arm. One should look at *this* end of the arm, the thing doing the craving. The process doing the craving is the delusion of self. When there is the delusion of self, there will always be craving. Craving is how the delusion expresses itself. When one sees with deep insight that the driver's seat is empty, that there is no "doer," then the delusion is exploded and craving soon stops. For there is nothing left to do the craving.

Some clever students ask me, if the driver's seat of our bus is empty, why should I bother practicing? What is the point of effort? The answer is that, because the driver's seat of your bus is empty, you have no choice but to practice! Effort is part of the journey. But always remember that striving is generated from many other causes, it does not come from your self.

The Buddha's Word on the One Who Knows

Even some good, practicing monks fail to breach illusion's last line of defense, the knower. They take "the one who knows," "the original mind," "the pure knowing," or some other descriptions of the citta as the ultimate and permanent reality. To be accurate, such concepts belong to the teachings of Hinduism and not to Buddhism, for the Buddha clearly refuted these theories as not penetrating deeply enough.

For instance, in the first sutta in the first collection of Buddhist scriptures, the *Brahmajāla Sutta,* the Buddha described in detail sixty-two types of wrong view *(micchā diṭṭhi).* Wrong view number eight is the opinion that the thing that is called *citta,* or *mind (mano),* or *consciousness (viññāṇa)* is the permanent self *(attā)*—stable, eternal, not subject to change, forever the same (DN 1,2,13). Thus maintaining that "the one who knows" is eternal is *micchā diṭṭhi,* wrong view, says the Buddha.

In the *Nidāna Saṃyutta,* the Buddha states:

> But, bhikkhus, that[17] which is called "mind" *[citta]* and "mentality" *[mano]* and "consciousness" *[viññāṇa]*—the uninstructed worldling is unable to experience revulsion towards it, unable to become dispassionate towards it and be liberated from it. For what reason? Because for a long time this has been held to by him, appropriated, and grasped thus: "This is mine, this I am, this is self."...
>
> It would be better, bhikkhus, for the uninstructed worldling to take as self *[attā]* this body...because this body...is seen standing... for [as long as] a hundred years, or even longer. But that which is called "mind" and "mentality" and "consciousness" arises as one thing and ceases as another by day and by night. (SN 12,61)[18]

However, just as the hard scientific evidence mentioned earlier cannot dislodge the view that it is oneself who is the doer, so even the hard scriptural evidence of the Buddha's own teachings is unable on its own to dislodge the view that "the one who knows" is the ultimate entity, the attā. Some even argue that these Buddhist texts must have been changed, solely on the grounds that the texts disagree with their view![19]

Such irrational stubbornness comes from *bhavataṇhā,* the craving to be. Bhavataṇhā is so strong that one is prepared to let go of almost everything—possessions, one's body, and one's thoughts—as long as one is finally left with something, some tiny spot of existence, in order to be. After all, one wants to enjoy parinibbāna, thoroughgoing extinction, having worked so hard to get there. Bhavataṇhā is why many great meditators are unable to agree with the Buddha and make that final leap of renunciation that lets go of absolutely everything, including the citta. Even though the Buddha said that "nothing is worth adhering to" *(sabbe dhammā nālam abhinivesāya)* (MN 37,3), people still adhere to the citta. They continue to hold on to the knower and elevate it to unwarranted levels of mystical profundity by calling it "the ground of all being," "union with God," "the original mind," etc.—even though the Buddha strongly refuted all such clinging, saying that all levels of being stink, the way even a tiny speck of feces on one's hand stinks (AN I,18,13).

One needs the experiences of many jhānas, combined with a sound knowledge of the Buddha's own teachings, in order to break through the barrier of bhavataṇhā, the craving to be, and see for oneself that what some call "the citta," "mind," "consciousness," or "the one who knows" is only an empty process, one that is fueled by the craving to be and blinded by the delusion of permanence, but which is clearly of the nature to cease absolutely and leave nothing at all remaining.

Deep Insight into the Citta

It is the mind, the citta, that rules all conscious activity. Sight might be assumed to be capable of seeing on its own, but in fact it is the mind sense, which immediately follows seeing, that makes knowing what is seen possible. Sight on its own does not register. As the Buddha said (SN 48,42), the mind can appropriate for itself any of the events in the five senses, as well as its own unique field of experience. Since the mind consciousness follows every recognizable event of the five sense consciousnesses, these five sense consciousnesses carry an illusion of sameness. There appears to be something similar in seeing, hearing, smelling, tasting, and touching. Once one has come face to face with the citta in jhāna, one recognizes that it is the accompanying citta that gives the illusion of continuity to the stream of consciousness.

The Granular Nature of the Citta

One now realizes that just as the stream of consciousness is granular, so is that component of the stream that is the citta. As noted earlier, sand on a beach appears continuous. Looking closely, however, one sees that the beach consists of tiny grains of silica. Looking even closer, one can see spaces between each grain, so that they aren't even touching. The citta has this same granular quality. Instead of appearing as a continuous entity, it is now clearly recognized as made up of series of individual "knowings," cittas or mind events, packed closely together and related to their neighbors by cause and effect. One can even discern that there is a gap between the mind events, between each knowing, where the citta has completely vanished from existence for a while.

That should be sufficient for deep insight to arise. Based on much experience of jhāna, one sees that even the undefiled citta is impermanent, a parade of individual mind-particles, and subject to cessation. One makes the great breakthrough and realizes that "the one who knows," "the knowing," "the mind," or "the undefiled citta" is merely a process empty of any essence or self. Moreover, it is a process driven by cause and effect: since all cittas are subject to arising, they are also subject to complete cessation. As the Buddha observed, "Whatever is of a nature to arise, all that is subject to cessation" *(yaṅkiñci samudaya-dhammaṁ, sabban taṁ nirodha-dhammanti)* (SN 56,11).

The Fading Away of the Citta

When one experiences not just the first jhāna but also several higher jhānas, one will have sufficient data to recognize that a feature of each higher jhāna is an incremental fading away *(virāga)* of the citta. As one proceeds through the jhānas and the immaterial attainments, that which knows is seen to experience less and less. One realizes that if the path into the first jhāna implies a letting go of the five sense consciousnesses, then the path through the ascending jhānas entails a letting go of the mind consciousness, the citta.

For instance, in the fourth immaterial attainment, the citta has almost entirely disappeared. That is why this state is called "neither perception nor nonperception." The citta, as it were, stands on the edge of its own ending. Once it proceeds beyond that edge, it is called *saññā-vedayita-nirodha,* "cessation of feeling and perception." Here, what was but a moment before the most refined manifestation of the citta possible is now extinguished. It vanishes, ceases—it "nibbānas."

Upon emerging from the state of cessation, either one is completely enlightened, an arahant, or else one is almost completely enlightened, a nonreturner *(anāgāmī).* The temporary extinction of that which knows, the citta, is so pronounced that deep insight must occur. One recognizes that everything has stopped, with nothing at all remaining. Such a deep insight has as its inevitable consequence the third or the fourth stage of enlightenment.

Even when one has not gone as far as this "attainment of extinction" *(nirodha samāpatti),* one may use the data of just one or two jhānas to infer that it is the nature of this citta to cease. One has already seen the first fadings of the citta, and now one can extrapolate to realize the full fading away of the knower. Moreover, the more the citta disappears, the more peaceful it is and the more sublime. Should one aspire to the most peaceful and most sublime, then one will direct one's mind to ceasing. As the suttas say, having experienced a jhāna, one realizes that "this full fading is the peaceful; this is the sublime, that is, the stilling of all formations, the relinquishing of all objects of attachment, the destruction of craving, fading, cessation, nibbāna. Standing upon that, one attains the destruction of the outflowings of the mind. But if he does not attain the destruction of the outflowings [as an arahant], he becomes a nonreturner" (MN 64,15).

Dependent Origination and the Pure Citta

What is the pure, undefiled, and radiant citta? In the suttas, the Buddha consistently described the mind on emerging from the jhānas as "pure and undefiled" (MN 51,24). A citta that is free of the five hindrances is also called "radiant" *(pabhassara)* (SN 46,33). Therefore, the pure, undefiled, and radiant citta, according to the Buddha, refers to the mind on emerging from the jhānas.

The deep insight that catalyzes enlightenment, according to many suttas, is the realization that even this purest, completely undefiled, and radiant citta is dependently originated, impermanent, and subject to extinction. For instance, in the *Aṭṭhakanāgara Sutta* (MN 52), Ven. Ānanda is asked what one thing does the Buddha proclaim as the door to enlightenment. Ven. Ānanda answered that the Buddha proclaimed eleven entrances to enlightenment, all requiring a jhāna as the trigger for deep insight: "He considers this and understands it thus: 'This first [or second, third, and so on] jhāna is conditioned and volitionally produced. But whatever is conditioned and volitionally produced is impermanent, subject to cessation.' Standing upon that he attains [full enlightenment or the state of the nonreturner]."[20]

In the simile of the grains of sand, one sees not only that the beach is comprised of individual grains that are not even touching but that a cause-and-effect relationship put the grains there in the first place. One understands how the sea deposits sand particles and takes them away, how it smoothes and packs the beach with sand. In the same way, when one looks closely at the purified citta, one can recognize the cause-and-effect relationship that produces this citta. One understands how craving and its partner, volition, deposit individual cittas (moments of mind) and take them away, how they smooth the citta and defile it, just as the polluted seawater can sometimes deposit oil and other flotsam on the sand. Here one discerns, in particular, how the craving to exist packs the sequence of individual cittas tightly into our stream of consciousness, filling in every empty space to give the illusion of continuity and permanence. Having seen this so clearly for oneself, one understands that even the pure citta is conditioned and impermanent. It is not an independent, self-sustaining essence. It is not the unconditioned. Having seen that the most purified and radiant form of knowing in all forms of existence is impermanent, one knows how much more so are all other forms of citta. One has experienced the deep insight that the citta, the one that knows, the mind, or whatever else one calls it, will not persist forever. When the causes that sustain the flow of mind moments cease, when the craving to be is destroyed, then the mindstream will run out of fuel. It will cease completely, and that is called parinibbāna, complete extinction.

Where Does the Pure Citta Go?—a Stupid Question

When the wanderer Vacchagotta asked what happens to the liberated mind *(vimutta citta)* after the death of an arahant, the Buddha replied using the simile of a fire (MN 72,19). A fire burns in dependence on its fuel. It is conditioned. When the fuel is used up, the fire is extinguished *(nibbuta)*. It makes no sense to ask where the fire goes after it has been extinguished. It likewise makes no sense to ask where the liberated citta goes after an arahant has been extinguished. That would be a stupid question. As we saw earlier, the famous bhikkhunī arahant Paṭācārā gained her deep insight that produced full enlightenment while watching an oil lamp being extinguished (Thig 116). She saw the essential similarity of the flame and the citta, how they are both dependently originated, and just as the flame had "nibbāna-ed," so the citta must do the same.

The liberated citta, like that of the arahant, can be compared to a shooting star. For untold millions of years, a piece of cosmic rock or ice had been going around and around our solar system, orbiting in the bright and dark spaces. Just like the stream of consciousness, the knower and the doer, have been wandering for untold millions of lifetimes, a piece of cosmic emptiness going around and around saṃsāra, being born and dying in the bright and dark worlds. Then the piece of rock or ice meets our planet, enters the atmosphere, and burns in brilliance as a radiant and pure shooting star before being extinguished forever. Just like that which we call a "person" meets the true Dhamma, the deep insight into the emptiness of the doer and knower, and the citta blazes in brilliance and radiance, with the certain knowledge that it will soon be extinguished—nibbāna-ed—forever.

As the famous *Ratana Sutta* (Sn 235) says:

> The old is destroyed, the new is not arising.
> Those whose minds [citta] are disgusted with future existence,
> Their seeds (of rebirth) have been destroyed, (and) they have no desire for growth.
> The wise are quenched, just like this lamp.[21]

Or as two great arahants in the Theragāthā said,

> Made to turn around, the citta will right here be destroyed!
> (Thag 184—Sivaka Thera)

> You, citta, will certainly perish!
> (Thag 1144—Tālaputa Thera)

Deep Insight and *Satipaṭṭhāna*

The Buddha taught the four focuses of mindfulness, or satipaṭṭhāna, as both a support for the attainment of jhāna as well as a means for gaining deep insight into no-self, anattā

The latter practice, penetrating no-self, relies on already having experienced a jhāna. This is why each satipaṭṭhāna begins with the prerequisite *"vineyya loke abhijjhā-domanassam,"* which, as explained in chapter 8, means having already abandoned the five hindrances. As the *Naḷakapāna Sutta* (MN 68,6) confirms, it is one of the functions of jhānas to stop these five hindrances from "invading the mind and remaining." One needs mindfulness empowered by jhāna for deep insight to occur.

The purpose of satipaṭṭhāna is revealed in the passage repeated at the end of each practice, where, having contemplated the causal arising and causal ceasing of these phenomena, one realizes that "there is just a body," "just vedanā," "just citta," or "just mental objects," all cause-and-effect processes that cannot be taken as me, mine, or myself. Thus "one abides not hanging on to anything *(anissita),* not taking up anything in the world" (MN 10). In other words, the function of satipaṭṭhāna is to win the deep insight into no-self, anattā.

In this chapter, I gave special attention to the fourth and the third satipaṭṭhāna. This is because the innermost and nearly inaccessible lair of delusion is where the doer and the knower reside. The investigation into the conditioned and empty nature of the doer belongs to the fourth satipaṭṭhāna. Deep insight into the impermanent and dependent nature of the knower is the whole of the third satipaṭṭhāna. So what I have described at length as deep insight is no more than the satipaṭṭhāna empowered by jhāna.

A Last Word from Ajahn Chah

When my teacher, Ajahn Chah, began feeling sick, we Western monks built a sauna for him at Wat Pa Nanachat. Ajahn Chah would come over from his own monastery, Wat Pa Pong, to take a sauna once a week. Thus, not only could we do service to our teacher, but our teacher could also do service to us by sharing some Dhamma teachings. In fact, he would usually give a talk to us each week before going to the sauna, with us monks accompanying him afterward to help him in the sauna.

On one occasion, Ajahn Chah had given such an inspiring talk that, instead of accompanying my teacher to the sauna as was my usual habit, I slipped around the back of the hall and sat in meditation. I had such a lovely meditation, so deep that I lost all sense of time. When I came out with a big smile on my face, I thought of my teacher. Perhaps there was still some time to go to the sauna and do some service, like rinsing his bathing cloth. So I walked to the sauna.

I was too late. Ajahn Chah had already finished, because I met him along the path leading to the sauna. He was returning to his car. Ajahn Chah stopped and looked right through me, with a gaze that only accomplished meditators possess. I assumed that he had noticed my relaxed features and smile and deduced that I had just emerged from a deep meditation. So it was that the great Ajahn Chah tried to enlighten me.

"Brahmavamso!" he demanded, with a thrust of his voice like a stab with a sword. "Why?"

I hesitated. I understood the question, but the answer was too distant from me.

So I replied, "I don't know, sir."

Ajahn Chah's probing features loosened, and he laughed.

"I'll tell you the answer anyway," he said. "Should anyone ask you 'Why?' the answer is 'There is nothing.'"

That blew me away. I was stunned. It impressed me so much that I can picture the encounter clearly even now as I write this, even though it was more than twenty years ago.

Ajahn Chah pressed me further, "Do you understand?"

"Yes, sir," I replied confidently.

"No you don't!" he laughed back, and then continued on his way to the car.

This was conveyed to me by the most compassionate and wise master that I have known. He summed up what this chapter on deep insight is all about. When probed with jhāna-empowered mindfulness, the big question "Why?" produces one and only one correct answer: "There is nothing"!

Do you understand?

No, you don't.

Enlightenment: Entering the Stream

14

This Dhamma that I have attained is profound, hard to see and hard to understand, peaceful and sublime, unattainable by mere reasoning, subtle, to be experienced by the wise. But this generation delights in attachment, takes delight in attachment, and rejoices in attachment. It is hard for such a generation to see this truth, namely, specific conditionality, dependent origination. And it is hard to see this truth, namely, the stilling of all formations, the relinquishing of all acquisitions, the destruction of craving, dispassion, cessation, nibbāna.

—*the Buddha, just after his enlightenment*[22]

ALTHOUGH ENLIGHTENMENT, which is the realization of nibbāna, is hard to attain, it is not impossible. There are monks alive today who have experienced the real thing. According to the Buddha's teaching to the wanderer Subhadda in the *Mahāparinibbāna Sutta* (DN 16,5,27), wherever the complete noble eightfold path is practiced well, there one will find stream winners, once-returners, nonreturners, and fully enlightened arahants. But where an incomplete path is practiced—where, for example, jhāna is discarded, leaving a sevenfold path, or all virtue (right speech, action, and livelihood) is discarded for a fivefold path—enlightened ones will not be found. Today a wholehearted commitment to a complete eightfold path is found in a few monastic communities that are devoted to both seclusion and sense restraint. Only there are enlightened ones found.

What Nibbāna Is Not

The above may be hard to accept, but it is true—just as the Buddha's teaching of nibbāna as cessation is hard to accept but true. In this chapter I will explain enlightenment as the Buddha meant it to be taught, that is, with precision and clarity. I will also describe the final parts of the process during which it occurs. But first I will comment on what nibbāna is not.

Dumbing Down Nibbāna

Whenever Buddhism becomes fashionable, there is a tendency to change the meaning of nibbāna to suit more people. The pressures born of popularity will bend the truth to make it more accommodating. Teachings are very well received when they tell people only what they want to hear. Furthermore, vanity induces some Dhamma teachers to explain nibbāna in ways that do not challenge their own unenlightened state. This all leads to a dumbing down of nibbāna.

One can read in modern Buddhist literature that enlightenment is nothing more than a passive submission to the way things seem to be (as distinguished from the way things truly are, seen only after jhāna). Or that the unconditioned is merely the easily accessible mindfulness-in-the-moment, within which anything goes—absolutely anything. Or that the deathless state is simply a nondual awareness, a rejection of all distinctions, and an affirmation that all is one and benign. The supreme goal of Buddhism then becomes little more than the art of living in a less troubled way, a hopeless surrender to the ups and downs of life, and a denial of dukkha as inherent in all forms of existence. It is like a neurotic prisoner celebrating his incarceration instead of seeking the way out. Such dumbed-down Dhamma may feel warm and fuzzy, but it is a gross understatement of the real nibbāna. And those who buy into such enchanting distortions will find they have bought a lemon.

Banana Nibbāna

When I was a teenager, I asked many Christian teachers to explain the meaning of God. Either they would tell me what it was not or they would give me an answer that was unintelligible. For example, they would say God is "the ineffable" or "the ultimate reality" or "the ground of all being" or "infinite consciousness" or "the pure knowing."

Later I asked many Buddhist teachers to explain the meaning of nibbāna. Either they would tell me what it was not or they would give me an answer that was unintelligible. For instance, they would say nibbāna is "the ineffable" or "the ultimate reality" or "the ground of all being" or "unbounded consciousness" or "the pure knowing." Then insight arose: I've heard such mumbo-jumbo somewhere before! For the very same reasons that I rejected meaningless descriptions of God as a youth, so even now I reject all the gobbledygook descriptions of the Buddhist nibbāna.

Some definitions of nibbāna are plain oxymorons, such as, for example, "nonmanifest consciousness" or "attuning to the ungraspable." Consciousness is that essential part of the cognitive process that makes experience manifest, so "nonmanifest consciousness" actually means "nonmanifest manifesting" or "unconscious consciousness," which is nonsense. One can only attune to what is possible for the mind to grasp, so the latter definition becomes "attuning to the unattunable" or "grasping the ungraspable." These and other similar descriptions are mere foolishness dressed up as wisdom.

The underlying problem is that it is very embarrassing to a Buddhist not to have a clear idea of what nibbāna is. It is like getting on a bus and not being quite sure where the bus is going. It is worse when your non-Buddhist friends ask you to describe where you are heading on your Buddhist journey. So, many Buddhists resort to obfuscation, meaning bamboozling their audience with unusual combinations of mystical-sounding phrases. For if your listeners don't understand what you're saying, then there is a good chance that they'll think it profound and consider you wise!

Such crooked descriptions of nibbāna are so lacking in straightforwardness, so bent out of line, that I call them "banana nibbāna." Experience tells us that, when one knows a thing well and has had frequent and direct experience of it, then one will be able to supply a clear, detailed, and straightforward description. Mystification is the sure sign that the speaker does not know what they're talking about.

Demystified Nibbāna

Here, I will give three complementary descriptions of nibbāna: (1) nibbāna as the highest happiness; (2) nibbāna as the complete ending of sensory desire, ill will, and delusion; and (3) nibbāna as the remainderless cessation of this process we call body and mind. These three depictions, all from the Buddha, give a clear and precise portrait of nibbāna. Once one has understood what enlightenment is, then one will easily recognize the path leading there, and all the teachings of the Buddha will become extraordinarily transparent.

The Highest Happiness

The Buddha said, "Nibbāna is the highest happiness" (Dhp 203, 204). This is, perhaps, the most helpful description of enlightenment. Not only is it straightforward and lacking in gibberish, it is also very appealing. It reveals why men and women have been striving for nibbāna throughout the past twenty-six centuries. We all want happiness, and if the highest happiness is on offer, then that's what we want. Thus Buddhism's perennial teaching is how to be happier and happier, until one reaches the summit of all happiness in this very life: nibbāna.

These days, I present the Buddha's special teaching of the four noble truths having rearranged them. I have found that if I begin with the noble truth of suffering, then my audience is turned off. They know enough about that already in their lives. They didn't give up their evening to come and listen to more suffering. As any salesperson knows, first impressions are paramount. Therefore I introduce the four noble truths as follows:

1. Happiness
2. The path leading to happiness
3. Unhappiness
4. The cause of unhappiness

This is essentially the same as the Buddha's teaching, but reordered for greater impact. Some might call this rearrangement "marketing," but it emphasizes the goal of Buddhism by placing it first.

Nibbāna portrayed as the highest happiness also reveals that the noble eightfold path is the way of ever-increasing happiness. Those who follow the path wholeheartedly get happier. As the Buddha said in the *Araṇavibhaṅga Sutta,* "One should know how to define pleasure, and knowing that, one should pursue pleasure within oneself."[23] One pursues such inner pleasure, which is jhāna, without fear until one reaches the highest happiness.

What is the highest happiness that you have experienced? Drugs? Sex? Music? Falling in love? Seeing the birth of your first child? You will find that the happiness of jhāna exceeds all of these. That is why one's first experience of jhāna blows apart all one's old conceptions about the meaning of happiness. Jhāna provides deep insight into happiness. Not that jhāna is the highest happiness, but it is so close that, as we said earlier, the Buddha called it *sambodhi sukha,* "the bliss of enlightenment."[24] From jhāna one proceeds to a happiness a little bit higher, and that is nibbāna.

Recent scientific studies support the assertions that meditation makes one happier and that Buddhist monks may be the happiest people of all.[25] Therefore, anyone who wants a really good time should be a really good meditator. And if one wants the highest happiness of all, then go for nibbāna.

The Complete Ending of Sensory Desire, Ill Will, and Delusion

The Buddha's chief disciple, Ven. Sāriputta, defined *nibbāna* as the complete ending of sensory desire, ill will, and delusion (SN 38,1). This story of the wishing game illustrates this definition well.

Five children were playing a wishing game. Each would be asked in turn, "If you had a wish, what would it be?" The child with the best wish would win. The first child said, "If I had a wish, I would wish for some chocolate ice cream," because it was a hot day and he liked ice cream.

The second child said, "If I had a wish, I would wish for an ice cream factory. Then I can have many ice creams, whenever I want!" The first child sat glumly, regretting that he had wished for only one ice cream and thinking how clever the second child was.

The third child said, "My wish is for a billion dollars. With a billion bucks, I can buy my own ice-cream factory, a candy store, and my own fast-food restaurant, then I can have a burger and double fries whenever I want, and my Mom won't be able to stop me! I'll also have enough money left over to buy anything else I want, as soon as I think of it." Now the second child felt stupid, having settled for only an ice-cream factory, while thinking how much smarter this third child was, wishing for a billion dollars.

The fourth child said, "If I had a wish, then I'd wish for three wishes! With my first wish, I'd get my ice-cream factory. With my second wish, I'd get a billion dollars, and for my third wish, I'd ask for three more wishes! That way, I can go on wishing forever." Even the child who'd wished for a billion dollars now felt beaten. All the first three children looked up to this fourth child as a genius. What could be superior to unlimited wishes?

The fifth child surpassed them all. He said quietly, "If I had a wish, I would wish that I was so content that I would never need any more wishes!"

That last child won the wishing game, just as those who sit perfectly still win the human race. He understood that the highest happiness, nibbāna, is the complete ending of all sensory desire, ill will, and delusion. Nibbāna is contentment at last.

There are two types of freedom found in the world: freedom *of* desire and freedom *from* desire. The first is symbolized by the fourth child's infinity of wishes, and it is the type of freedom that is worshipped in our materialistic societies as the ultimate goal. Modern governments strive to give their people unlimited freedom of desire, with wealth, rights, and liberty. However, their people are mostly dissatisfied. The second type of freedom is symbolized by the fifth child's eternal contentment. Only spiritual paths like Buddhism worship freedom from desire. Nibbāna is the perfect form of this second type of freedom; for the complete ending of sensory desire, ill will, and delusion is the freedom from *all* desire. It is the ending of craving. Peace. Enlightenment.

The Remainderless Cessation of Body and Mind

In the time of the Buddha, even simple villagers understood the meaning of nibbāna. For *nibbāna* was the word in common usage for an oil lamp being extinguished (see *Ratana Sutta*, Sn 235). When the oil was used up, or the wick had burned out, or a wind had carried the heat away, the villagers would say that the flame had "nibbāna-ed." *Nibbāna* was the word in ordinary usage that described the remainderless ending of a natural process, whether it was a simple flame, or this complex body and mind...or a fashionable curiosity box:

I was told that in the late 1970s in California it was trendy to have a small metal box on one's coffee table as a conversation piece. The rectangular box was plain on all sides except for a simple switch on the front. When one's guest inquired what the box did, they were invited to turn it on. As soon as the switch was flicked on, the whirring of a motor and the rumbling of cogwheels could be heard from inside. Then a flap would rise up on one side, and a mechanical arm would emerge from within. The metal arm would extend, bend around the corner to the front, and then turn off the switch. Then it would retreat back inside its box, the flap would close, and all would be quiet once again. It was a box whose sole purpose was to switch itself off. To me, it is the most wonderful metaphor for nibbāna!

The purpose of this process we call "body and mind" is to switch itself off. Peace at last.

Of course, one is capable of appreciating the delightful accuracy of this metaphor only if one has had direct experience of the utter emptiness of this whole process called "body and mind." The crucial deep insight is that there is no one in here, out there, or anywhere, for that matter. The doer (will) and the knower (consciousness) are just natural processes. When one penetrates to the heart of this insight, then there is nothing at all to lose and nothing to be annihilated. Only when there is some persistent entity there to begin with can we use the word *anni-hilate*. But for the remainderless ending of an empty natural process, we use the word *cessation*. Nibbāna is the empty and natural process of body and mind doing its cessation thing.

> Mere suffering exists, no sufferer is found;
> The deeds are, but no doer of the deeds is there;
> Nibbāna is, but not the person that enters it;
> The path is, but no traveler on it is seen.
>
> (Vsm 16,90)

The First Experience of Nibbāna— Stream Winning

After much wholehearted practice of the complete noble eightfold path, there comes a time when one reflects back on what it all means. After a recent experience of jhāna, one has the superpower mindfulness that is capable of holding any object for investigation motionless for long periods of time. The hindrances of restlessness and sloth-and-torpor are well gone. The mind is brilliantly clear and still. It is charged with inner happiness, so potently present that it easily overcomes whatever fear arises as mind-fulness goes deep into unfamiliar places. It is bliss that makes the mind courageous, heroic, and unstoppable in its quest for truth. At other times, one came close to the elusive "way things truly are," but fear, desire, and aversion turned the mind away. But now, after dwelling in jhāna, there is no desire, no aversion, and no vested self-interests to protect. Using the recollection of the jhāna for one's data, one bores relentlessly into the center of things. Bold and brilliant, the mind breaks through to the origin of experience, what I have called the citadel of the self, ruled by the two lords the doer and the knower. There, one sees for the first time, with unambiguous certainty, that this citadel is completely empty!

Such experience of deep insight is totally different than anything one can imagine. As the Buddha said in the *Sappurisa Sutta,* in reference to jhāna but equally applicable to stream winning, "For however they imagine it will be, the experience is always other than that" (MN 113,21). There occurs a tremendous paradigm shift. Just as the shifting of the earth's tectonic plates produces a massive earthquake, so the shifting of fundamental standpoints for one's views is like a terrific earthquake in the mind. Many ancient and cherished constructions of concepts and views come crashing to the ground. Such high-powered deep insight feels like an explosion in the mind. For a while, one does not know where to stand. One is certain one hasn't gone mad. In fact, the mind feels more sane than it ever has felt before. It is so clear, still, and blissful. One of the necessary signs of deep insight is the ensuing long period of sustained and delicious bliss. After his enlightenment, the Buddha is said to have sat without moving for seven days, made motionless by the extreme bliss of liberation (Vin 1,1,1).

After some time, maybe even days, it is as if the dust finally settles. Euphoria's blinding light diminishes enough for one to discriminate again. One looks to see what edifices are left standing and what is no longer there. If it is stream winning *(sotāpatti)* one will distinctly see that all illusions of a self or of an essence, personal or universal, have been completely annihilated, now and forever.

After *sotāpatti,* it all seems so obvious. The wonder is that one was so densely stupid as to not see through this blatant deception even earlier. This truth of no-essence is explicitly articulated again and again in the Buddha's teachings. Now one realizes that, because of wishful thinking, denial, and the other five hindrances, one had been filtering all that one had read, bending and interpreting it, to get only what one wanted to hear from the Buddha's words. Delusion is so incredibly powerful, much more pervasive than most people know. As Voltaire quipped, "The only way to comprehend the mathematical concept of infinity is to contemplate the extent of human stupidity."

Now the illusion is revealed, and delusion begins to unravel. Having penetrated to the core of anattā, one is now able to know the full extent of dukkha. Previously, one would recoil from accepting that all things are dukkha. This was because the illusion of self demanded at least one corner of existence where dukkha doesn't apply, some heavenly realm of perfect happiness, whether it be the "original mind," "merging with the one," or whatever other spiritual fantasy is on offer. Everything else might be dukkha, but not this one exempt niche that the illusion of self reserves for its ultimate "retirement home." But once one has seen the absolute emptiness of all phenomena, both inner and outer, then one has no need of such a retirement home. The vested interest in one's own continuance is destroyed. Denial is undermined. One now agrees fully with the Buddha's explicit teaching that *"sabbe sankhārā dukkhā"* (Dhp 278), all phenomena are suffering, the whole unredeemable lot.

Furthermore, seeing the body and mind as void of a persistent entity means that this whole process can come to a remainderless end without anything being lost. It is fascinating to observe so many sincere Buddhists wanting to keep something for themselves after enlightenment. Preserving something for oneself is called "attachment," even when it is clinging to something refined. However, after stream winning, all such attachments that arise from a view of the self are finally eliminated. One realizes that all experiences are only phenomena that arise due to causes and, therefore, must one day come to a complete cessation. And this includes the body and mind. The full understanding of anicca, as said in the previous chapter, is not merely seeing things rise and fall like waves on the ocean but seeing the whole ocean disappear together with the landmass that contains it. To know anicca fully, one must see such cessation. And this knowledge follows seamlessly from the uncovering of anattā, no-self. Thus, in the suttas, one finds many a new stream winner expressing their attainment in the words:

Whatever arises, all that will [one day] completely cease.

(SN 56,11)

Thus, the full penetration of anattā permits the mind's full penetration of dukkha and anicca as well. The event of stream winning is the realization that all experience, including that which knows the experience, is anicca, dukkha, and anattā, "subject to cessation, suffering, and without a persisting essence." These famous three characteristics of existence pervade everything. Thus it is also the nature of body and mind to cease one day with nothing remaining.

Making Something Out of Nothing

As I've just noted, some people are so attached to existence that they see nibbāna as a kind of retirement home for the one who knows. Such people will assume "nowhere" to be a place name, "emptiness" to be a precious solid entity, and "cessation" to be the beginning of something wonderful. They try to make something out of nothing.

It is a problem with language that when we describe what a thing is not, what qualities are absent, then the negation or the absence can easily be misunderstood as a thing in itself. For example, in Lewis Carroll's *Through the Looking Glass*,[26] the White King asks Alice whether she could see either of his messengers on the road. "I see nobody on the road," said Alice. "I only wish I had such eyes," the king remarked in a fretful tone, "To be able to see Nobody! And at that distance too! Why, it's as much as I can do to see real people, by this light!" Then, after a messenger did arrive, the king asked him, "Who did you pass on the road?" "Nobody," said the messenger. "Quite right," said the king, "this young lady saw him too. So of course Nobody was slower than you." "I do my best," the messenger said in a sullen tone, "I'm sure nobody walks much faster than I do!" "He can't do that," said the king, "or else he'd have been here first."

There is a similar story in Buddhism, regarding an early episode in the life of the great disciple of the Buddha, Anuruddha. As a result of a great act of good kamma in one of Anuruddha's previous existences, in this life he would always receive the goods he wanted (Dhp-a 5:17). One day, the young Anuruddha was playing at marbles with his friends and gambling the contents of his lunch basket on the result. Unfortunately, he kept on losing until he had no lunch left. Being from a very wealthy family, he ordered his servant to take his lunch basket back home and bring back some more cakes. Soon after the servant returned, he lost these cakes too. So, for a second time the servant was sent back home for more food, and a second time Anuruddha lost the cakes gambling at marbles. He ordered the servant a third time to take the basket back to his house and ask his mother for some more cakes. However, by now his mother had run out of cakes. So she instructed the servant to return to her son with the empty lunch basket and tell Anuruddha, "*Natthi* cakes!" *Natthi* is the Pāli word for "there isn't any."

While the servant was taking the empty basket back to Anuruddha, the *devas* (heavenly beings) realized that if they didn't intervene, Anuruddha would not receive something he wanted. Since this could not happen because of the good kamma Anuruddha had done in a previous life, the devas secretly inserted some heavenly cakes into the empty basket.

When the servant arrived, he handed the basket to his young master, saying, "Natthi cakes, sir!" But when Anuruddha opened the basket, the aroma of the heavenly cakes was so enticing that he couldn't resist trying one. They were so delicious that he asked his mother to give him only natthi cakes from then on.

In truth, "natthi cakes," when devas don't get involved, means no cakes at all. Just as *ajātaṁ,* when wishful thinkers don't get involved, means nothing born at all, *abhūtaṁ* means nothing come to be, *akataṁ* means the absence of anything made, and *asankhataṁ* means the absence of anything conditioned, which four Pāli terms are famous synonyms for nibbāna in the *Udāna* (Ud 8,3). Translators add an unwarranted spin when they render these negatives (indicated by the privative prefix *a-* in Pāli) as if there were something there, by translating them as "the unborn," "the unoriginated," "the uncreated," "the unconditioned," much as the White King takes "nobody" to be a person's name.

Two Triggers for Stream Winning
and Five Supporting Conditions

The Buddha said on many occasions that sammā samādhi, or jhāna, was the immediate cause for "seeing things as they truly are," *yathā bhūta ñāna-dassana* (AN V,24; V,168; VI,50; VII,61; VIII,81; X,3; XI,3). So why is it that not everyone who experiences a jhāna becomes a stream winner?

The answer is that in addition to jhāna one also needs an adequate understanding of the Buddha's teachings. In chapter 12, I gave the simile of the flashlight and the map. Imagine three men searching for treasure in the forest at night; the first man has a flashlight but no map. The second man has the map but no flashlight. And the third man has both a flashlight and the map. Only the third man will find the treasure. In this simile, the flashlight stands for the radiant mind empowered by jhāna, the map represents an accurate working knowledge of the Buddha's teachings, and the treasure refers to stream winning. Only when one has been instructed in Dhamma and has experience of jhāna will one discover nibbāna.

In the *Mahāvedalla Sutta*, Ven. Sāriputta stated that there are two "triggers" for the arising of right view, which is another way of saying for the attainment of stream winning. Those two triggers are "the words of another" *(parato ghosa)* coupled with "work of the mind that goes back to the source" *(yoniso manasikāra)*. Ven. Sāriputta continued by saying that these two triggers are supported by five conditions: virtue *(sīla)*, learning *(suta)*, discussion *(sākacchā)*, jhāna *(samatha)*, and insight *(vipassanā)* (MN 43,13–14).

The "work of the mind that goes back to the source" refers to insight based on jhāna. In the simile of the thousand-petaled lotus within whose center lies the most precious of jewels, nibbāna, the task of the meditator is to gently open this lotus layer by layer until one reaches its heart. This describes what is meant by "work of the mind that goes back to the source." The function of jhāna is to bring one sufficiently close to that source. The function of insight is to realize the complete emptiness inside. Both jhāna and insight must be founded on virtue. For if one's virtue is not pure, then the nimitta will be dull or not arise at all, making jhānas unreachable. Thus, the second of Ven. Sāriputta's triggers for stream winning—work of the mind that goes back to the source—comprises the three supporting conditions of virtue, jhāna, and insight, all rolled together as yoniso manasikāra.

The "words of another" is the other necessary ingredient for stream winning. In the template of the five supporting conditions, this is represented by learning and discussion. Just reading the texts or listening to discourses from accomplished monks and nuns is not enough. One also needs to discuss what one has read and heard with a competent teacher to make sure that one has understood it correctly. In our universities we have a system of both lectures and tutorials or seminars that corresponds well with suta and sākacchā.

More profoundly, the "words of another"—spoken or written—must come from a noble one if they are to be effective. The noble ones are those who are stream winners, once-returners, nonreturners, or arahants. They have seen anicca, dukkha, and anattā to their very depths. They have had direct personal experience of nibbāna, so they know exactly what they're talking about. Hearing the Dhamma from a genuine noble one is so crucial, according to the suttas, that without it stream winning is impossible (AN X,61). A noble one and an ordinary person might be expounding exactly the same message, but the audience recognizes intuitively that there is a mountain of difference. It is where the teaching is coming from that makes the difference. When the discourse comes from a noble one, it is alive and thrilling. When it comes from an ordinary person, it is just interesting at best. Thus it is that even in Theravāda Buddhism there is something similar to the tradition of transmission, usually associated with Vajrayāna and Mahāyāna, although in Theravāda it is demystified and clearly explained as the inherent power in the teachings of a noble one. Moreover, such teachings and discussion, the words of another, are only half of what is required for stream winning to happen.

Thus the path to stream winning requires cultivating with diligence the five supporting conditions of virtue, learning, discussion, jhāna, and insight, making sure that learning and discussion, which combine as "the words of another," originate from a noble one. Let virtue and jhāna be one's foundations for insight, so that one fulfills "the work of the mind that goes back to the source." Then, when one brings close together these two, the words of another and the work of the mind that goes back to the source, it is like bringing gunpowder and a flame close together. When they touch, a huge explosion occurs. That is deep insight. When the smoke clears away, then one will discern that all illusions of a self are completely destroyed. And that is stream winning.

The Saddhānusārī and Dhammānusārī— Stream Winning without Jhāna?

A recurring topic of debate among our Sangha is, can one attain to stream winning without any experience of jhāna? As should be obvious from what has been written so far, I cannot see a possibility of penetrating to the full meaning of anattā, dukkha, and anicca without the radical data gained in a jhāna experience. Yet, there are some stories in the Tipiṭika (the "Three Baskets" that comprise the Pāli canon) that suggest it might be possible.

The most compelling passage that I have come across is the story of the thirty-one murderers sent by Devadatta to kill the Buddha without leaving a trail. The first murderer was to kill the Buddha, the next two were to kill the assassin, the next four had to kill those two, the following eight would slay the four, and the final sixteen would finish off the eight. That way, it would be difficult to trace who killed the Buddha. However, because of the powerful presence of the Buddha, none were able to fulfill their task. Instead, each group asked for forgiveness from the Buddha and were given a discourse on Dhamma. Hired killers are not known for their virtue, let alone any practice of jhāna, yet each one of these thirty-one would-be murderers attained to stream winning after hearing the Buddha's teaching (Vin 2,7,3,7–8).

Perhaps the anomaly can be explained through introducing here the two types of people on the path to stream winning: the *saddhānusārī*, or "mostly-by-faith follower," and the *dhammānusārī*, or "mostly-by-wisdom follower" (MN 70). The five spiritual faculties of faith, energy, mindfulness, samādhi, and wisdom are what power the mind toward enlightenment. When samādhi and the resultant wisdom are weak, however, then faith and the resultant energy can compensate. One whose faith and energy are the main driving forces toward stream winning is called a *saddhānusārī*, and one for whom samādhi and wisdom are the main forces is called a *dhammānusārī*. Both, of course, need mindfulness. Perhaps, then, one with very strong faith in the Buddha's teachings, and with the enormous energy that flows easily from such faith, can attain to stream winning without any jhāna. As the old proverb says, "Faith can move mountains."

However, such a faith needs to be extraordinarily uncompromising to move the Mount Everest that is delusion and attain to stream winning without any jhāna. The level of faith required is like that of the young man in the following story adapted from the commentaries (Dhp-a III, 417–21). A young man begged an accomplished master to accept him as a disciple. The master refused, protesting that disciples are just a headache since they never do what they're told. The youth insisted that he had such strong faith in this master that he would follow his every instruction. So the master decided to test him. He ordered the youth to walk in a straight line due east, neither stopping nor changing direction, no matter what. Thus the student set off walking due east. When he came to a prickly bush, he just went straight through. When he came to some paddy fields, he trudged through the mud in a straight line, instead of zigzagging on top of the dikes. And when he came to a big lake, he simply continued walking, not deviating even one degree in his direction. Soon the water reached to his waist, then to his neck, and then up to his nose! He still continued walking. Just before the water covered his ears and stopped him from hearing, the master shouted for him to stop and come out of the water. After that, the young man became his disciple. It is easy to teach such a student who is willing to give up their life to follow their teacher's instructions. That is the level of faith required to be a *saddhānusārī* and attain to stream winning with no experience of jhāna. I don't see much possibility for this in these skeptical times.

Such an intense degree of faith should be invested only in a noble one. Faith without wisdom is a gamble. For this reason the path of wisdom based on jhāna, the way of the *dhammānusārī,* is the recommended path.

On a related issue, the suttas are explicit that it is impossible to attain to nonreturning, let alone to become an arahant, without any experience of jhāna, any more than one can reach the heartwood of a tree without first going through its bark and then its sapwood (MN 64; see also AN V,22; VI,68; VIII,81; IX,12).

Causality and Some Consequences of Stream Winning

The Buddha said, "One who sees dependent origination sees the Dhamma; one who sees the Dhamma sees dependent origination."[27] One of the inevitable consequences of stream winning is the full understanding of dependent origination. Before the breakthrough to Dhamma, the knower and the doer were both seen as one's self, or part of that self. After stream winning, they are seen as mere natural processes, not ruled by a person, but ruled by the impersonal law of cause and effect as perfectly described in dependent origination.

Stream winners clearly comprehend the causes that generate the acts of knowing and doing. They also comprehend the consequences of knowing and doing. In particular, they realize how craving for sensual pleasure *(kāmataṇhā)* and craving to be *(bhavataṇhā)* propel this mental process of knowing, not only from moment to moment but also from life to life. Indeed, the stream winner understands that one of the main functions of dependent origination is to explain how rebirth happens without a self or a soul. It is, for the most part, these two types of craving that create the fuel *(upādāna)* for more existence *(bhava)* such that a rebirth *(jāti)* occurs. Or, if looked at in a parallel way, it is the illusion of a self and the denial of dukkha—in other words, delusion *(avijjā)*—that motivates kamma *(sankhāra)* to give the support for more consciousness *(viññāṇa)* to sprout in a new life cycle. Thus, the stream winner has no doubt that rebirth happens, just as the Buddha said. Moreover, the stream winner knows *why* rebirth happens.

Stream winners also have full penetration of the twelve factors of dependent origination in their ceasing mode, what I call *dependent cessation*. Having seen what keeps this impersonal process of body and mind going, they also see how it can cease without any remainder. They also see that from the moment of their attainment the process of cessation has begun. For them, the process of being has been fatally wounded, and the cessation of their existence is now irreversible.

When stream winners see anicca fully, they realize that body and mind can cease with no remainder. When they see anattā fully, they understand that there is nothing lost in such a final cessation, since there was no persisting thing there to begin with, only a process. And when they see dukkha fully, it invariably gives rise to an urgency to bring the process to an end. This is just like having an apple and finding that it is rotten through and through, with no part worth saving. An urgency would then arise to throw the apple away. After stream winning, it is this understanding of such thoroughgoing dukkha that takes the lead, driving the body-and-mind process to cessation.

Revulsion

Revulsion *(nibbidā)* to one's predicament sets in. Just as the Buddha often taught, the inevitable consequence of seeing things as they truly are, that is, stream winning, is the arising of revulsion (SN 12,23). When one finally sees the apple as rotten, revulsion causes one to discard it.

It is to be emphasized that there is nothing personal in such revulsion, for all views of a self have been eliminated. Nibbidā is an impersonal phenomenon that arises naturally after stream winning, whether one wants it or not (cf. AN XI,2). It is nature, Dhamma, that's all. Moreover, such a sense of revulsion is one of the signs of stream winning. One who has seen the Dhamma fully, in particular dukkha, will experience the urge to find release, just like the prisoner who was born and raised in jail would want to get out soon after he realizes his awful predicament. It is delusion *(avijjā)* and craving *(taṇhā)* that tie one to the wheel of saṃsāra, and it is revulsion *(nibbidā)* that flings one off. Nibbidā is saṃsāra's ejection seat. Before stream winning, the conditioned process of doing was under the influence of delusion, and so was mostly engaged in acquiring and socializing. After stream winning, the process of doing comes increasingly under the guidance of Dhamma, especially the knowledge of dukkha, and therefore inclines more and more to renunciation and solitude.

Fading Away

Further along the causal sequence of cessation—along the "law of nibbāna," one might say—nibbidā generates fading away *(virāga)*, especially the fading away of sensory desire and ill will. Once one has seen that the world of the five senses is permeated so thoroughly by dukkha, then there is nothing there for one anymore. As the mind rejects that world, not because one wills it but because it is a part of an inevitable process, then that world literally fades away from the mind. Later the world of the mind will also fade away, since that is permeated with dukkha too. Depending on such factors as the strength of one's experience of stream winning—that is, how deeply one's understanding of dukkha, anattā, and anicca has penetrated one's habitual tendencies—so long will it take for the process of cessation to culminate in the experience of *vimutti,* "full deliverance." And since this process is governed by natural laws, its duration has a limit.

Seven Lifetimes at Most

The law of nibbāna is such that, at the very most, the process of cessation will crescendo to a finale at the end of six more lifetimes.[28] Understanding that the doer is not a self, but simply part of a causal process, will make it clear that stream winners cannot choose, for instance, three more lives or the whole six. The matter is not under their control anymore. It is like getting on the bus to nibbāna. Once on this bus, one can neither get off nor control the driver. The nibbāna bus goes according to its own schedule, and only to the terminus! So it should be apparent that having reached the stage of stream winning, one is incapable of resolving to postpone one's impending enlightenment out of compassion for other beings. It is now too late for bodhisattva vows. The law of nibbāna, this natural process of cessation, has passed the point of no return. It is unstoppable now. It will be nibbāna in seven lifetimes at most. Good-bye!

Onward to Full Enlightenment 15

···

THERE ARE FOUR LEVELS of enlightenment: the stream winner *(sotāpanna)*, the once-returner *(sakadāgāmī)*, the nonreturner *(anāgāmī)*, and the fully enlightened one *(arahant)*. The stream winner is one who has seen the Dhamma, attained correct view *(diṭṭhipatta)*, and must win full enlightenment within seven lifetimes. The once-returner has progressed from stream winning to see much of sensory desire and ill will fade away, so much so that they will return to a human existence only once more, at most. According to the commentary on the Aṅguttara Nikāya, all once-returners arise in the Tusita heaven after this life and are then reborn in the human realm for their last life.[29] Nonreturners have advanced even further to completely eliminate all desire within the world of the five senses and ill will. Should they not win full enlightenment at the time of their death, then they will arise in the pure abodes *(suddhāvāsa)* to attain full enlightenment there. They are never again reborn in this human world. Finally, arahants, fully enlightened ones, have completed the task and have nothing further to achieve. This is their final existence.

The Seven Shipwrecked Sailors

These four stages of enlightenment are further explained in the Buddha's simile of the seven shipwrecked sailors in the *Udakūpama Sutta* (AN VII,15). Even though this sutta makes no direct mention of sailors or a shipwreck, this detail (added by me) is a reasonable assumption to account for the seven men of the sutta being in the water a long way from land.

Seven sailors found themselves in the sea after a shipwreck. The first sailor went straight down and drowned. The second man floated for a while, and then sank to his death. The third floated on the surface and remained with his head above water. The fourth, while remaining with his head above water, looked around and saw the safety of land in the not too far distance. The fifth, also having floated and spotted land, was well on his way swimming to the shore. The sixth sailor, having kept above water and seen land as well, had swum almost there and was now standing in the surf, wading to shore. The seventh shipwrecked sailor, having floated, seen land, swum, and waded to shore, was now sitting happily on dry land, relaxed and safe.

The Buddha explained the meaning of the simile as follows:

The first shipwrecked sailor, who went straight down and drowned, represents someone who has done lots of bad kamma. They go straight down to the lower realms after death.

The second shipwrecked sailor, who floated for a while and then went down to his death, represents someone who had the seven spiritual strengths, but then lost them. The seven spiritual strengths *(satta balāni)* are moral shame *(hiri),* fear of the kammic consequences of wrongdoing *(ottappa),* faith, energy, mindfulness, samādhi, and wisdom (these last five being the standard five spiritual faculties or strengths). Having carelessly let them disappear, through lack of practice, they also go down to the lower realms after death.

The third sailor, who remains afloat, represents someone who maintains these seven spiritual strengths. They keep their head above water, so to speak, in spite of the ups and downs of life.

The fourth sailor, who looks around while afloat and sees the safety of land, represents the stream winner, one who has seen the safety of nibbāna.

The fifth sailor, who is swimming to the shore, represents the once-returner, one who has partially eradicated sensory desire and ill will.

The sixth sailor, who is so close to the land that he can stand and wade the rest of the way, represents the nonreturner, one who has eliminated all desire and ill will within the world of the five senses. The majority of their work is done, and they stand very close to nibbāna.

The seventh former shipwrecked sailor, who has reached the safety and comfort of dry land, is the fully enlightened one, the arahant.

This illuminating simile of the Buddha contains much valuable information about these four stages of enlightenment. First, it emphasizes again the importance of the five spiritual faculties of faith, energy, mindfulness, samādhi, and wisdom for attaining stream winning, while adding two vital ingredients, moral shame and fear of wrongdoing. These two qualities, in Pāli *hiri* and *ottappa,* are called by the Buddha "guardians of the world," because they protect virtuous conduct (AN II,1,9). Second, the simile shows the difference between the stream winner and the arahant: the stream winner has only *seen* nibbāna, whereas the arahant has *reached* nibbāna. In another simile from the suttas, stream winners are like thirsty persons who can see water in a deep well but have neither bucket nor rope to reach it, whereas arahants have buckets and ropes, draw up water, and quench their thirst (SN 12,68). Third, the simile illustrates what the stream winner needs to do next to proceed to full enlightenment, and how their practice progresses through once-returning to nonreturning and then to full enlightenment. Now I will explain what that practice is.

The Vipallāsa and Purifying One's Thought

The practice leading from stream winning to nonreturning is, of course, the noble eightfold path. At this stage, the eightfold path truly deserves the designation "noble," since it is now being pursued by a noble one. The first factor of this path, right view, has now come to perfection. Once this foundation stone of the noble eightfold path has been set in place by the stream winner, only then can the rest of the path be brought to perfection (AN X,121). From then on, the main focus of work for the stream winner is on perfecting the second factor of the path, *sammā sankappa,* or right thought.

It is thoughts of sensory desire *(kāma-sankappa),* ill will *(vyāpāda-sankappa),* and cruelty *(vihiṃsa-sankappa)* that must now be completely abandoned to reach nonreturning. Effort, mindfulness, and samādhi must now combine to purify thought. It is only after stream winning that one can begin to root out, once and for all, these insidious mental defilements *(kilesa)* that have been distorting the thought process over countless lifetimes. For this reason, only after stream winning is the student called by the Buddha a *sekha,* "learner"; only then does the training start in earnest.

To explain more deeply what needs to be done and why, I need to introduce the Buddha's teaching of *vipallāsa,* "the distorting of the cognitive process" (AN IV,49). Here the cognitive process is regarded as threefold: consisting of view, perception, and thought. The Buddha observed how views fashion perceptions, perceptions fashion thoughts, and thoughts fashion views. Thus, incorrect view will distort perception to suit itself, resulting in mistaken perceptions. Perceptions are the building blocks of thoughts (MN 18,16). So, from mistaken perceptions one constructs erroneous thoughts. These thoughts are then employed to justify one's views. Thus, these erroneous thoughts reinforce our original wrong view. So continues the seemingly unending, self-sustaining, vicious circle of wrong view leading to mistaken perception leading to erroneous thought leading to wrong view leading to mistaken perception....The unfortunate aspect of this distortion of the cognitive process is that most people can't see it happening. They presume that raw perception, the primary evidence supplied by the senses, is always accurate. It explains beautifully why everyone thinks they are right!

A distressing, modern-day example of this is the common attitude of ex-partners during their divorce. One starts out with the view that one's ex is a pig. Driven by this wrong view, one will perceive only their piglike behavior. Anything about them that isn't porcine will be blocked out by denial, or be interpreted to appear very piggish. All that is allowed to manifest as perception is their pig nature. So, based on the evidence of one's own perception, which one takes as authentic data drawn from raw experience, one will reasonably keep thinking of one's ex as a swine. Thus one's rational thinking process confirms what one knew all along. See, they are a pig! In this way, wrong view is justified, and the vicious circle of cognitive distortion continues unrecognized.

A more subtle example comes from out-of-body experiences, the sort where one floats out of one's body, travels down a tunnel to a light, through that light to meet a divine presence, who then announces that it's not one's time yet, and one returns to tell the tale. Of interest here is the identity of this divine presence. From what I have read and heard, devout Christians report meeting Jesus, while some Catholics claim it was the Virgin Mary, whereas Chinese Buddhists insist they met the goddess of mercy, Kuan Yin, while some Hindus were received by Lord Krishna...and the atheist is convinced that the presence he met was the recently deceased Uncle George!

What is happening? Do all these divine beings have a peek to see who's coming before deciding whose turn it is? "Here comes a Buddhist from Hong Kong. This one is for you, Kuan Yin." Please excuse my cheekiness, for I don't mean to offend anyone's beliefs. I only mean to demonstrate the implausibility of such a scenario. What is really happening is that each person's experience (which is in fact but a reflection of the radiance of their own mind) is distorted by their religious views, or lack of them, which bend perception to fit their belief system. Unaware of this process of distorting, they take their perceptions at face value. The Christian is overjoyed to have met Jesus, the Catholic is so inspired to have witnessed the Blessed Virgin...and even the atheist is delighted to have caught up with dear old Uncle George. It is no wonder that, as a result, they each firmly believe that theirs is the only truth.

The Fourfold Delusion

The Buddha was specifically concerned about the cognitive distortion that sustains the delusions of a self, pleasure, permanence, and beauty (AN IV,49). For instance, when one holds the view that there is indeed a self "in here," then that wrong view will distort perception to make it appear as if there *is* a self. Then one will think in terms of me, mine, and a self, thereby reinforcing that wrong view. Should that view of a self be challenged, one will resort to reasoning—that is, thought—and back it up with what one takes to be raw experience: one's perceptions. To such a one, it is blatantly obvious from reason and experience that there is indeed a self, and even the argument from a buddha will not sway them. It needs the revolutionary new perceptions derived from jhāna to overthrow their delusion.

Let's take another example. Most people hold the view that sex is pleasurable. This view is held so widely that, were I to suggest this is wrong view, many of my readers will regard me not just as a weird monk but as downright crazy—or "a few pieces of cloth short of a full set of robes," as we monks say. Because this view is held so strongly, sex actually does appear pleasurable, for pleasurable sexual experiences are the only data allowed to enter perception. Based on such experiences, one thinks about sex—thinks of it as pleasurable and thinks about it often! That is why the view that sex is pleasurable is taken as fact. The Buddha said that this is wrong view (MN 22,3). Mere words, though, will never break such a deeply rooted, self-sustaining vicious circle of delusion. Again, it is the force of jhāna that will explode the myth of sex as pleasure.

In summary, the Buddha explained that delusion *(avijjā)* is fourfold: taking what is not a self to be a self, what is transient to be permanent, what is suffering to be pleasure, and what is disgusting to be beautiful. Each of these four misapprehensions manifest at all three levels of cognition, view, perceptions, and thought. That is the problem.

This fourfold delusion is broken at the stage of view. Through using jhāna to suppress the five hindrances and provide undistorted perceptions, one is able to see things as they truly are. Right view becomes established at stream winning. A stream winner will never again hold the four wrong views: of a self in what is not self, of permanence in what is transient, of pleasure in what is suffering, and of beauty in what is disgusting. But this does not mean that a stream winner is exempt from lustful perceptions or angry thoughts. Once view has been purified, perception and thought do not immediately fall into line. For the sekha, or learner, sometimes perceptions and thoughts are fashioned by the right view attained at stream winning, and sometimes they are fashioned by former distorted views, what we call "habitual tendencies." It takes a while, sometimes seven lifetimes, to overcome old habits. Nonetheless, when sekhas do have thoughts of, say, lust, they regard it as a temporary lapse of mindfulness—that is, they understand that their mind has briefly disconnected from right view and fallen back into long-ingrained habits.

The purification of perceptions and thoughts from sensory desire and ill will, then, is the route from stream winning to nonreturning. This is done by keeping in mind the Dhamma that was realized at stream winning, until it is constantly present, what is called "unbroken mindfulness." Such continuous mindfulness is made possible only through jhāna and right effort, supported by virtue. This is what was meant by "swimming to the shore" in the simile of the seven shipwrecked sailors. Effort, mindfulness, and jhāna gradually overcome all thoughts of sensory desire, ill will, and cruelty *(micchā sankappa),* to the point where they can never arise again. The second factor of the noble eightfold path, right thought, is completed. One is a nonreturner. Now all that is left to do is to wade the short distance to land.

The Nonreturner

Once the first two factors of the noble eightfold path are perfected, the next three factors of right speech, right action, and right livelihood must also come to perfection. This is because all actions of body and speech originate in thought. So, when thought has been purified of sensory desire and ill will, speech and action are also purified of the same two defilements. Furthermore, the Buddha stated that the nonreturner is fully accomplished in virtue, fully accomplished in samādhi, but only moderately accomplished in wisdom (AN III,85).[30] Thus the final three factors of the noble eightfold path, which are together represented as samādhi (as at MN 44,11), have also been perfected. The nonreturner, then, has purified the path. All the factors are in place. All that is left is the goal, realizing nibbāna.

So what does a nonreturner look like? In the suttas, the most detailed descriptions of nonreturners concern laypersons. In the Aṅguttara Nikāya (AN VIII,21), Ugga of Vesāli had four young wives before he attained to nonreturning! Afterward, he informed all his wives that he could not remain as their husband anymore, and he asked them to choose either to remain in the house as his "sisters," to return to their former families, or to take another husband, as each saw fit. Nonreturners, by nature, are celibate. The nonreturner's inherent humility also led Ugga to treat all members of the Sangha—even those monks less attained than he was—with utmost respect.[31] In the Saṃyutta Nikāya, Citta the householder, another nonreturner, could attain the four jhānas to whatever extent he wished.[32] In the Majjhima Nikāya, Ghaṭīkāra the potter was also a lay nonreturner (MN 81). He was prevented from becoming a monk only because of his duty to look after his blind and aged parents. He kept the five precepts, was celibate, ate only in the morning, and would have nothing to do with money. Thus he kept much the same precepts as a *sāmaṇera,* or novice monk. Having made some pots, he would announce, "Let anyone who likes leave some food, and let them take away whatever they like," and that was how he provided for himself and his parents.[33] In the Aṅguttara Nikāya (AN VII,50), Nandamātā was a lay female nonreturner. When the king's soldiers killed her only son in front of her, she bore no ill will toward her child's killers. She also could attain any of the four jhānas at will. Thus, even laypersons who were nonreturners behaved as though they were not of this world.

To return to the system of the vipallāsa explained above, for the nonreturner, delusion *(avijjā)* still operates but only at the levels of perception and thought. View remains forever freed from delusion. Therefore the nonreturner sometimes perceives and thinks with desire, but no longer for the world of the five senses; the nonreturner retains desire for the world of jhāna and the world of the immaterial attainments. Also, the nonreturner sometimes perceives and thinks in terms of "I am" (e.g., SN 22,89). Such perceptions and thoughts regenerate the doer, causing discontent and consequent restlessness. Thus the nonreturner is said to be tied by the five higher fetters: delusion *(avijjā),* desire for jhānas *(rūpa-rāga),* desire for immaterial attainments *(arūpa-rāga),* conceiving "I am" *(māna),* and restlessness *(uddhacca).*

In practice, nonreturners have to continue along the path, using the combination of right effort, mindfulness, and jhāna to keep in mind those insights first seen at stream winning. In particular, they keep in mind that dukkha extends to jhānas, and permeates the immaterial attainments also, to the point where revulsion *(nibbidā)* turns the mind away from these existences too. They also keep in mind the Dhamma of anattā, no-self, until that becomes constantly established at the levels of perception and thought. When this has been completed, then the mind has been fully purified. One is an arahant. As the well-known summary of Buddhism states:

> Not to do any evil,
> To cultivate good
> *To purify the mind,*
> This is the teaching of the buddhas.
>
> (Dhp 183)

Fast-Tracking Full Enlightenment

Sometimes, noble ones go from stream winning straight to full enlightenment, bypassing the stages of the once-returner and nonreturner. Using the simile of the seven shipwrecked sailors, it is as if they swam straight to the land without ever standing in the surf. Perhaps, having swum so close, they are picked up by a strong wave and gently deposited on the beach.

An example of this is the full enlightenment of the Buddha's chief attendant, Ven. Ānanda. After the final passing away of the Buddha, a meeting of senior monks was arranged to collect the Buddha's teachings and preserve them. It later became known as the First Council (Vin 2,11). Five hundred monks were invited, of whom 499 were arahants. The exception was Ven. Ānanda. So the evening before the meeting, Ven. Ānanda resolved to meditate earnestly throughout the night, trying his best to gain full enlightenment. At dawn he could see no progress. So he gave up. He let go. And a few moments later, he became the five-hundredth arahant!

This remarkable event can be explained using the simile of the donkey and the carrot. Many years ago in southern Europe, villagers would use donkey carts for transportation. Donkeys, being notoriously stubborn, had to be tricked into pulling the heavy carts. The owner would attach a long stick to the cart, so that it extended a couple of feet in front of the donkey's head. A string was tied to the front end of the stick, and a big juicy carrot tied to the end of the string. Motivated by desire to eat the carrot dangling on the end of the string just in front, the donkey would move forward and thereby pull the cart. The carrot would also move forward, at the same speed. Thus the owner would get his donkey to pull the cart without wasting too many carrots.

Buddhist donkeys, however, know how to get that carrot! They run like hell after that carrot, putting maximum effort *(viriya)* and concentration *(samādhi)* into moving that cart as fast as they can. Of course, the carrot moves just as fast, always remaining a couple feet in front of the donkey's mouth. At this point, the Buddhist donkey lets go of desire. They suddenly stop! Because of momentum, the carrot swings even further from the donkey, arcing up further than it has ever been before. But this donkey has faith *(saddhā)* and wisdom *(paññā)* and so waits patiently with mindfulness *(sati),* since effort and concentration have done their work. Patiently observing, the donkey sees the carrot swing away to the extreme, and then sees it begin to swing back again. "Rising and falling," notes the donkey. Soon the carrot has fallen back to its usual position but, oddly, it is now traveling toward the donkey and at some speed. Practicing patience, the donkey does nothing. It is the carrot that does all the work as it comes closer and closer. At the right moment, the donkey simply opens its mouth and the big juicy carrot comes in *all by itself.* Crunch! Munch! Mmm! That tastes sweet! This is how donkeys who know the Dhamma catch the carrot.

In Ven. Ānanda's story, he had pursued the carrot of nibbāna so energetically throughout the night. But however hard he chased that carrot, full enlightenment was always just out of reach. When he gave up and stopped to take a short nap, nibbāna swung even further away for a few moments. And then nibbāna, like the carrot, came to Ven. Ānanda! According to the well-known account, before Ven. Ānanda's head had touched the pillow, his mind had swallowed sweet nibbāna.

The Arahant, or Fully Enlightened One

Full enlightenment means that one will never again hold the view that there is a self, nor perceive in terms of a self, nor think that anything is me, mine, or a self. Since there is no longer any idea of "me" or "mine," an arahant does not store up possessions as other people do. For instance, when my teacher Ajahn Chah was at the height of his fame and still very active, he asked me to go up to his room for something. It was the first time that I had seen his living quarters, and I shall never forget the experience. Even though prime ministers, powerful generals, and wealthy businesspersons presented all sorts of gifts to Ajahn Chah, he kept nothing for himself. His room was empty but for a rolled-up grass mat, his alms bowl, and a couple of robes. It would have taken him less than a minute to pack up all his possessions and go. The room appeared as if there was no one living in there, which well reflects the mind of an arahant.

Nine Things an Arahant Cannot Do

There are nine things that an arahant, by nature, cannot do: store up possessions, intentionally kill any form of life, steal, perform sexual intercourse, tell a deliberate lie, and act improperly out of desire, out of ill will, out of delusion, or out of fear (AN IX,7).[34] For instance, since sensory desire has been totally transcended, there is no spark left to ignite the passion for sex. All arahants are "potently impotent."

Furthermore, the arahant has eradicated, once and for all, the three kinds of conceit *(māna):* "I am better," "I am worse," and "I am equal." In Buddhism, even cringing self-disparagement of the "I am hopeless" type is seen as an inverted form of conceit. Arahants, inherently, cannot perceive in terms of "I am" anymore (SN 22,89). They see the body and mind as an impersonal process. To them, it makes as little sense to compare one process with another as it does to compare the value of a piece of wood to that of a mango.

On the subject of the three forms of conceit, it is at full enlightenment that all personal comparisons cease. Old and troublesome controversies, such as whether an arahant is superior to a bodhisattva or vice versa, all disappear. An arahant lives a truth, that of no-self, beyond such measuring. Elitism has no part in full enlightenment. Thus one can expect genuine humility from an arahant, as the following story demonstrates.

Ven. Sāriputta was a famous arahant, acknowledged by all as exceptionally wise. One morning he went on his alms round improperly dressed. A very young upstart of a novice noticed the fault and publicly admonished the great monk. Instead of responding something like "Who do you think you are, you little squirt, to tell me!" Ven. Sāriputta quietly checked to see if he was indeed untidily dressed. On seeing that it was true, Ven. Sāriputta went behind a bush, adjusted his robes, and then came back to thank the little novice, addressing him with great respect as "my teacher." That is graceful humility, a sign of an arahant (Th-a 2,116).

The Arahant and the Outlaws

The arahant, being beyond all perceptions of self, feels no need to be popular. Their minds are freed from the need to impress. Nor will they ever experience fear, since they have nothing left to lose. The following verses from the *Theragāthā* (verses 705–25) describe such a fearless one, the arahant Adhimutta Thera, and his dialogue with robbers:

705 *The Robbers:*
　　　"Those whom we killed for sacrifice,
　　　Or for their wealth against their will,
　　　All trembled, babbling with fear.

706 "But you don't seem to be afraid,
　　　With your complexion brightening;
　　　Serene and calm, you don't lament
　　　When faced with greatest danger, death."

707 *Adhimutta:*
　　　"There is no suffering inside the mind
　　　When longing has been left behind;

And truly, Chief, all fears are overcome
In one who has forever cut his bonds.

708 "When that which leads one to future birth
Has been destroyed, and when phenomena
Are seen with wisdom as they really are,
There is no fear at death; a burden is put down.

709 "The holy life has been well lived by me;
The path has been developed to the end.
I have no fear of death, just as
I would not fear destruction of disease.

710 "The holy life has been well lived by me;
The path has been developed to the end.
Existences are seen as pointless and banal;
I have spat out the poison that I used to drink.

711 "For one who has reached the further shore,
For whom there's no more 'taking up,' whose task is done,
In whom the outflows of the mind have ceased,
There is delight at the life's concluding end,
As one delights at freedom from the chopping block.

712 "I have attained the highest truth, supreme;
The world has nothing left to offer me.
At death there is no grief, it brings relief,
Like being rescued from a burning house.

713 "The mighty sage has made it clear to us:
'Whatever here has come to be,
Wherever else existence is obtained,
All that is not created by a ruling god.'

714 "Whoever knows this as the Buddha taught,
     Does not take up existence, as one won't
     'Take up' a red-hot glowing iron ball.

715 "For me there is no 'I have been,'
     Nor does the thought occur that 'I will be.'
     When these formations terminate and cease,
     Regarding them, what is there to lament?

716 "Just pure arising of phenomena,
     The pure persistence of formations through a cause,
     Seen as it truly is, there is no fear, O Chief.

717 "When one with wisdom looks upon this world
     As one would look upon a heap of grass and sticks,
     One can't find any ownership;
     There won't be grief, because there is no 'mine.'

718 "I'm weary of this corpse, and I'm fed up;
     Existence lost its spell, and there will be
     No other corpse when this one here breaks up.

719 "Do as you please, do what you have to do.
     But on account of this cadaver here,
     No hatred or affection will ensue."

720 At these hair-raising and extraordinary words,
     The robbers, throwing down their swords, said this:

721 "Dear Sir, what have you done, and who has been your
          instructor,
     Whose teaching leads one to such freedom from all sorrow?"

722 *Adhimutta:*
>   "All-knowing and all-seeing, the Conqueror and Victor,
>   Of infinite compassion has been my instructor;
>   He is the teacher of the world and its physician.

722 "He taught this matchless Dhamma leading to extinction,
>   Which when pursued will lead to freedom from all sorrow."

723 Now having heard these words, well spoken by the sage,
>   With swords put down, and with their weapons laid aside,
>   Some robbers there and then desisted from their trade,
>   While others left the world, to live the holy life.

725 Gone forth in the religion of the Blessed One,
>   Developing the factors of enlightenment,
>   The "powers," wisdom, and the higher mind,
>   With joyful hearts, and with their faculties matured,
>   They came to touch the unconditioned state; nibbāna.
>
>   (Translated by Ajahn Cattamalo)

What Motivates Arahants?

One explains the state of full enlightenment not just by listing the things that arahants are incapable of doing, but also by depicting the kind of behavior that they do perform. In essence, their behavior consists of acts of loving-kindness, compassion, sympathetic joy, and equanimity. It is these four "sublime abidings," or *brahmavihāras,* that motivate every action of an arahant, whether it be teaching or serving, eating or resting, or whatever else they are called upon to do.

I count it as my most fortunate blessing to have lived as a monk in Thailand from 1974 to 1983 and met such arahants. One that I will always remember was reputed to possess many psychic powers. Psychic powers often come with full enlightenment, but not always (SN 12,70). In particular, this great monk was said to read minds. Suspecting this might be true, I was hesitant—actually I was terrified—of meeting such an arahant.

My young monk's mind was no more fit to be read by a great monk than a raunchy novel was, and certainly not in public! But when I entered the presence of such a being, or I should say a "nonbeing," all my fears evaporated in a instant. I felt so calm, so safe and accepted, in spite of all my faults. It is because arahants don't look down on anyone (the three conceits have been eliminated) that one feels so at ease with them. All that they emanate is their compassion and wisdom. Being with a genuine arahant is the most comforting and encouraging of encounters.

Sometime later, a fellow monk gave the following unusual but precise metaphor for an arahant. He told me that it is as if people have many sharp, invisible, spiritual spikes protruding from their bodies. Some people's spiritual spikes are so extensive and razor sharp that, when they enter a room, everyone in that room feels very uncomfortable. One often gets wounded in their presence. Most people's spiritual spikes are not so long or sharp. One can get close to them but, if one comes too close...ouch! one gets scratched. Some exceptional people have very few spikes, and those they do have are short and blunt. They seem so full of love that one wants to get close to them. But even with these people, if one comes really close, then too one can get scratched. They also have personal territory to protect. Then lastly, there is a rare and special class of being that has no spiritual spikes at all. They are the arahants. "They are just so soft and cuddly!" someone once said to me, impertinently though quite understandably. An arahant is like the perfect spiritual grandfather, all wise and gentle, with absolutely no trace of anger, one who keeps your well-being as their only concern. When one comes into the presence of such an arahant, one never wants to leave.

The End of All Suffering

That is what an arahant is like, should one be fortunate enough to meet one. They appear to be the happiest people in the world (MN 89,12). But what is the inner experience of an arahant? Are they free from all suffering?

The answer, which comes as a surprise for some, is no! Arahants are not yet free from all dukkha. In order to explain the difference between an arahant and all others, the Buddha taught the simile of the two darts (SN 36,6). Should one be struck by a dart, or an arrow, they would experience much suffering. Should they be struck immediately afterward by a second dart, then they would experience twice as much suffering or more. In this simile, the two darts are bodily and mental feeling *(vedanā).*

When most people experience a painful bodily feeling, it is followed immediately by a painful mental feeling. It is like being struck by two darts in quick succession. But for arahants (and nonreturners),[35] when they experience a painful bodily feeling, it is not followed by a painful mental response. It is like being struck by only one dart. The fully enlightened ones have removed the dart of mental suffering, but they still must experience the dart of bodily suffering. Even the Buddha had to experience bodily pain (DN 16,4,20). Indeed, during the last few months of the Buddha's life, he said that only when he entered "the signless samādhi" *(animitta ceto-samādhi)* was he free from bodily discomfort (DN 16,2,25).

Of course, the dart of bodily suffering is very small compared to the totality of mental suffering that has been removed. That is why arahants are the happiest beings alive. The suffering that remains, though, is important. It both defines the inner experience of the arahant and provides the main cause for their parinibbāna, or complete extinction. For example, when the arahant Vajirā was challenged to say who she was, she explained how the body-and-mind process named "Vajirā" looked from inside the mind of an enlightened one:

It is only suffering that comes to be,
Suffering that stands and falls away.
Nothing but suffering comes to be,
Nothing but suffering ceases.[36]

Such an insider's view of an arahant's mind is confirmed by the Buddha in the *Kaccānagotta Sutta* (SN 12,15), where he states, "What arises is only suffering arising, what ceases is only suffering ceasing."[37] As explained earlier, it is because dukkha permeates every level of existence, even that of an arahant, that revulsion *(nibbidā)* arises and then causes the body-and-mind process of the arahant to come to a complete end.

So full enlightenment is not the end of all suffering! Instead, it is called *sa-upādisesa-nibbāna,* or "nibbāna with existence remaining." The arahant is at the very last stage of being, the level where they know two things. First, they know the causes of rebirth, mostly craving for sensual pleasure *(kāmataṇhā)* and craving to be *(bhavataṇhā)*. Second, they know that these causes have all been destroyed. Why crave "to be" when one has realized that even being an arahant is dukkha? Thus the arahant is said to have destroyed the seeds (Sn 235), the "spiritual genes," that reproduce dukkha from life to life, *and they know it has been totally destroyed*. That is the unique knowledge of the arahant. For them, it is only a matter of a short time until they reach *an-upādisesa nibbāna,* or "nibbāna with no existence remaining," otherwise known as parinibbāna, or complete extinction. In the timeless words from the *gāthā* of the arahant Sankicca Thera:

> I do not long for death, for life I have no yearning;
> Like a workman, waiting for his wages, I await my time. (Thag 606)

Parinibbāna

That moment when arahants receive their "wages," the final end of all suffering, is parinibbāna. It is the end of existence, *bhavanirodha* (SN 12,68). From the time when full enlightenment occurs until their parinibbāna, the arahant is the greatest benefit to the world (*Ratana Sutta,* Sn 233). They teach by example, through direct experience of nibbāna, and are living embodiments of the Dhamma. The Buddha's own forty-five years from full enlightenment to parinibbāna still remain the most powerful period of this age. Those years still echo like thunder in countries far distant from the fertile Ganges plain, and their brilliance even illuminates our time, some twenty-six centuries remote, like a massive supernova showering its light across the millennia. It was long ago that the Buddha set in motion the wheel of the Dhamma. Through the succeeding centuries it has been the arahants who have kept that wheel turning. Like the Buddha, the first arahant of this age, all arahants merely show the way. It is up to their listeners to walk the journey. That way continues to be shown, and it remains well traveled even today. There being nothing more they can do to help all sentient beings, all buddhas and all arahants attain parinibbāna. What was only "dukkha arising and dukkha passing away" now ceases forever.

So what follows after parinibbāna? After the moment of complete extinction, all knowing *(viññāṇa, citta, and mano)* and all that can be known *(nāma-rūpa)* cease, and with them all descriptions and words cease as well. There is nothing more to say. It doesn't even make any sense to say there is nothing (e.g., AN IV,174), lest someone misunderstands "nothing" to be something's name.

How to Tell If Someone Is Enlightened

An often-asked question is, how can one verify that someone is enlightened? The answer is that one cannot know for sure. Only the buddhas have that ability (AN VI,44),[38] for it is the sixth of the ten powers of a buddha (AN X,21).[39] In the time of the Buddha, only he would confirm another's attainments. Even great arahants like Ven. Sāriputta had to ask the Buddha on this matter (SN 35,87).[40]

However, even though one is unable to know for sure that someone *is* enlightened, it is possible to know for sure that certain types of people are *not* enlightened. The four stages of enlightenment are each defined by clear signs, so, if any of the essential signs are missing, then one can be certain that they have not reached that level.

The Essential Signs

For stream winning, the essential signs begin with the "four characteristic qualities of a stream winner." They are as follows: unshakable faith in the enlightenment of the Buddha; unshakable faith in the excellence of the Buddha's teaching, the Dhamma; unshakable faith in the worthiness of noble ones in the monastic Sangha; and a high level of moral conduct that is "dear to the noble ones" (DN 16,2,9; SN 55,1).

The *Kosambiya Sutta* (MN 48) gives more detail on what that level of conduct is: Should they break a precept then, by nature, they will always reveal it to their teacher, or to a fellow student, and restrain such misbehavior in future.[41] Furthermore, the stream winner has eradicated *sakkāya diṭṭhi,* "personality view," meaning that they never regard *any* of the five *khandhas* (body, feeling, perception, mental formations, and consciousness) as a self, as a possession of a self, as containing a self, or as being contained in a self (MN 44,7; SN 22,1). Since it is such personality view that creates all sixty-two of the wrong views listed in the *Brahmajāla Sutta* (SN 41,3), the stream winner can hold none of those views (DN 1). This is why the stream winner is called "one complete in right view" *(diṭṭhi-sampanna)* (AN VI,89–95). Therefore all stream winners necessarily hold the view that rebirth exists (MN 60,11) and kamma exists (MN 60,19). Lastly, stream winning is an event (AN III,12), so the stream winner should be able to point out the time and the place that it occurred.

So, for example, if someone has no respect for the Sangha, or claims not to believe in rebirth, or holds the view that the mind *(citta)* or mentality *(mano)* or consciousness *(viññāṇa)* is everlasting (wrong view number eight in the *Brahmajāla Sutta,* DN 1,2,13), then one can know for sure that this person is not a stream winner.

This standard is based on clear statements in the suttas. If someone objects to this standard, saying that they do not respect what the suttas say about stream winning, then that is another sure sign that they are not a stream winner; for all noble ones respect the Buddha's teaching and receive inspiration therefrom (MN 48,13–14).[42]

For once-returners, all the signs of stream winning must be present, plus a lessening of sensory desire and ill will. This stage is so hard to define precisely that I have said little about it in this chapter. For instance, in the Aṅguttara Nikāya (AN VI,44) there is a story of two brothers, Purāna and Isidatta, who were both declared as once-returners by the Buddha, although the former was celibate and the latter was sexually active.[43] It was a case in point, showing that only a buddha has the ability to know for certain the attainments of another.

For nonreturners the signs are much clearer. All the qualities of the stream winner must be present, plus a complete absence of sensory desire and ill will. Thus a nonreturner is incapable of even fantasizing about sex (inferring from AN VI,63),[44] let alone performing any sexual act. So someone who is sexually active is certainly not a nonreturner, and the same goes for someone who is obviously angry.

For the arahant, the signs are clearer still. All the qualities of the stream winner and the nonreturner must be present, plus qualities such as the nine things that an arahant is incapable of doing, such as storing up possessions (AN IX,7).[45] The arahant also has a natural humility due to the absence of the three "I am" conceits (SN 22,89). Another unique quality of the arahant is their fearlessness in the face of death (such as in the story of Adhimutta Thera given earlier in this chapter). So if you see someone who has many possessions, is proud, or fears death, then you know that person is not fully enlightened.

That is how one can know that someone is *not* at this or that stage of enlightenment. However, just because certain wrong views or behaviors are not apparent does not mean that they are eradicated. Sometimes they are suppressed by jhāna, sometimes by will. For example, if one could read another's nonenlightened mind just after it emerges from jhāna, then it would appear so clear of defilements as to be indistinguishable from the normal mind of an arahant. That is one of the reasons why only a buddha can know for certain the attainment of another. Everyone else can only know for sure that certain types have yet to reach such and such an attainment.

The Two Temple Boys

A helpful story on this point concerns an incident that occurred two decades ago to one of the most highly regarded meditation teachers of our time. Two temple boys with little education asked this famous teacher for some instruction in meditation. Every few days the young boys would report their progress, which was outstanding. In a very short time, these two youths from a poor village had outstripped all the monks. Those who were there at that time later told me that the atmosphere in that monastery was electric. Two boys of exceptional spiritual ability had come to their forest monastery, as if by chance, and were now well on the way to fulfilling their brilliant karmic potential. The monks' inspiration soon reached a rare peak when their learned meditation master solemnly confirmed that both boys had reached full enlightenment. The monks were thrilled to hear that two new arahants had appeared in the world. It is understood in the Theravāda tradition, with some justification (Miln 7,2), that should a layperson attain to full enlightenment, then they must quickly join the Sangha or else they will pass away in a matter of days. So certain was this great teacher of the boys' attainments that he had them both ordained that very day. Sometime later, one of the boys was taken to see a doctor about some minor ailment. The doctor prescribed surgery. Not understanding that surgery was done under an anesthetic, the boy "arahant" became alarmed. He was clearly afraid. As mentioned above, genuine arahants have no such fear. Thus it became clear, first with one boy and then with the other, that they were not fully enlightened after all. One of the most accomplished meditation masters in his country had been completely mistaken. If such a learned and competent teacher can make such an error, so can we.

Some people assume that persons with psychic powers must be at some high stage of enlightenment, but they are misinformed. The Buddha's cousin, Devadatta, had amazing psychic powers, but he wasn't even a stream winner. Later, he lost his powers and tried to kill the Buddha (Vin 2,7,2,5). Psychic powers are not a reliable sign of enlightenment.

In the *Sunakkhatta Sutta* (MN 105), a layman asked the Buddha about the monks who, he heard, had claimed full enlightenment in the presence of the Buddha. He wanted to know whether or not all those monks were arahants. The Buddha replied that some of them were arahants; some were not.[46] Thus, what someone claims about their own attainments was unreliable even in the time of the Buddha. In fact, it is an offense against the *vinaya* (the monastic precepts) for a monk or a nun to claim a stage of enlightenment to a layperson (*pācittiya* 8). So a person in robes who makes such a claim in public is deliberately breaking their precepts, making their claim even more dubious. When establishing the monastic precept, the Buddha had recognized how easy it was to overestimate one's own attainments. So it is best to keep quiet about them, except to one's teacher. As one nun said, "If you become enlightened, don't tell anyone, or else you'll spend the rest of your life having to prove it!"

When assessing one's own progress, it is advisable to know the signs of each stage of enlightenment first and then investigate, without vanity and over a long period of time, to see which signs are there and which signs are missing. One should not rush into claiming any stage of enlightenment; rather, one should wait, perhaps for years, before one is sure. One should let ongoing experience test the attainment, as shown in the following story.

The Monk Who Was Unafraid of Tigers

In late 1980 in the remote Thai mountain monastery of Poo Tork, the great forest monk, Tan Ajahn Juan, related this monk's tale to me.

Late one afternoon, a forest monk entered a poor village in the middle of a jungle. It was the custom then for monks who wandered in search of solitude to announce their arrival in the nearest village, so that the devout Thai villagers could expect them for alms round on the next morning. The villagers promptly warned the monk of a ferocious tiger roaming the surrounding jungle that had already killed and eaten many of their water buffalo and even some of the villagers.

"I am no longer afraid of death," boasted the monk. For he sincerely thought that he was already enlightened.

The villagers didn't believe him.

"Show me where the tiger track is," said the monk defiantly. "I will meditate there all night."

The villagers led the monk deep into the jungle to a place where the tiger's track crossed one of their own paths. It was a long way from the village. The confident monk calmly set up his monk's mosquito net and umbrella, and then shooed away the villagers so that he could meditate in quiet. The villagers were impressed.

In the forest tradition of Northeast Thailand, many monks meditate using the mantra "buddho." As one breathes in, one mentally notes "bud," then as one breathes out one notes "dho": "bud-dho, bud-dho," along with the breath.

Once the darkness settled most of the jungle insects, the monk became very peaceful. "Buuuuuud—dhoooooo," he noted as his breath grew smooth, slow, and refined. Then he heard a sound of some animal moving in the jungle. As he paid attention to that sound, he noticed his breath get a little shorter, "buuud—dhooo."

The sound increased. Not daring to open his eyes, he mentally assessed that the sound must be from a largish jungle animal coming in his direction. His breath was now very loud and very short, "bud-dho, bud-dho, bud-dho."

The sound increased. This must be a huge animal. So he opened his eyes. In the place of "bud-dho, bud-dho," he found his mantra automatically change to "ti-ger, ti-ger"! Not far away, and coming straight toward him was this gigantic monk-eating tiger. Losing all of his mindfulness, except for his new mantra, he leapt out from under his mosquito net and began running to the village. "TI-GER! TI-GER!" His new mantra grew louder the faster he ran.

Now, it is against the monastic rules for a monk to run, and there is a good reason for this. The reason is that a monk's robes have no buttons or zips but are held together only by ingenious folding and lots of mindfulness. When a monk runs, robes are apt to become undone. Then they slip down, trail behind on the ground, and eventually fall off completely. And this is precisely what happened to that monk who thought he was so enlightened that he had no fear of tigers.

He arrived in the village shouting his mantra at the top of his voice, "TI-GER! TI-GER!" and woke everyone up. He was by this time as bare of robes as his head was bare of hair. Those villagers never forgot that forest monk whose claim to be fearless was exposed, along with other embarrassing things, that night.

Conclusion,
Letting Go to the End

♦ ♦ ♦

Summary of the Method

THE METHOD is one of renouncing attachments, otherwise
known as letting go. Such renouncing begins with generosity, which is why we don't have any donation boxes in our Buddhist
centers; instead we call them "letting go boxes." Then one renounces
those actions of body or speech that cause harm to another or to oneself,
which is another way of saying that one lives morally by following the
precepts. After this, one renounces thinking and the body, together with
the five senses, through the practice of Buddhist meditation. Then one
renounces the doer to enter the world of jhāna, the jewel box within
the heart of meditation. Lastly one renounces the delusion of a persisting
essence, a me, mine, or self, thus removing the wrong view that sepa-
rates this world from nibbāna.

This book has focused on the renunciation that is called meditation.
The first stage was renouncing the paradigm of time to enter the meditation state of timelessness, or present-moment awareness. Then one
learned to renounce the tyranny of inner speech, thinking, in order
to enter the bright, sacred peace of silent present-moment awareness.
Next, one developed the way to partially renounce the body and its
five senses by focusing on just one bodily function, the breath, to the
point where nothing else remained. Then one completely renounced
the body and the five senses to reach, via the beautiful breath, the stage
of the nimitta. Soon, one proceeded to renounce the doer in order to
enter the jhānas. Then one gradually renounced the only thing left,
the knower, or mind, to gain access to the delicious higher jhānas and

through them the gossamer-like immaterial attainments. In summary, Buddhist meditation is a gradual method of renunciation. One may now appreciate why the Sangha, the community of Buddhist monks and nuns, comprises what are called renunciants.

Please don't be scared by the word renunciation. The way of renouncing is also the way of happiness. As one gradually lets go, happiness gradually increases. In the suttas, the Buddha describes this path of meditation as a natural process:

> For one who is virtuous, there is no need to will, "May I be free from remorse." Freedom from remorse arises automatically in one who is virtuous.
>
> For one free from remorse, there is no need to will, "May I be glad." Gladness arises automatically in one who is free from remorse.
>
> For one who is glad, there is no need to will, "May I be joyful." Joy arises automatically in one who is glad.
>
> For one who is joyful, there is no need to will, "May my body be tranquil." Tranquillity arises automatically in one who is joyful.
>
> For one who is tranquil, there is no need to will, "May I have inner happiness." Inner happiness arises automatically in one who is tranquil.
>
> For one who is happy, there is no need to will, "May my mind enter samādhi." Samādhi [jhāna] arises automatically in one who is inwardly happy.
>
> For one who has jhāna, there is no need to will, "May I see things as they truly are." Seeing things as they truly are [wisdom] arises automatically in one who has jhāna. (AN X,2)

Thus, from harmlessness (virtue) one gets gladness, joy, tranquillity, inner happiness, the bliss of jhāna, and the freedom that flows from wisdom. These are all different forms of happiness occurring in a gradual and natural progression. The process of renunciation, or ever-increasing happiness, culminates here in seeing things as they truly are, which is enlightenment. And enlightenment is the greatest happiness of them all.

In the *Dhammacetiya Sutta* (MN 89,12), King Pasenadi remarked how much he enjoyed visiting the Jeta Grove monastery because he would always see happy, smiling monks. The Buddha acknowledged that this is how it is when one successfully develops one's meditation.

So the method described in this book is a happy path, a blissful path, a blow-your-mind-with-ultimate-ecstasy path! The more one renounces what is only suffering, the more one experiences real happiness. So much for the method. Now for the goal.

Goals

"The best of all communities," in the Buddha's opinion, "is where the elder monks are frugal and diligent, not neglecting time in seclusion, and where their energies are aroused to attain what is yet to be attained, to understand what is not yet understood, and to realize what is still to be realized" (AN III,93). So it is clear that the Buddha taught that there were goals to achieve. His disciples were well aware that there were spiritual attainments to be worked for. The very highest rewards were on offer, but only to those committing everything to the task. The suttas make clear that Buddhist practice is unsuitable for those who are lazy. Only the arahants have nothing more to do (MN 70,12), and even those fully enlightened ones often tirelessly work for the ultimate welfare of others.

In this book I have promoted the attainment of many spiritual goals. They are some of the most sublime achievements accessible to people in today's world. Moreover, they include the most wonderful goal of all, full enlightenment, which is the same achievement as the Buddha's.

Some say that there is nothing to attain. Those who follow such misinformed advice, of course, achieve nothing. Just their foolishness remains, as thick as ever. And this is seen by others in the turmoil that unabandoned greed and ill will create in their lives. To be born as a human being is a very precious opportunity for progress on the path of wisdom, but sadly it is all too often wasted in languid lounging or pointless pursuits. As for the Buddha, he advised that one should practice the training with the same sort of urgency as if one's clothes were on fire.[47] So much for wasting time.

Goals and No-self

Buddhist goals are infinitely different from worldly goals. Whereas mundane goals usually strengthen the sense of self and are bound up with acquisitions, Buddhist goals lead only to selflessness and to the abandoning of all possessions. This is the fundamental difference that makes aspirations to attain Buddhist goals so distinct from the cravings of the world.

Wise teachers rightly warn against striving for worldly goals, for in the end it invariably leads to frustration. Either one fails to achieve the goal and gives up, or else the achievement when won is experienced as much less than expected. As Oscar Wilde famously said, "In this world there are only two tragedies. One is not getting what one wants, and the other is getting it."

The spiritual goal of jhāna can be achieved only through great skill in letting go. One does not acquire anything in the achievement, except for the knowledge of what it is like to be free from one's body as well as from thought. Moreover, deep insights based on such experiences of profound letting go are incapable of leading to pride. How could they? These are realizations that undermine the very illusion of a self from which arrogance arises. Wherever no self is seen, pride cannot stand.

So the goals recommended in this book are very different from the goals that are pursued in the world. Since these goals that the Buddha praised lead only to spiritual positives, they deserve to be placed in the forefront, as focuses of one's aspirations, and developed without fear. Only when one has such a clear goal will there be the possibility of spiritual progress.

To illustrate how Buddhist goals differ from worldly goals, imagine a football team comprised of highly attained Buddhists. Since letting go is their prime concern, they would be constantly and joyfully passing the ball to their opponents. Since compassion is their practice, should the opposing team have difficulty scoring a goal, then the Buddhists would kindly help them. And since generosity is their very nature, the more points that they give away, the better their kamma. Then, at the end of the season, should the Buddhist team be banished from the league, they would rejoice in the similarity of their plight to being expelled from saṃsāra!

Real Buddhists do think differently. Their goals are never at another's expense. They aspire to give away all possessions, and they delight in losing things.

Raising the Bar

In this book, I have recommended the goals of jhāna and the four stages of enlightenment. The Buddha, as we saw, called these *uttari-manussa-dhamma,* "states that surpass normal human experience." By raising the bar regarding what meditators should aspire for, I am urging meditators to stretch high. A good coach always extends their students beyond their presumed limits in order to excel. And why not excel in the highest and best goals of all, those proclaimed by the Buddha? It is still possible to achieve uttari-manussa-dhamma in this very life. This book challenges you to try.

As well as championing these attainments, I have described the path in detail. This path focuses mainly on the causes and less on the results. For when one gazes too long and longingly on the great goal, one neglects investing time and energy into cultivating the causes that generate the goal.

For example, someone bemoans the fact that the dishes in their kitchen are all so dirty. "Oh! When will my dishes be clean? I want all my dishes to be sparkling!" But they become discouraged when they see the size of the task. Someone else considers, "How can my dishes become clean?" and then begins the work that is the cause of clean dishes—washing them! Soon, as regularly happens when one does the washing up, the dishes become clean and sparkling. The goal is achieved.

Similarly, someone bemoans the fact that they have yet to reach jhāna. "Oh! When will my mind reach bliss? I want my mind to sparkle in jhāna!" But they are discouraged by the size of the task. Someone else considers, "How can this mind enter a jhāna?" and then begins the work that is the cause for entering jhāna—letting go of the doer and the five senses. Soon, as regularly happens when one follows with precision the instructions of the Buddha, one's mind enters jhāna and sparkles. The goal is achieved.

Raising the bar is not the cause of frustration. Wrong attitude is the cause. Spending too much time longing for the goal and not enough time working on the causes—that is what causes frustration and disables achievement.

Unearthing Attachments

When aiming for jhāna one will encounter many hurdles. These obstacles are one's attachments. Those without attachments can enter any jhāna without difficulty, as a natural abiding for their mind. Aiming for jhāna unearths these attachments. When aiming for something less, one does not meet the root attachments and may think they do not exist. So aiming for jhāna also serves the purpose of digging deep enough to uncover these root attachments, confront them, and then transcend them by entering the jhāna.

It is easy to delude oneself that one is free of attachments. Some cigarette smokers delude themselves into thinking that they can give up smoking at any time, but they just don't plan to give it up today. Until one has tried to give up smoking, one is unaware of the power of the addiction. In the same way, until one has tried to reach jhāna, one cannot comprehend the subtle force of one's attachments. Furthermore, when one has tested one's freedom from attachments by the ability to enter a jhāna, only then can one be sure that one has dealt with them all.

For example, most meditators do not realize how attached they are to sound. Even though background speech is none of their business, nor is the sound of the traffic outside, most find it impossible to turn off their hearing and pay no attention to sound. They are unable to let it go because of their strong attachment to hearing. They identify with being the one who hears. Letting go of sound and enjoying total silence, then, is like letting go of part of their identity. That is *attachment*. To enter the states of deep meditation, one must center the mind beyond the reach of all sound, untying this knot of attachment until one is incapable of hearing anything. In the *Mahāparinibbāna Sutta,* the Buddha was in such a state of nonattachment while meditating at Ātumā that he heard nothing during a violent thunderstorm (DN 16,4,33).

Most people are deeply attached to thinking. That is why they cannot stop thinking when they need, for instance, to go to sleep. Most people celebrate thought and value their ideas as their most personal property. Thinking is the tool by which they control their own world, both outer and inner. Letting go of thought and entering into mindful silence means dropping the attachment to control of their domain. Such letting go is terrifying to control freaks, and all who cannot enter jhāna are in fact control freaks! They are attached to controlling and thereby to thinking. But when one has the guts to let go of this commentary of inner control, that is, thinking, one experiences the bliss of inner silence. Only then does one comprehend that thinking is an attachment that blocks peace of mind.

Clinging to this body and its five senses, to this doer and its thinking, is the root attachment blocking jhāna. Just as one proves nonattachment to cigarette smoking by giving it up, one proves nonattachment to the body, the five senses, and thoughts through entering a jhāna.

Stories of Letting Go

The instructions in this book take the meditator beyond these root attachments. You enter inner realms where the five senses cannot disturb you and where thoughts cannot move, but where mindfulness glows blissfully. Here are some stories about letting go.

Striking a Deal with My Mind

I spent my sixth rains retreat as a monk completely alone in a remote mountain hermitage in the highlands of northern Thailand. After a while my meditation began to fall apart. The harder I tried to subdue my restless mind, the more vigorously it wandered. Unmonkish thoughts of lust and violence would overwhelm my defenses and play at will with my mind. Soon, it was getting out of hand, but I had no companion to help me. One day, in desperation, I made a solemn resolution before the great Buddha statue in the main hall. I made a deal: for one hour every day, from three to four every afternoon, I would permit my wanton mind to think whatever it liked. Sex, violence, romance, even the most deviant fantasies would be allowed in that hour. In return, I asked that my mind stay with the breath for the rest of the day.

It did not work quite as I'd planned. For most of the first day, my mind was as rebellious as ever. It refused to agree to follow my breath. It kicked and bucked violently like a wild horse at a rodeo. Then at three in the afternoon, to keep my agreement, I gave up the struggle. I leaned against the wall of my hut to rest my aching back, stretched out my legs before me to ease my sore knees, and gave permission to my mind to do whatever it wanted. To my astonishment, for the next sixty minutes my mind followed every breath with the greatest of ease. It seemed as if it didn't want to do anything else, only be with the breath! That experience taught me the difference between letting go and trying to let go. It was one of the most dramatic lessons in letting go.

Further along the path leading to jhāna, there are some more advanced lessons in letting go. One misses these lessons if one does not aim for reaching jhāna. One can learn to let go so completely of the five senses that they totally disappear for a while, as I discovered to my great relief in my first year as a monk.

Ajahn Mosquito

It was my kamma to be one of the first six monks sent by Ajahn Chah to establish his training monastery for his Western monks. The dense piece of rain forest that would become Wat Pa Nanachat had no halls, no huts, no toilets, not even sleeping platforms. We all had to sleep on the jungle floor with only a mosquito net as protection from whatever crawled or slithered in the shadows of the jungle undergrowth. Even worse, at dusk every day we would sit for several hours in the open under the trees for the evening service. Together with Ajahn Chah and some fifty or sixty villagers, we would chant first and then meditate for one hour. Unfortunately, this was the time in the sultry jungle that the mosquitoes would assemble seeking out their dinner. I was their supper! There were no mosquito coils or repellent in those early days. Moreover, as a Buddhist monk I couldn't swat them. They had free rein. We just had to endure it, defenseless and bald.

Together with a young American monk, I would play a game of counting how many mosquitoes would bite my bare flesh at the same time, to see which one of us could count the most. I would count to sixty or seventy before stopping, because the bites were too close to count separately. It was unbearable, and I often prepared to run. But when I opened my eyes, I would see Ajahn Chah and all the villagers sitting so still that my pride would not permit me to flee. So I took the nightly torture until I learned how to let go of my body. Soon I could let go so effectively that I couldn't feel my body anymore. I went deep within my mind, at peace, happy, well beyond the reach of those irritating mosquitoes. It was my means of escape. I now thank those benevolent mosquitoes for teaching me how to let go.

It is of interest to realize that when one faces one's death, one will have to let go of this very same body. By learning to let go of one's body well before the time of death, by aiming for jhāna, one overcomes all fear of the dying process. One learns to let go of the five senses whenever one wants. One then has the power to be unmoved by disturbing sights, to be quiet in booming noise, and to be totally at ease amid piercing pain. When one has learned the lesson in letting go that severs the connection between the mind and the five senses, then one has learned how to let go of attachment to the body.

Learning How to Do Nothing

Letting go, slowing down, and stopping are not only essential for attaining enlightenment, but also crucial to surviving ordinary life. Stress, which is caused by not knowing how to do nothing, is the quintessential weapon of mass destruction. So many diseases, both mental and physical, are caused by stress. Even three and a half centuries ago, the French philosopher Blaise Pascal recognized this when he said, "All the troubles of man come from his not knowing how to sit still."

Some of the time there is nothing to do. Yet at such times you are unable to do nothing. You have forgotten how. So you struggle meaninglessly. If you were wise, when there's nothing to do then you do nothing! It makes so much sense.

We all need to learn how to do nothing so that at the right times we can rest and relax. Fortunately, for those with no opportunity to go to a monastery, teachers are available in great numbers in most modern cities. They are found at the major crossroads. They are traffic lights. When the red light appears it says "Stop!" That's letting go practice. Have you learned how to do nothing at the red traffic lights? Or does only the vehicle stop while you speed on? If so, then an opportunity is being wasted. At the red light, you can open your mind to the present and allow unexpected beauty and peace to appear all around you. I have heard, but not yet seen, that in the capital city of spiritual India, New Delhi, when the red light appears it shows the five letters *r, e, l, a,* and *x: relax.* They are not stoplights, they're relax lights. What a great idea. If it ain't true, it ought to be!

If you don't take time to learn how to do nothing, if you are unable to relax at the red traffic lights of life, then you will soon be *forced* to stop in an early grave. As the old saying goes, "Death is nature's way of forcing you to slow down." I recommend meditation over a premature death.

Letting Go of the Water Buffalo

When one hasn't yet learned how to do nothing, how to let go and relax, one generates more problems in life than are necessary. The following story occurred when I was a monk in Northeast Thailand, and it shows how letting go can save a lot of unnecessary pain and injury.

Early one morning a local rice farmer tied a rope around the neck of his water buffalo and led it out of his village to the paddy fields to graze. As he was passing by our monastery, his buffalo took fright and began to run away. The villager held on to the rope in an attempt to restrain the frightened animal. As the buffalo charged off, the rope wound around the farmer's finger and took the top third of his finger off! We saw the poor farmer as he came into our monastery for help. His finger was all bloody with a stump of bone showing above the ripped flesh. We took him immediately to the local hospital, fixed him up, and he was soon back at work with one finger shorter than before.

The moral of this story is that if anything as strong as a water buffalo wants to run off, it is sensible to let them go. Water buffalo don't go far, only a couple of hundred yards, and then they stop. Once they've calmed down, the farmer can easily walk after them and bring them back safely. That way many fingers are saved. There are many people who act like a water buffalo sometimes. It may be your partner, your son, or your mother-in-law, who gets out of line. When they're rampaging it is sensible to let them go. You'll only injure yourself painfully if you try to rein them in. Wait and do nothing. Soon they'll calm down, and then you can do something.

For instance, a meditator recently asked me how she could control her "water buffalo" of a mind during meditation. "Let it go," I answered, "Soon it will stop and come back to you." I reminded her of another anecdote from a disciple who had a six-year-old son. One day her son was so upset that he announced to his mom, "I'm leaving home!" The very wise mother, living in a safe neighborhood, said "OK!" and helped him pack his small bag, even making him some sandwiches for his life's journey. She waved him off at the door. Of course, the six-year-old only went a couple of hundred yards down the road before he missed home. Then he promptly turned around and walked back into his waiting mom's arms.

The meditator with the uncontrollable mind couldn't stop giggling as I told that anecdote. She explained that the very same thing had happened to her when she was seven years old in Singapore. She told her mother that she wanted to leave home. Not only did her mother pack her bags but she gave her a little money as well. She didn't even manage two hundred yards away from her door before she returned. Now she knows how to deal with a "water buffalo" mind.

When any problem is as strong as a water buffalo, then let it go. Situations change, fires burn out, and floods recede. When the water buffalo stops charging, then you can do something effective to solve the crises of life. So learning how to let go and relax is not only for the purpose of enlightenment, but it is also for the purpose of surviving life.

Life Ain't Heavy (When You Know How to Let Go)
Leaving aside the crises of life, even on ordinary days meditation helps one carry the burden. Following my teacher, Ajahn Chah, I often

explain the meaning of meditation, together with its benefits, by holding up a glass of water at arm's length.

"How heavy is this cup?" I ask. Before anyone can answer, I continue, "The longer I hold it, the heavier it feels. If I keep holding my glass for ten minutes, then it starts to feel heavy. If I remain holding it thus for twenty minutes, then my arm will begin to ache. And if I am still holding this glass of water at arm's length after one hour, then not only will I be in great agony, but I will also be a very stupid monk. So what should I do when my glass becomes too heavy to hold comfortably?"

"Put it down," they answer. Of course. The problem is not the weight of the glass. It is holding the glass for too long, not knowing how to let it go and rest one's arm for a while. You only need to put down the glass for a few minutes. Then, having rested, you pick it up again and carry it easily.

In the same way, the problem of stress has nothing to do with the weight of your duties. The problem is that you hold on to your responsibilities too long, not knowing how to put them down for a while and rest your mental faculties. You only need to let go of your concerns for a few minutes to reap the benefits of relaxation. Then, having rested in meditation, you can pick them all up again. Now they actually feel lighter. You can carry them further, without any stress, until the next time that they need to be put down.

Putting down your heavy glass for a few minutes, or letting go of all your worries for a short while, is an ability learned through meditation. Meditation is *the* training in letting go. So meditation is not being irresponsible and abandoning your duties forever. It is not goofing off. Meditation is the exercise that empowers you with the ability to put down your burden, however heavy, whenever you want, to rest a while so as to pick up that duty later with greater efficiency. Life isn't heavy when you know how to let go.

Total Listening

I passed by my monastery's kitchen one morning and looked through the window. I saw six of our supporters all talking as they prepared our daily meal. There were just six in that room, and all had their mouths open. I began to wonder, if all six people were speaking at once, who was left to do the listening? No one was doing the listening! All were doing the talking. What a waste of breath their talking was!

Unfortunately, the above story is symptomatic of our modern life. Too many are doing the talking, leaving hardly anyone left to do the listening. Marriages break up because of lack of communication. Teen-agers turn wild because they feel they're not understood. Clients go elsewhere because their needs are not heard. And nearly all of us grow old still not comprehending the true meaning of life. Why? Because we never learned how to listen totally.

To listen totally, you must shut up. Really shut up. You are either listening or talking; it is impossible to do both at the same time. Here, I don't just mean stopping your external speech, but I mean quieting the inner speech as well. When you are quiet within, only then can you really listen. To listen totally, you have to listen with everything you've got.

It is amazing what information can be gleaned when you listen from the place of inner silence. Some others become convinced that you are psychic and can read their minds. But it is only the power of total listen-ing. It should be obvious that when you need to pick up more of the "signal," then you must lessen the "static" of inner speech. Through such training in mindful silence, all barriers to communication are fully dis-solved. You become effortlessly sensitive to the people around you. You generate happy harmony in your family and rich success in your business.

From the place of total listening, you might even hear your own body trying to tell you something. Before coming down with a sickness, the body always gives many warnings. However, very few of us listen to our bodies' signals, because we are too busily engaged in our inner conver-sation. Even when our bodies scream a desperate warning, begging for a rest, we are too busy thinking to hear the S.O.S. Then we get cancer, heart disease, or some other terminal ailment. Meditators, on the other hand, learn to listen to their bodies from the place of mindful silence. They hear the needs of their bodies, like they hear the needs of their families, and end up living long, happy lives with both.

Total listening generates insight. From silence, you get to know the true nature of things. And the very best insight is realizing life's meaning. Wouldn't it be so wonderful if we all would put aside for a while every dogma, both religious and personal, and just listen to the throb of life with an alert, silent mind? Then we would totally listen to the teaching of life. Life is constantly, patiently, and gently offering us her wisdom, but we are too busy talking to ourselves to ever listen totally. No wonder so few of us ever understand.

Passing Life's Exams

My final examinations at Cambridge University in 1972 were in theoretical physics. It was a tough time. All my university career came down to these last series of exams. All that went before counted for nothing. This was it, pass or fail. My exams consisted of a three-hour written paper in the morning and another three-hour paper in the afternoon, one day after another without any break. I was told that every year at Cambridge at least one student committed suicide during the final exams. Such was the stress. However, I had a competitive edge over my fellow students that enabled me to do well; I had learned how to meditate.

After the morning exam, I never went for my lunch. Instead, I went to my room, sat down on a cushion, and began meditating. The first thing that I became aware of, as you would expect, was the morning examination just completed. I started to worry whether I had answered a question correctly or whether I should have added more explanation. I soon became obsessed with the past, which for me meant the morning exam. It is easy to say that the past is gone, that my morning's exam can't be changed now, and that it makes no sense to worry about it. However, for some it is not that easy to think so sensibly. Most of us worry about the past nevertheless. Fortunately, due to my training in meditation, I found that I could let go of the past. I stopped worrying about the morning exam. Guess what came into my mind next?

Taking over the whole of my thoughts came the afternoon exam due in less than an hour. Should I open my eyes, pick up a book, and do more revision? Often in the past I had done last-minute cramming before an important exam. I don't know if it is the same for others, but whatever I revised at the last minute never came up in the exam. Revising now was a waste of energy. This was rest time, not exam time. Again, my meditation training came to my rescue, and I let go of the future. Meditating between exams in my college room, I entered the rest state of present-moment awareness.

Once in the present, I was shocked. I noticed for the first time that my body was trembling. I had never considered myself to be a nervous person, but there I was, shaking with fear. My nervous trembling was quite understandable given that I was in the middle of my final exams. What shocked me most was that I hadn't noticed it. I had been so pre-occupied with my exams that I had paid no attention at all to what my body was doing. In present-moment awareness I began total listening, and I heard my body plead for some rest. By paying gentle attention to my body, it soon calmed down. The trembling stopped. My body was still. Then I could hear my mind pleading.

I noticed I was tired. I became aware how mentally drained I was. I had been too busy to notice this before. Now it became clear to me that, as I put it, I had run out of brain juice. Totally listening to my mind, I heard it ask me to rest and not do anything. So I just sat there. Gradually my mental energy came back. Ajahn Chah later confirmed that mental energy grows out of stillness. By the end of my thirty-minute-long med-itation, I was relaxed, bright, and full of energy. My friends later told me that I was the only student to enter the exam hall with a smile on his face. They thought I was cheating and had found out the answers beforehand. I had found the answers, but not to the questions in the exam paper. I had found the answers to stress, and I did very well in those exams.

Life—at school, college, or thereafter—is full of exams. There are many tense days when one is tested sharply and probed very deeply. The experience I've just related is an example of how this meditation helps one pass life's exams, at the university or at the job interview, in one's relationships or in illness, wherever one is put to the test. The smartest examination technique for life is to learn how to let go and fully relax. In other words to learn meditation.

A Holy Place in Your Home

Meditation training is not just for those chasing enlightenment but also for those who are chasing a happier, more meaningful life. If you do not live in a monastery, it is a great help to have a holy place in your house.

It is not that difficult to create an in-house holy place. Many modern houses have family rooms, guest rooms, rumpus rooms, as well as several bathrooms. Wouldn't it be shrewd to include one holy room? If a spare room is not available, then you can always use a quiet corner of your bedroom. Mark out the private corner with your favorite cushions. Then surround it with just the right amount of spiritual symbols and peaceful posters to give it a mood of serenity. Use that corner regularly for your meditation or for listening to or reading something inspiring. Never do anything worldly in your holy corner and always avoid talking there. As the months flow past and the years trickle by, you will discover a gentle "energy of stillness" build up in that space. It soon matures into a special sacred spot. Meditation becomes much easier there because you have made it a place of spiritual power. You have created an authentic holy place in your own house.

One Australian disciple followed my advice and set up a holy place in a corner of her bedroom. She would meditate there regularly, often alongside her husband. One day, she told me, her two young children had a heated argument just outside her front door. Her seven-year-old daughter began crying, ran into the house and into her parents' bedroom. There she sat on her mom's meditation cushion in the holy place, calming her tears. The small girl had never gone there before. Intuitively she found her home's place of peace, the sanctuary in which to heal the unbearable hurt in her little heart. The holy place had become a valuable resource for her whole family.

Even in a busy office, one can create a holy place. I heard of one successful lawyer who desperately needed to meditate at lunchtime to alleviate his considerable stress. He had difficulty finding a private spot where his clients couldn't see him and where the phone wouldn't tempt his ears. There was a small cupboard in his office full of papers and files. So he cleared out that cupboard completely and made it into his holy place. Every lunchtime, his secretary would lock him in his cupboard for thirty minutes meditation. Should a client drop in or the telephone ring, his secretary would gleefully say, "I'm sorry, he's unavailable. He's in his cupboard!" She willingly locks him in his holy place because she knows from experience that he is a much kinder boss in the afternoon having been in his cupboard. He also knows from experience that half an hour spent in meditation is time soon made up through increased efficiency and sharpness of mind. Meditation is an investment of min-' utes that always returns many hours.

Letting Go beyond Measure

The renowned British scientist Lord Kelvin once said, "If you cannot measure, you cannot control." He meant, of course, that in order for science to effectively control our world, we must first learn how to accurately measure natural phenomena. Lord Kelvin's insight into the need for precise measurement was crucial to the growth of technology and to its success in controlling some of the unpleasant aspects of nature.

That gem of truth, however, can also be used the other way round: "If you cannot measure, you cannot control." If one stops all measuring, then control becomes impossible. Abandoning measurement generates letting go.

While in meditation, do you measure your progress? Do you think, "This is a bad meditation" or "This is a good meditation"? You learn from experience that such measuring of good or bad generates controlling, and that leads to doing something. If you gauge your meditation as bad, then you will struggle to make it good. If you count your meditation as good, then you will strive to make it even better. Having measured, you end up with more doing. Letting go is forgotten, and thus you fall away from the path of peace.

Consider what would happen if there were no measuring at all within your meditation sitting. How would it be if there were no assessments of the type "This is a good meditation," "This is a bad meditation"? When you give up all measuring, you relinquish control. Your mind becomes the same as a beginner's mind, one that has yet to learn the measuring scale. Such a mind easily lets go and becomes very peaceful. When you don't calibrate your meditation, the doing stops. Peace grows, happiness blossoms, wisdom ripens. Finally, the fruit of enlightenment drops in your lap.

Abandon measuring time, and you automatically rest in the timelessness of the present moment. Discard measuring with names, and effortlessly the thinking process stops as you enter into mindful silence. Drop measuring the breath as in or out, long or short, rough or smooth, and the breath disappears to reveal the luminous nimitta. Release the nimitta from the measurement of bright or dull, and you enter the jhānas easily. Renounce measuring the mind with perceptions, and the mind rises smoothly through the immaterial attainments. Stop measuring the citta, and the whole of saṃsāra, including the mind, finally ceases altogether. Nothing is left now, not even nothing.

If you follow the path of meditation, your inner happiness rises like a tide that never ebbs. Mindfulness becomes energized as you struggle less with your inner world. Insights appear in abundance like luscious fruits on a heavily laden tree, too many to pluck and eat all at once. You realize so clearly that the path to peace is this letting go that you learned in meditation. Or you can call it the path of unconditional loving-kindness. Such mettā softens your judgments of yourself and others. Judging and measuring fade away like the phantoms they always were. In the final disappearance of all measuring, words are stolen away, for language is nothing more than the measuring scale for life. As peace reaches its apex, as happiness crystallizes into a radiant gem at the summit, when measuring finally implodes—the mind disappears as well. One realizes at last that the mind was the measurer.

This is cessation, the ending of everything without any remainder. Nibbāna is where all words lose their meaning because all measuring has stopped. When great sages point to where there is no long or short, no present, no past, no future, no here or there, no birth or death, everything having stopped, this is what they are pointing to. The final mental object, that which signs off from saṃsāra once and for all, and which signals the end of all name-and-form, is absolute cessation. Parinibbāna *is* the last word.

Notes

◆ ◆ ◆

1 Unless otherwise specified, all translations from the Pāli are my own and therefore will differ in places from other English translations.

2 This booklet has been reprinted in English eight times, and it has also been published in German, Sinhalese, Czech, and Russian.

3 Here I am using Bhikkhus —āṇamoli's and Bodhi's translation of the Majjhima Nikāya, *The Middle Length Discourses of the Buddha* (Boston: Wisdom Publications, 1995), p. 340.

4 Lewis Carroll, *The Complete Illustrated Works of Lewis Carroll* (London: Chancellor Press, 1982), p. 65.

5 Jacobo Timerman, *Prisoner without a Name, Cell without a Number* (London: Weidenfeld and Nicolson, 1981).

6 See *upādāna* in *Buddhist Dictionary: Manual of Buddhist Terms and Doctrines,* by Nyanatiloka, 4th rev. ed. (Kandy: Buddhist Publication Society, 1980), p. 228.

7 I have dealt at length with the relationship between *pīti-sukha* and the breath in chapter 7 on ānāpānasati above.

8 I am using the translation here from the *Numerical Discourses of the Buddha: An Anthology of Suttas from the Aṅguttara Nikāya,* trans. and ed. Nyanaponika Thera and Bhikkhu Bodhi (Walnut Creek, CA: Altamira Press, 1999), p. 36.

9 Sound can disturb the first jhāna, but when one actually perceives the sound one is no longer in jhāna.

10 Here I am citing Bhikkhu Bodhi's translation in *The Connected Discourses of the Buddha* (Boston: Wisdom Publications, 2000), pp. 1252ff.

11 Here I am using —āṇamoli and Bodhi, *Middle Length Discourses,* p. 508.

12 Sam Parnia and Peter Fenwick, "Near Death Experiences in Cardiac Arrest: Visions of a Dying Brain or Visions of a New Science of Consciousness," *Resuscitation* 52 (2002): 5 (abstract).

13 Pim van Lommel et al., "Near-Death Experience in Survivors of Cardiac Arrest: A Prospective Study in the Netherlands," *Lancet* 358 (December 15, 2001): 2044.

14 Ibid., p. 2043.

15 Sam Parnia et al., "A Qualitative and Quantitative Study of the Incidence, Features and Aetiology of Near Death Experiences in Cardiac Arrest Survivors," *Resuscitation* 48 (2001): 154.

16 Benjamin Libet, "Unconscious Cerebral Initiative and the Role of Conscious Will in Voluntary Action," *Behavior and Brain Sciences* 8 (1985): 529–39 (with commentaries, pp. 539–66, and *Behavior and Brain Sciences* 10 [1987]: 318–21).

17 In Pāli, "that" *(yam)* is singular, which means it refers to one and the same thing, which people call by three different names.

18 Here I am using Bodhi, *Connected Discourses*, p. 595.

19 For example, the former president of the Pali Text Society, Mrs. Rhys Davids, in her introduction to the first English translation of the Aṅguttara Nikāya, argued that anattā and the undesirability of craving were both "monkish teachings" and not the Buddha's teachings (pp. xiv–xv). More recently, Thich Nhat Hanh wrote in his book *The Sutra on the Full Awareness of Breathing* that "thus we can infer that the four Meditative States [jhānas]…were instituted after the death of the Buddha" (p. 20).

20 Ñāṇamoli and Bodhi, *Middle Length Discourses,* pp. 454–58.

21 Here I am using K. R. Norman's translation of the *Sutta Nipāta, The Group Discourses,* rev. ed. (Oxford: Pali Text Society, 1995), p. 26.

22 Ñāṇamoli and Bodhi, *Middle Length Discourses,* p. 260.

23 Ibid., p. 1083.

24 Ibid., p. 557.

25 Goleman, Daniel, narrator, *Destructive Emotions: How Can We Overcome Them? A Scientific Dialogue with the Dalai Lama.* (New York: Bantam Books, 2003), pp. 338–39. This passage relates a presentation by researcher Richard Davidson of the University of Wisconsin–Madison.

26 Carroll, *Complete Illustrated Works,* pp. 193–94.

27 Ñāṇamoli and Bodhi, *Middle Length Discourses,* p. 283.

28 In Pāli, "seven" lifetimes is meant to be counted including this present lifetime as the first. The stream winner has at most six more lifetimes.

29 *Manorathapūraṇī* (commentary on *Aṅguttara Nikāya*), 3:374. The sutta in question is AN 6,44.

30 See also Nyanaponika and Bodhi, *Numerical Discourses of the Buddha,* p. 71.

31 See also ibid., pp. 205–6.

32 Bodhi, *Connected Discourses,* p. 1329.

33 Ñāṇamoli and Bodhi, *Middle Length Discourses,* p. 674.

34 See also Nyanaponika and Bodhi, *Numerical Discourses,* p. 231.

35 See also Bodhi, *Connected Discourses,* p. 1433n236.

36 See also ibid., p. 230.

37 See also ibid., p. 544.

38 See also Nyanaponika and Bodhi, *Numerical Discourses*, p. 162.

39 See also ibid., p. 243.

40 See also Bodhi, *Connected Discourses*, p. 1167.

41 Ñānamoli and Bodhi, *Middle Length Discourses*, p. 422.

42 See also ibid., p. 423.

43 Nyanaponika and Bodhi, *Numerical Discourses*, pp. 159ff.

44 See also Nyanaponika and Bodhi, *Numerical Discourses*, p. 171.

45 See also ibid., p. 231.

46 Ñānamoli and Bodhi, *Middle Length Discourses*, p. 861.

47 Here I am using Bodhi, *Connected Discourses*, p. 1859.

Bibliography

✦ ✦ ✦

Buddhist Texts in Pāli

The Aṅguttara Nikāya. 5 vols. London: Pali Text Society, 1888–1961.

Buddhaghosa, Ācariya (fifth century C.E.). *The Commentary on the Dhamma-pada (Dhammapada-aṭṭhakathā).* 4 vols. Edited by H. C. Norman. London: Pali Text Society, 1906.

———. *Manoratha Pūraṇī: Buddhaghosa's Commentary on the Aṅguttara Nikāya.* 5 vols. London: Pali Text Society, 1940–73.

———. *The Visuddhi-Magga of Buddhaghosa.* Edited by C. A. F. Rhys Davids. London: Pali Text Society, 1975. Originally published 1920–21.

Dhammapada. Edited by O. von Hinüber and K. R. Norman. Oxford: Pali Text Society, 1994.

Dhammapāla, Ācariya. *Paramattha-dīpanī, Theragāthā-aṭṭhakathā: The Commentary of Dhammapālācariya.* 3 vols. Edited by F. L. Woodward. London: Pali Text Society, 1940–59.

The Dīgha Nikāya. Edited by T. W. Rhys Davids and J. Estlin Carpenter. 3 vols. London: Pali Text Society, 1890–1911.

The Jātaka. Edited by V. Fausboll. 6 vols. London: Pali Text Society, 1963.

The Majjhima Nikāya. 3 vols. Edited by V. Trenckner (vol. 1) and Robert Chalmers (vols. 2, 3). London: Pali Text Society, 1888–99.

Milindapañho. Edited by V. Trenckner. London: Pali Text Society, 1880.

The Saṃyutta Nikāya. Edited by M. Leon Feer. 5 vols. London: Pali Text Society, 1884–1998. Vol. 1 rev. ed. by G. A. Somaratne, 1998.

Sutta Nipāta. Edited by Dines Andersen and Helmer Smith. New ed. London: Pali Text Society, 1913.

The Thera- and Therī-gāthā: Stanzas Ascribed to Elders of the Buddhist Order of Recluses. Edited by Hermann Oldenberg and Richard Pischel. 2nd ed. by K. R. Norman and L. Alsdorf. Oxford: Pali Text Society, 1966.

Udāna. Edited by Paul Steinthal. London: Pali Text Society, 1885.

The Vinaya Pitakam. Edited by Hermann Oldenberg. London: Pali Text Society, 1929–64. Originally published 1879–83.

Buddhist Texts in English Translation

Bodhi, Bhikkhu, trans. *The Connected Discourses of the Buddha: A New Translation of the Saṃyutta Nikāya.* 2 vols. Boston: Wisdom Publications, 2000.
———, ed. *In the Words of the Buddha: An Anthology of Discourses from the Pāli Canon.* Boston: Wisdom Publications, 2005.
Buddhaghosa, Ācariya, and Bhikkhu —ānamoli, trans. *The Path of Purification (Visuddhimagga).* 5th ed. Kandy: Buddhist Publication Society, 1991.
—ānamoli, Bhikkhu, and Bhikkhu Bodhi, trans. *The Middle Length Discourses of the Buddha: A New Translation of the Majjhima Nikāya.* Original translation by Bhikkhu Ñānamoli, edited and revised by Bhikkhu Bodhi. Boston: Wisdom Publications, 1995. Additional revisions, 2001.
Norman, K. R., trans. *The Group of Discourses (Sutta-Nipāta).* Vol. 2. Rev. trans. Oxford: The Pali Text Society, 1992.
Nyanaponika Thera and Bhikkhu Bodhi, trans. *Numerical Discourses of the Buddha: An Anthology of Suttas from the Aṅguttara Nikāya.* Selected and translated by Nyanaponika Thera and Bhikkhu Bodhi. Walnut Creek, CA.: Altamira Press, 1999.
Walshe, Maurice, trans. *Thus Have I Heard: The Long Discourses of the Buddha, Dīgha Nikāya.* London: Wisdom Publications, 1987. Repr. as *The Long Discourses of the Buddha: A Translation of the Dīgha Nikāya.* Boston: Wisdom Publications, 1995.

Other Buddhist Works

Brahm, Ajahn. *Who Ordered this Truckload of Dung: Inspiring Stories for Welcoming Life's Difficulties.* Boston: Wisdom Publications, 2005. Also published by Lothian in Australia under the title, *Opening the Door of Your Heart.*
Nyanatiloka and Nyanaponika. *Buddhist Dictionary: Manual of Buddhist Terms and Doctrines,* 4th rev. and enlarged ed. by Nyanaponika. Kandy: Buddhist Publication Society, 1980.

Other Works

Carroll, Lewis. *The Complete Illustrated Works of Lewis Carroll.* London: Chancellor Press, 1982.
Goleman, Daniel, narrator. *Destructive Emotions: How Can We Overcome Them? A Scientific Dialogue with the Dalai Lama.* New York: Bantam, 2003.

Libet, Benjamin. "Unconscious Cerebral Initiative and the Role of Conscious Will in Voluntary Action." *Behavioral and Brain Sciences* 8 (1985):
529–39, with commentaries: pp. 539–66; 10 (1987): 318–21.

Parnia, Sam, and Peter Fenwick. "Near Death Experiences in Cardiac
Arrest: Visions of a Dying Brain or Visions of a New Science of Consciousness." *Resuscitation* 52 (2002): 5–11.

Parnia, Sam, D. G. Waller, R. Yeates, and P. Fenwick. "A Qualitative and
Quantitative Study of the Incidence, Features and Aetiology of Near
Death Experiences in Cardiac Arrest Survivors." *Resuscitation* 48 (2001):
149–56.

Timerman, Jacobo. *Prisoner without a Name, Cell without a Number.* London:
Weidenfeld and Nicolson, 1981.

Van Lommel, Pim, Ruud van Wees, Vincent Meyers, and Ingrid Elfferich.
"Near-Death Experience in Survivors of Cardiac Arrest: A Prospective
Study in the Netherlands." *Lancet* 358 (December 15, 2001): 2039–45.

Index

The index includes subjects, proper names (such as people, places, etc.), and some Pāli words. In addition it provides access to some of the more important similes, stories, and personal anecdotes that appear in this book. English headings have been preferred except in cases where there is no equivalent for a Pāli term or where the Pāli term has been used exclusively in the text. Pāli terms are shown in italics.

About the Author

✦ ✦ ✦

 AJAHN BRAHMAVAMSO MAHATHERA
(known to most as Ajahn Brahm),
born Peter Betts in London in 1951,
is a Theravada Buddhist monk. Ajahn
Brahm grew up in London and earned
a degree in Theoretical Physics from
Cambridge University. Disillusioned
with the world of academe, he trained as a monk in the jungles of Thailand under Ajahn Chah. A monk for over thirty years, Ajahn Brahm is
a revered spiritual guide and the abbot of Bodhinyana Monastery, in
Serpentine, Western Australia—one of the largest monasteries in the
southern hemisphere. He is also the Spiritual Director of the Buddhist
Society of Western Australia, and spiritual adviser and inspiration for
Buddhist centers throughout Asia and Australia. His winning combination of wit and wisdom makes his books bestsellers in many languages,
and on his teaching tours Brahm regularly draws multinational audi-
ences of thousands.

Other Books by Ajahn Brahm

✦ ✦ ✦

DON'T WORRY, BE GRUMPY
Inspiring Stories for Making the Most of Each Moment

"I love a Dharma book that I can open randomly to any page and know I'll find a valuable teaching. This describes the delightful new book *Don't Worry, Be Grumpy*. With every story, the irrepressible Ajahn Brahm gently challenges our conventional views, giving us a fresh perspective imbued with wisdom and compassion."—Toni Bernhard, author of *How to Be Sick*

WHO ORDERED THIS TRUCKLOAD OF DUNG?
Inspiring Stories for Welcoming Life's Difficulties

"A splendid collection of 108 Buddhist-based tales with lasting, gentle, pervasive teachings. Brahm weaves a long, rich tapestry of understanding using short threads of stories only a couple of pages long. Especially resonant if slowly savored, this is a wonderful collection that can be enjoyed by a broad audience."—*Publishers Weekly*

THE ART OF DISAPPEARING
The Buddha's Path to Lasting Joy

"This book is an invaluable companion for your journey to your true self, the not-self that lies at the end of the Buddha's path."—*BuddhaSpace*

About Wisdom Publications

Wisdom Publications is the leading publisher of classic and contemporary Buddhist books and practical works on mindfulness. To learn more about us or to explore our other books, please visit our website at wisdomexperience.org or contact us at the address below.

Wisdom Publications
199 Elm Street
Somerville, MA 02144 USA

We are a 501(c)(3) organization, and donations in support of our mission are tax deductible.

Wisdom Publications is affiliated with the Foundation for the Preservation of the Mahayana Tradition (FPMT).